NURSES AND DOCTORS AT WORK

This book is to be returned on or before
the last date stamped below.

NURSES AND DOCTORS AT WORK

Rethinking professional boundaries

Deidre Wicks

OPEN UNIVERSITY PRESS

Buckingham

For Roy, Otto and Claude

Open University Press
Celtic Court
22 Ballmoor
Buckingham
MK18 1XW

email: enquires@openup.co.uk
world wide web: http://www.openup.co.uk

and
325 Chestnut Street
Philadelphia, PA19106, USA

First published 1998

A catologue record of this book is available from the British Library

ISBN 0 335 20273 X (pbk)
ISBN 0 335 20274 8 (hbk)

Library of Congress Cataloging-in-Publication Data applied for

Set in 10.5/12 pt Sabon by DOCUPRO, Sydney
Printed and bound in Singapore.

Contents

Acknowledgments

This book is an edited and largely rewritten version of my PhD thesis. I owe a debt of gratitude to past supervisors, Bob Connell and Ken Johnston, who helped significantly with the development of the thesis. Thanks are due to the staff of various organisations and libraries: The National Library of Australia, The Mitchell Library, Sydney Hospital Library, Royal Australian College of Physicians, London School of Economics, Royal College of Nursing, Greater London Record Office and the archivists at St Bartholomew's Hospital (London).

An undertaking to ensure that individuals and workplaces would remain anonymous unfortunately prevents me from directly thanking many of the key people involved in the research. Notwithstanding these restrictions, I want to give special thanks to the Director of Nursing and the Chief Executive Officer at the hospital where the fieldwork took place. They facilitated my entry and gave me every support. I owe an enormous debt of gratitude to the nurses and doctors who gave me their time and their trust during the fieldwork and interviews. It has been their working lives which have provided me with the ongoing motivation for the project. I hope that the result is worthy of their time and their trust.

I am very grateful for the support provided by Elizabeth Weiss at Allen & Unwin, as well as her critical comments on the manuscript which resulted in many improvements. I would also like to thank the anonymous reviewers sought out by Allen

& Unwin and Open University Press. This is yet another layer of work for pressured academics and I want to let them know that I appreciate the time and effort which went into their very useful comments. Very special thanks go to my former Head of Department, colleague and friend, Lois Bryson, who conscientiously and generously read and commented on the entire manuscript. Her thoroughgoing commitment to academic professionalism has long been an inspiration. Naturally, the flawed creation before you is ultimately my own responsibility.

Friends and family provided support and encouragement during the long haul. Special thanks go to my parents, Laurel and Mick Wicks, and to Marlies and Bert Green, Paula Rix, Suzanne Mullen, Debbie Malcolm, Susan Eade, Stephen Troy, Brian Duke, Bronwyn Ridgeway and lastly and importantly, Wendy Elphink. A special thanks also goes to my original mentor and friend, Rosemary Lewins. They have all helped in innumerable large and small ways.

Lastly, and most importantly, I want to thank my partner, Roy Green, and my sons, Otto and Claude. My boys have been a constant, shining balance to the rigours and loneliness of intellectual work. Roy has helped in every imaginable way, from long discussions and editing chapter drafts, to finding books and providing constant encouragement and practical support. The book is dedicated to my lovely boys.

Abbreviations and rankings

Australian title/English title

NUM	Nurse Unit Manager/Senior Sister
DON	Director of Nursing/Matron
Intern	Intern/Junior House Officer
RMO	Resident Medical Officer (Resident)/Senior House Officer
SRMO	Senior Resident Medical Officer (Senior Resident)/Senior House Officer
Registrar	Registrar/Senior House Officer, Registrar
VMO	Staff Specialist, Specialist, Visiting Medical Officer, Consultant/Consultant
GP	General Practitioner
ICU	Intensive Care Unit
TLC	Tender Loving Care

Introduction

At some point in their lives most people will get sick. And at some point every person will die. These are moments of great vulnerability and it is during these times that people have requirements of other people that go beyond the normal expectations of social and family obligations. At such times there are essentially three things that we want. The first is to be well again. To this end people will travel, pay money or goods in kind and place their trust in those who claim expert knowledge or influence with higher powers. The second is to be as free as possible from the impact of symptoms, especially pain. The third is to be comfortable and clean. The process of disintegration in human beings is messy. As we disintegrate, our solid body begins to dissolve. It may turn into liquid, become foul-smelling and ugly to look at. While other animals accept this, humans—having the gift or curse of self-consciousness—find it both repulsive and frightening. We want this burden removed; we want to smell and remain as normal and intact as possible until we die. If we are fortunate (or loved or powerful or rich), these wants and needs translate into work from other people. This work has variously been called caritas (care), healing, or more recently the provision of health care services.

This book is about the social organisation of these historically durable healing tasks. In modern Western societies, most of this work is performed by doctors and nurses. What they actually *do* is highly socially constrained and constructed through social processes of gender and other power relations. Both of these occupations, as we know them today, are relatively new. As they are presently constructed, both are interdependent. While they are both subject to extensive analysis and critique, they are universally accepted as the appropriate occupations to deliver the bulk of health care services. In this book, I want to question this blind acceptance of a division of labour which is based on a nineteenth century conception of master/servant gender appropriateness. Of course, neither doctors or nurses need necessarily behave in a nineteenth century way (although some do). A modern veneer of respect, politeness and sometimes camaraderie, often quite genuine, smooths most interactions. Nevertheless, at its heart, the relationship is based on a division of knowledge, power and authority which constantly threatens to overflow and to bifurcate the essential experience of being sick and wounded or dying. While it may be functional in terms of getting health care work 'done' it is dysfunctional (in the sense that it limits human potential) in almost every other way. Indeed, it can, and I believe should, be construed as itself a wounded relationship.

I have chosen to look at the relationship and the work that it constructs primarily through the eyes and standpoint of nurses. I do this for two reasons. Firstly, as a feminist, I work from the position that women's voices and women's lives have been underrepresented in history and that it is important, indeed essential, that we constantly work to correct the historical record. This is especially so in the area of health care where the voices of working nurses have only rarely been heard. Secondly, and more particularly, it is nurses who perform the vast bulk of health care work and who spend the majority of their time actually being with the sick, injured and dying. If the aim is to understand the nature of health care work and make some record of it, then it makes sense to focus on these workers. At the same time, it is essential not to see doctors and medical work solely through the eyes of nurses. It is important to recognise the agency of both nurses and doctors in the making of the sexual division of labour and the health care practices which are constructed within this division.

My impetus for writing this book has come from several sources. Firstly, it arose from my own early experiences as a nurse-in-training and then, briefly, as a registered nurse. During these periods of my working life, I was struck by the contrast between my own (and others') experience of the work, and the way it was viewed by the 'outside' world. On the one hand, there was my own direct experience of the centrality of nurses' work to everything that went on in hospitals, to the dark and terrible secrets of sick and dying bodies, to the sometimes agonisingly slow road to recovery. On the other hand, there was, despite the recognition and gratitude from individual patients, an almost total public denial of the truth of this. Status and pay rates were low and working conditions poor. In particular, I was nonplussed by the patronising and disrespectful attitudes of many doctors toward nurses. It was as though the importance of nursing work was a secret held by nurses and patients and of which others did not know, did not believe or were somehow ashamed. Nurses were regarded as sexy and cute or large and ferocious but always and above all, the carriers of bedpans.

It was to try to understand this and other mysteries that I turned to a study of sociology and particularly the sociological literature on nursing. While this addressed many issues, it was ultimately a sense of dissatisfaction with the existing sociological literature on nursing which led to the formulation of the rationale for this book. There are contributions from many theoretical approaches within sociology on nursing. Firstly, there is a whole tradition which is based broadly on a symbolic interactionist approach (Goffman 1961, 1963; Buckenham & McGrath 1983). While this approach gives a good sense of the lived and negotiated reality of nurses as social actors, it misses out on the 'bigger picture' where ingrained and unequal patterns of social interaction take on a firmness, indeed a stability, which belies the notion of free choice and negotiation.

Secondly, there have been the 'critical' approaches to nursing which emphasise social structure and which are derived either from Marxist approaches (with an emphasis on the political economy of health care) or from feminist approaches which emphasise the structural nature of the sexual division of labour based on an ideology of the naturalness of female nurses and male doctors (see Navarro 1977; Waitzkin 1981, 1983; Willis 1983 for Marxist approaches and Ehrenreich & English 1973; Gamarnikow 1978; Game & Pringle 1983; Versluysen 1980, Witz 1992, 1994; Davies 1995 for feminist approaches).

It has, without doubt, been the contributions from a feminist perspective which have provided the richest analyses and interpretations of the working relationship between nurses and doctors. But while these accounts have provided a crucial sense of the pervasiveness and intractability of social structure to explanations of the doctor/nurse sexual division of labour, they have done so at a price. In particular, there has been a tendency to view nurses as an undifferentiated bloc of subordinated women. So while these approaches have caught the patriarchal nature of the 'bigger picture', they have missed out on the details of everyday working life, its inconsistencies, its reversals and contradictions.

Since undertaking the research for this book, some important studies have been published on nurses and the nurse/doctor relationship from the ethnographic research tradition. These include: Mackay 1993; Walby et al. 1994; Porter 1995; and Svensson 1996. These works, in particular Walby et al., have provided extensive and rich documentation on the ideas and attitudes of nurses and doctors toward each other and the day to day reality of hospital work. Generally however, these works do not develop their material within a framework which prioritises gender. The exception is Porter (1995) who, through an approach known as critical realist ethnography, attempts to combine elements of structuralism with elements of ethnography.

Nurses and Doctors at Work also attempts to deepen our sociological understanding of nursing's relationship with medicine but it takes a very different approach from Porter. Significantly, Porter takes the structures of class, race and patriarchy as given, whereas I am investigating the *process* of structuration in relation to gender, as it is expressed and 'made' in the daily interactive work processes of nurses and doctors. Let me say at this point that attempting to understand and elucidate the everyday reality of health work in terms of gender is no easy task. In attempting to avoid pitfalls and open up new areas for analysis, I have not succeeded in neatly packaging 'gender' for this book. I do hope, however, that I have shown how gender enters into, constructs, negates and shapes a large proportion of *what* happens and *how* it happens on a typical hospital ward.

My aim in writing this book has been to provide an account of nurses at work and of the nurse/doctor relationship in a way that acknowledges the centrality of gender at the same time as acknowledging nurses and doctors as active social agents, who are not deterministically caught in an inevitable cycle of social reproduction, but who are capable of both challenging the dominant hierarchical structure and resisting its effects. Ultimately, it is this perspective, and in the end this belief, which allows for the possibility that the work of healing might be organised in a more humane and less divided way. In addition, this book aims to clarify and enrich sociological theory by demonstrating the way that an eclectic or inclusive approach to theoretical application may elucidate and deepen our understanding of the social world—in this case, the social world of the hospital. The book focuses on hospital work, not because I consider it more important or more effective than public health or community health work, but because it is, in a very real sense, a 'hot house' for the nurse/doctor relationship. In the hospital ward of a teaching hospital, nurses and doctors must meet, communicate and relate on a daily basis. There is no avoiding it; there is no choice. They must meet and they must make the relationship work. Just *how* they do this is the subject of this book.

The organisation of the book is as follows: Chapter 1 outlines some of the theoretical issues which are relevant for an understanding of nursing work and the sexual division of labour more generally. Readers with no particular interest in theory may choose to skip this chapter and move straight on to the empirical studies. Chapter 2 examines some historical themes which are relevant for an understanding of the present-day relationship between nursing and medicine. Chapters 3 to 7 consist of a presentation and analysis of the research findings of an ethnographic study into the work of nurses and doctors undertaken in a regional city hospital. In these chapters, I pick up and further develop the significant themes explored in a historical context in chapter two. Finally, in chapter eight, I draw out the implications of the book's findings and explore some different possibilities for health and healing organisation for the future.

THE RESEARCH STUDY

I have chosen to search out and analyse medical and nursing discourses from both the past and present as a way of getting 'inside' power relations between and within the knowledges and practices of medicine and nursing. There has been an almost exclusive focus within feminist literature on the 'outside', 'big picture' political process of medical dominance over nursing, and the consequent neglect of the role of agency in the everyday practice of power relations between the two occupations. This is not to say, of course, that wider political processes are not important, but it is the everyday agency of individuals and groups which 'make' the power structures of the immediate and the long-term structures or what Braudel called the *'longue durée'* (Braudel 1972 quoted in Clark 1990). Essentially, the book is concerned with *how* this happened, and how it *continues* to happen, in the context of nursing and medicine. For this reason, the analysis of discourses will make connections with the historical political, economic and cultural influences which are the concrete expression of the way practice has shaped and constrained the current and future discourses of health care.

Two specific times and places provide the material on which this book is based. Firstly, we move backwards and forwards between nineteenth century Britain at the time of the Nightingale reforms and seventeenth century Britain and Europe at the time of the 'scientific revolution'. This is historical sociology rather than orthodox, chronological history and is used to investigate the role of structure and agency in the making of the 'modern' occupations of nursing and medicine that we know today. Secondly, an ethnographic study of the everyday world of work in a modern teaching hospital is undertaken. In this study, I explore the possibility of the survival of the marginalised, healing discourses analysed in chapter 2 and the place these discourses might have in relation to agency and resistance in making the sexual division of labour. The material for these chapters was derived from a period of ethnographic fieldwork in a teaching hospital which encompassed participative and non-participative observation over a six month period. During this period I was based in a general medical ward. In addition, I conducted in-depth, semi-structured interviews with a sample of all the health care staff attached to or connected with the ward as well as others who visited. These included 20 nurses, including the Nurse Unit Manager (Senior Sister) and the Director of Nursing, the Chief Executive Officer of the hospital, a physiotherapist, an occupational therapist, a social worker, and seven doctors—one Staff Specialist (Consultant), one Registrar, two Visiting Medical Officers (Consultants) and three Resident Medical Officers (House Officers)—as well as with patients where this was possible and appropriate. The purpose of the design was to explore medical and nursing discourses for evidence of compliance with and resistance to the dominant discourses of bio-medicine and to examine the effects of this on nurse/doctor relations.

Chapter 1

A new framework

This book is about nurses, nursing work and the different and sometimes competing frameworks that nurses call upon to name and perform that work. Because nursing work so frequently intersects with medical work, it is also, inevitably, about doctors, and about the complex relationships between nurses and doctors and between nursing and medicine.

In the following chapters I describe an approach to the sexual division of labour between doctors and nurses which takes into account the actions—or the active agency—of the participants in building their occupations and working relationships. At the same time I demonstrate some of the many factors that have facilitated or hindered these actions in various times and places. In other words, I examine the way that nurses have *made* nursing, but not always in conditions of their own choosing and not always in the direction that they would have most preferred.[1] In theoretical terms, the attempt to balance these tensions is usefully understood in terms of the sociological debate concerning structure versus agency. While some theories emphasise the power of social structure to direct and limit people's lives, others emphasise the ability of individuals to choose their life directions and conditions.

Finding a way through this confusion is clearly important for us to understand a group of (mostly) women workers whose lives are, at least to some extent, shaped and directed by the social structures of class and gender. The challenge is to keep

1

hold of a sense of social forces as powerful, directing, limiting and sometimes frightening, while at the same time refusing to see nurses solely as the passive or misguided victims of these forces. In order to meet this challenge, it is necessary to develop a theoretical approach which has the theoretical sensitivity to be able to hold this and other issues in a kind of tension while at the same time refusing to see nurses solely as passive or misguided victims. Such a theoretical approach is explained by Bryan Turner as a theoretical 'strategy of inclusion'. Turner has counterposed this approach to the more usual 'strategy of annihilation', whereby a theorist adopts a particular theoretical paradigm and then proceeds to destroy all others as incompatible with their preferred position (1992, p. 235). This approach would appear to be especially apt for the kind of multi-dimensional research presented here.

Such an approach needs to build on the strengths at the same time as overcoming the weaknesses of past accounts and analyses of nursing. Before outlining such an approach, a brief review of the existing literature on the subject for both its strengths and omissions will show what questions concerning nurses and doctors have been addressed and which remain unanswered or not yet even posed. Every framework or *discourse* (in the sense that Foucault uses it) permits and constrains what questions can be asked and therefore what questions will be examined. In regard to the sexual division of labour between nurses and doctors it is now time to extend the framework within which this relationship has been explored. This will allow us to pose new questions and to explore undiscovered dimensions of this complex and multi-layered relationship. In the review which follows, I focus on feminist approaches as it is from within this tradition that the concept of a sexual (or gendered) division of labour has been developed and put to use as a tool for understanding the relationship between nurses and doctors. I also outline some recent developments in feminist theory which have the potential to enrich our understanding of the sexual division of labour between doctors and nurses. These include the concept of discourse derived from post-structuralism, and insights and concepts derived from feminist critiques of science and psycho-analysis. Finally, I introduce aspects of a theory of structuration into a feminist theoretical framework capable of explaining and illuminating aspects of both the long history as well as the routine day to day practice of nurses and doctors at work in a hospital.

FEMINISM AND NURSING

Feminist analyses of nursing have brought long overdue attention to the gender dimension of nursing and to the gendered underpinning of the division of labour between doctors and nurses. Most of the pre-feminist literature focused on either the efforts of nursing as an occupation to *professionalise,* or on the *meaning* of interactions between staff and patients which underlies a symbolic interactionist perspective. The division of labour itself, the fact that nurses did some things and doctors strictly did others, was either ignored or was seen as necessarily and desirably functional for the efficient carrying out of health care work, or as the 'natural' expression of the true natures of men and women into their 'complementary' occupations. When feminist theory arrived on the scene in the 1970s, it shone like a beacon onto the nurse/doctor relationship and illuminated the unequal and often exploitative power relations which underpinned the ostensibly complementary gender dimension of the division of labour. It raised vital questions such as who gives the orders and who takes them, who does the stimulating work and who does the drudge work, who gets paid more and who gets paid less (Young 1980). This was an important theoretical and political breakthrough. Yet it is something of a paradox that in achieving this significant contribution to an understanding of the gender politics between doctors and nurses, feminist approaches emphasised the power of the social structure of gender to such an extent that nurses began to appear as either hapless victims or as misguided collaborators in a patriarchal system. A brief overview of the most significant contributions will illustrate the point.

WOMEN HEALERS AND NURSES

One of the first and certainly one of the most significant contributions appeared in the early seventies when two

American writers, Barbara Ehrenreich and Deirdre English, turned conventional theories on their head with their polemical pamphlet, *Witches, Midwives and Nurses: A History of Women Healers* (1973). These authors examine the way that women were systematically excluded from formal health delivery and suppressed as informal healers and midwives. The focus for these authors is on the social and political processes involved in the development of the sexual division of labour. They also make an implicit connection between the suppression of witches in Europe and the 'invention' of modern nursing in the nineteenth century (1973:34). Their emphasis on organised male power—essentially the church, the state and the medical profession—was an important counterbalance to traditional histories which glorified the rise of the medical profession and the demise of 'ignorant' quacks. Nevertheless, there are some substantial problems with their work which are relevant for a more thorough understanding of nurses, doctors and women healers.[2]

Ehrenreich and English claim that nursing as a paid occupation was 'invented' in the nineteenth century. They argue that before this, in the early nineteenth century, 'nurse' 'was simply a woman who happened to be nursing someone—a sick child or an aging relative' (1973:35). However, as far as Britain is concerned, there are many records of women being paid for nursing work in homes and institutions prior to the nineteenth century. In fact, as we shall see in the following chapter, it is apparent that nurses *co-existed* with women healers and other 'empirics' (practitioners whose practice is based on observation rather than theory) for long periods in Britain. It is not enough to imply, as Ehrenreich and English do, that the nurses who worked in the 'refuges for the dying poor' were not really nurses (1973:35). They were really nurses, and it is important to understand the type of nursing work they did so that we can understand more fully the massive reorganisation that followed.

Ehrenreich and English also present an oversimplified schema which presents women healers (prior to the invention of nursing) as the 'people's doctors', while male professionals 'served the ruling class' (1973:5). This is only partly true. In eighteenth century England there were also significant numbers of male practitioners who treated low- to middle-income earners (Loudon 1986:102; Porter 1987:22). There were also male apothecaries and early general practitioners who would travel for hours on horseback to care for sick and isolated patients for hours or even days at a time (see chapter 2, 'Nurses making nursing'). To omit or ignore these facts is to ignore contradictory and competing tendencies *within* organised male medicine. The victory of a certain type of scientific medicine (hospital/laboratory medicine over bedside medicine) was a long and disjointed process which took place over a long period. A key point of this book is that this process took place within formal male medicine as well as between it and the 'wise women' or informal women healers.

A related but more general problem concerns the way in which Ehrenreich and English view struggle in health care as something that took place in an earlier period between traditional women healers and formal male practitioners. According to this analysis, the defeat of the women healers ushered in an epoch of capitulation on all fronts to organised, scientific male medicine. For instance, they are critical of middle-class reformers, like Nightingale, and of nineteenth century feminists who 'did not challenge nursing as an oppressive female role' (1973:38). Again, all of this is partly true, but it overlooks much that is crucial to a dynamic analysis of nursing. By viewing the nineteenth century formation of modern nursing only in terms of capitulation and defeat, the authors tend to devalue modern nurses and nursing work. It is also possible to view nurses' different forms of accommodation, their seizing of limited opportunities, their non-compliance and resistance, as creative, often artful, strategies, which have allowed them not only to do their work but to carve out significant areas of practice within the dominant power relations.

PATRIARCHAL OPPRESSION AND NURSING

One of the most influential writings on nursing and its relationship to medicine is Eve Gamarnikow's 'Sexual division of labour: The case of nursing' (1978). Writing from a feminist perspective, Gamarnikow challenged accounts of the sexual division of labour which are based on 'naturalism' or biological determinism (that is, accounts which are based on the idea that it is women's biological destiny to nurture and care for others). She argued for a materialist analysis which locates the sexual division of labour as a *social* relation, that is, one which has been socially and historically constructed. This was such a significant breakthrough that sociological analyses continue to refer to this article to establish a position which runs counter to biological or naturalist accounts of the nurse/doctor relationship (see, for example, Versluysen 1980; Game & Pringle 1983; Willis 1983; Lawler 1991; Hazelton 1990; Porter 1995). It is widely regarded as *the* foundation on which any critical sociological account of nurse/doctor relations must be built.

However, upon closer examination it can be seen that Gamarnikow's account is based on a theoretical tradition which sees patriarchy (or the system of male power) as the key determinant of women's subordination. The effect of this emphasis on the determining power of patriarchal ideology has been the representation of nurses as an undifferentiated bloc of subordinated women. Individual or collective acts of agency and resistance have either been ignored or minimised as insignificant or as yet another variant of 'complaint' among nurses (see Turner 1986). The emphasis on an all-pervasive ideological structure has also had the effect of denying nurses' subjectivity, for in accounts based on the power and pervasiveness of structure, the voices of nurses have rarely been heard. (There are some exceptions, however, notably the work of Game and Pringle 1983; Porter 1995).

Yet Gamarnikow's contribution was pivotal for a reassessment of the conventional literature on nurse/doctor relations. Indeed, the emphasis on power relationships in general, and patriarchy in particular, opened up the traditional nurse/doctor relationship of dominance and subservience to a sophisticated and long overdue sociological critique. Nevertheless, an emphasis on structural reproduction and an inferred passivity on the part of nurses runs the danger of indirectly contributing to the status quo by emphasising the inevitability and hopelessness of the situation. Indeed, other accounts within this paradigm read as though there is simply 'no way out' for nurses (for example, see Short and Sharman 1989). What I am suggesting here is not the need for a return to voluntarism, but rather a reading of historical and more recent events which allows some space for nursing *agency* in both its collective and individual forms.

Recent developments in feminist theory have provided the tools for new ways of examining and conceptualising both the form and content of nursing work, and the division of labour with medicine.

PROFESSIONS AND NURSING

A recent development in feminist analysis which has developed the theme of active agency on the part of nurses has come from an unlikely quarter: the sociology of the professions. This has historically been an area which has provided little joy to nursing. In its traditional form, the sociology of professions set up an (ever changing) 'checklist' of criteria of what constituted a profession. It will come as no surprise to the reader to learn that nursing (like every other female occupation) never quite made it and therefore became relegated to the nether world of the 'semi-professions' as a 'stunted occupational subspecies' (Salvage 1988:517). The response of many nursing theorists was to develop yet another set of criteria or 'traits' which could then be used to demonstrate that nursing did in fact meet the criteria and therefore ought to be recognised as a true profession (see for example, Katz 1969). It was clearly an uncomfortable position for nursing, whose spokespeople were constantly on the defensive in a theoretical world seemingly dominated by 'gatekeeping' sociologists.

Recent work by Anne Witz has broken with this mould. Witz has grappled with the issue of gender and the professions directly and has developed a very different approach to inter-pretations both of the past as well as analyses of the present and future (Witz 1992, 1994). She puts the case for a theory of professionalisation 'that can cope with the fact that women as well as men have engaged in professional projects' (Witz 1992:37). In terms of the history of modern nursing, she has analysed the various political strategies of nursing leaders as strategies of 'dual closure'. This term refers to the double focus of the strategy. On the one hand, members of the group resist domination from above and seek to extend their territory, on the other, they seek simultaneously to close off the occupation and restrict entry to its ranks (Witz 1992:201). Witz goes on to argue that the group of initiatives which surfaced in the 80s in Britain known as 'Project 2000', which sought to sever the link between nursing education and the staffing needs of hospitals, was the realisation of the professional project envisaged by Mrs Bedford-Fenwick and her followers one hundred years ago (Witz 1992:202). While this represents historical continuity in nursing's occupational strategy, Witz also suggests that there is a new element. This new element is the emphasis on the *content* of nursing work which, she argues, represents a bid to establish practitioner *autonomy* in the daily practice of nursing work (Witz 1994:26); This strategy and the type of practice that is envisaged for nursing has come, at least in the United Kingdom, to be called 'the New Nursing' (Salvage 1992; Wicks 1997). While this contribution has re-focused attention on the gendered nature of professional projects and on the agency of nurse leaders, it does so within a framework which is strongly schematic and which misses out on the detailed, lived reality of the everyday working life of nurses. In particular, it subsumes nurses' desire for more autonomy in their daily work into a coherent strategy for professional status. While these goals are frequently related, they are not necessarily always connected.

Also grappling with the issue of gender and the professions is the recent work of Celia Davies which focuses, as its title suggests, on *Gender and the Professional Predicament in Nursing* (1995). Unlike Witz, who sees professional strategies as having relevance for nursing, Davies suggests that nursing's role has been to bolster the concept of profession for others such as doctors, who use the activities of nursing to present themselves as rational and in control. She goes on to argue that nursing's long term project may actually be to challenge the gendered basis of the concept of a profession—a concept which has worked against nursing.

Davies's book is an important contribution to the recent literature on nursing which attempts to use feminist theory to elucidate the 'predicament' of nursing. It is especially useful because of the variety of empirical data it analyses. Through this analysis, it reveals some of the key ways that gender has worked against nursing and so shows the importance of analysing gender and nursing at many different levels or sites.

The problems that Davies's book encounters have great relevance for this book. On the one hand, Davies's use of

Chodorow (1978), Gilligan (1982) and Bologh (1990) contrib-
utes to an understanding of the way masculinity and femininity
are implicit in the division of labour between doctors and
nurses (see also Wicks 1994 and below for a discussion of
Chodorow in relation to this issue). On the other hand, her
definition of gender in terms of masculine and feminine inter-
twined 'cultural codes' creates as many problems as it solves.
These problems arise from the distinction that Davies makes
between real women and men on the one hand, and masculinity
and femininity (with their historical burden of cultural codes)
on the other. Whenever this distinction is made (and it is the
same as that made by Althusser between real men and women
and their class positions; see Connell 1983), the question arises:
what is the relationship between real men and women and the
cultural codes of masculinity and femininity? Where do the
cultural codes come from? The danger here is that 'cultural
codes' can become both the expression of gender and the
explanation for it. The problem then, is the development of
a theory where the 'metaphorical terms for a relationship'
are extended into 'abstract categories' until these analytic
categories

> . . . as so often in idealist thought, have, almost unnoticed,
> become substantive descriptions, which then take habitual
> priority over the whole social process to which, as analytic
> categories, they are attempting to speak. (Raymond Williams
> quoted in E.P. Thompson, 1978)

In order to avoid this problem, we need an account of
gender where the historicity of the daily practice of gender
takes centre stage. At the same time, we want to retain a sense
of social structure, but structure as 'structural actuation', in
other words, a social structure which is capable of any number
of alternate possibilities (Thompson 1978:302).

These are significant and ongoing problems for social theorists and will be grappled with throughout this chapter and
applied throughout the book as a whole. At this point, however, I want to step back from specific feminist approaches to
nursing, to examine some important developments within feminist theory and social theory more generally. These
developments have the potential for fruitful application to

nursing and to the nurse/doctor relationship. At base, they are all concerned with different dimensions of the operation of power, an issue which is always present in the nurse/doctor relationship. Let us begin at the beginning, at the earliest stages of gender development.

GENDER CONSTRUCTION

Feminist interest in the processes of the unconscious, especially in relation to the construction of gender identity, is important in order to understand the ways that nurses and doctors themselves 'make' the sexual division of labour. While a complete account of the feminist re-assessment and reformulation of psychoanalytic theory is not appropriate here, some insights and developments are pertinent. The work of Nancy Chodorow (1978), in particular, is useful for an analysis of some of the less visible dynamics of the nurse/doctor relationship.

Chodorow has developed an alternative (to the Freudian) theory of the psychodynamic construction of masculinity and femininity. She examines the way that the sexual division of labour in childcare leads to an attachment to the mother, which results in different forms of separation from the mother for male and female infants and different implications for male and female identity. She argues that the process of primary attachment to the mother results in 'blurred boundaries' for girls who grow up with a strong need for 'completion' in other close relationships. Boys, on the other hand, have to make a traumatic 'double separation' from the mother, first as a separate child and then on another level as a *male* child. The male child then lives with the constant tension of the attraction of 'completion' in the mother and the fear of loss of masculine identity and independence if he does not thoroughly and completely separate. She argues further that this process is a cause of the tenuousness of masculine identity and a fundamental cause of the rejection of the feminine both within the male himself and at a more general level in the social and cultural devaluing of women (1978:92–110). All of this has important implications for any strategy for change in the sexual division of labour at work. Chodorow's redevelopment of psychoanalytic theory certainly provides another dimension to our understanding of the reasons for girls' attraction to jobs which involve nurturing and 'mothering' and boys' attraction to more overtly instrumental and competitive work situations. Chodorow achieves this without falling into the trap of a theory of *essential* femininity or masculinity (or the idea that males and females are born with essential, ingrained characteristics). At base, her explanation is a social and cultural one.

Chodorow's work is relevant for an understanding of the sexual division of labour between nurses and doctors and also for the insights it provides into the tensions within nursing and medical knowledge and their respective labour processes. There has been a recent application of Chodorow's theory to an examination of men who become nurses by Christine Williams (1989). Her study tends to validate Chodorow's theory, particularly in relation to the type of work male nurses choose within nursing. She states: 'Male nurses go to great lengths to carve for themselves a special niche within nursing that they define as masculine' (1989, p. 14). Another useful contribution from the feminist tradition has been the concept of 'emotional work' developed by Arlie Russell Hochschild (1983). In her book, *The Managed Heart*, Hochschild argues that women tend to find themselves in jobs that not only require nurturing skills but also require (as part of the nature of the work), skills of status enhancement for others. The author teases out this concept to show that rather than being an inherent, feminine characteristic, it is in fact *work*, and it is work which carries its own little-recognised occupational hazards. Hochschild herself puts it in the following terms:

> Those who perform emotional labour in the course of giving service are like those who perform physical labour in the course of making things: both are subject to the rules of mass production. But when the product—the thing to be engineered, mass-produced and subjected to speed up and slow down—is a smile, a mood, a feeling, or a relationship, it comes to belong more to the organisation and less to the self. (1983:198)

While Hochschild concentrates on flight attendants and their work, her theory is also relevant for nursing work, where it adds a new dimension to the notion of 'burnout'.[3] However, there is a significant difference in my application of the concept

in that it is expanded to identify the pleasures as well as the
pain of emotional work.

CRITIQUES OF SCIENCE

Another area of feminist theory which has the potential to
elucidate 'hidden' aspects of the relationship between nurses
and doctors comes from feminist critiques of science. These
contributions examine different aspects of gender and power
as they relate to the emergence and dominance of a particular
form of scientific knowledge. As it is one of the key points of
this book that the sexual division of labour is constituted at
the level of knowledge as well as practice, and that this
dimension of domination is visible as the victory of scientific
medicine over older, holistic traditions, a feminist critique of
scientific knowledge adds an important tool for understanding
the work of nurses and doctors.

Sandra Harding, however, points to the lack of a fully
developed feminist theory for the critique of the natural sciences. She argues that there are at least five research programs
which illuminate the extent to which scientific knowledge is
gendered (1986:20–24). The program of most value for my
purposes (the fourth program) is described by Harding as
follows: '[T]he related techniques of literary criticism, historical
interpretation, and psychoanalysis have been used to "read
science as a text" in order to reveal the social meanings—the
hidden symbolic and structural agendas—of purportedly value-
neutral claims and practices' (1986:23). Central importance is
attached in this program to the explication of discourses,
especially discourses which rely on metaphors of gender politics, in the writings of the founders of modern science and in
the current writings of scientists and scientific apologists. These
discourses are the mechanism which both reveals and constructs social relationships of power, including relationships of
gender.

A key work in this field and one of great interest is Caroline
Merchant's *The Death of Nature* (1982). In this book Merchant
carefully documents a gendered language of power and dominance which is to be found in the writings of the 'father' of
modern science, Francis Bacon. This 're-reading' of Bacon and

subsequent discovery of a coherent, gendered view of the relationship between a potential, masculine 'knower' and a passive, female 'nature', provides the basis for a startling and perceptive analysis of the origins of modern science (1982:168–172). Her work also provides an original, materialist analysis of British and European history which looks at the interplay of ideas and the changes in the physical and social environment.[4] She examines the way that the ideas and images of dominance, rape and torture came to replace older, organicist traditions and created a sympathetic context for the subsequent full-scale exploitation of nature. At the same time, Merchant also examines the way that actual changes in the physical environment (such as the draining of the Fens in England) influenced ideas, attitudes and even intellectual movements. This dialectical account of human/natural history is very firmly based on an active view of human agency:

> The replacement of the older, 'natural' ways of thinking by a new and 'unnatural' form of life—seeing, thinking, and behaving—did not occur without struggle. The submergence of the organism by the machine engaged the best minds of the times during a period fraught with anxiety, confusion, and instability in both the intellectual and social spheres. (1982:193)

Merchant's work is useful because her scholarly research and documentation of older, organicist philosophies and traditions, and her account of their struggle and defeat, provide the inspiration for the presentation in the following chapters on continuities between these older traditions and current marginalised, but resilient, forms of oppositional knowledge, language and practice.

Other writers who fall within Harding's 'fourth program' include Keller (1985) and Jordanova (1986). In the work of Evelyn Fox Keller (1985), we find another detailed explication of a profoundly gendered language in scientific writings of the seventeenth century. She argues that we cannot understand the values, aims and goals embodied in the scientific enterprise without attending to the role played by metaphors of gender. Like Merchant, she pays particular attention to the writings of Francis Bacon. Her work is especially interesting because, while she provides ample evidence of symbols and metaphors of

domination—force and rape in the language of the 'founding
fathers' of modern science—she also provides evidence of other,
more gentle discourses which continue to exist in scientific writings to the present day. These other discourses though, 'persist
throughout history only sotto voce, as minor themes made inau-
dible by the dominant rhetoric' (1985:125). Nevertheless, they *do*
persist and, significantly, she shows that neither the ideas nor the
values of the dominant ideology have been uniformly embraced
by the community of working scientists. Keller's work is important
for the evidence she offers, and the insights she provides, into the
existence of competing and contradictory discourses within scientific knowledge and practice. The ongoing critique of Western
science and scientific medicine undertaken by these and other
writers, along with the exposition of the centrality of gendered
metaphors of domination and control in the language of science
provided a fruitful path for further exploration in their application
to the discourses of medicine and nursing. It is important to note
however, that while the concept of 'gendered metaphors' is useful
for explicating the hidden face of gender within science, it has the
same theoretical problems as the concept of 'cultural codes'
discussed in relation to Celia Davies's work earlier, i.e. who
constructs them, where do they come from and what is the *process*
of their construction. So far, I have examined various aspects of
feminist theory which can all be squarely placed within a 'modernist' feminist tradition. However, some of the insights and
concepts from post-structuralism have been taken up by feminists
and used to analyse instances of the operation of power in gender
relations. Concepts from post-structuralism will also be put to
use in the analysis of nursing and medicine which follows.

POST-STRUCTURALISM AND NURSING

Having left one 'unhappy marriage' (with Marxism), it seems
that many feminist theorists are prepared to experiment with
the possibility of a new relationship with post-structuralism, in
particular, with the concept of discourse (Weedon 1987; Barrett
1991; Pringle & Watson 1992). As we shall see, this new
merger solves some problems but leaves others unresolved.
Barrett and Phillips (1992:2) have recently argued that the
theoretical and paradigmatic critique of modernist feminism

which has taken place over the last twenty years represents a 'paradigm shift' because of the way that the founding principles of contemporary, Western feminism have been questioned. Central to this questioning has been a critique of three of the assumptions of '1970s feminism'. These are, first, the notion of women's *oppression*, second, the assumption that it is possible to specify a *cause* for the oppression and, third, consensus around the notion that the cause lies at the level of *social structure*, be it patriarchy, class or a combination of the two. Crucial to this process of critique has been the appropriation and development by feminists of post-structuralist and post-modernist ideas (Barrett 1992:207). Significantly, these have included the rejection of theoretical universalism and the subsequent view that analyses of power ought to proceed from the micro level (Pringle & Watson 1992:64). Of particular importance have been the importations into feminist analysis from the work of Foucault.

The work of Foucault has been crucial for making links between discourse, knowledge and power. For Foucault (1970, 1972), discourses are ways of constituting knowledge, social practices and forms of subjectivity. However, discourses always function in relation to power relations and, as Foucault has stated many times and in many ways, wherever there is power there is also resistance (Foucault 1977:142). Foucault's view of power, specifically his conceptualisation of a power that is productive as well as repressive, that circulates (in a capillary fashion), that exists in action and provides 'spaces of freedom' ('loopholes') within the ruling relations, seemed to have potential for the analysis of an area of women's work that is usually presented as structurally powerless (Foucault 1977:142,151). The point of entry for such an analysis of power is the concept of discourse, used in the Foucauldian sense, as a network with its own history which proscribes and enables what can be said. In this case, I am interested in the bio-medical discourse of scientific medicine. While this is a prime example of a powerful and pervasive discourse, it is not without historically specific resistances and challenges. This has been well documented by historians, anthropologists and sociologists who have written on the status of the bio-medical paradigm in relation to other kinds of healing knowledge (see for instance, Doyal 1979; Engel 1977; Ehrenreich & English 1973; Willis 1983; Salmon

1984). Throughout the book I explore the extent of the dominance of this model of knowledge in relation to nursing knowledge and practice. In particular, I am interested in the extent to which nurses are immersed in and constitute the dominant discourse and the extent to which and in what ways they resist it.

Feminist post-structuralists have taken from Foucault a concern with the local and the specific as a guide to research. After his oft quoted statement 'that there are no relations of power without resistances', Foucault goes on to argue:

> [T]he latter are all the more real and effective because they are formed right at the point where relations of power are exercised; resistance to power does not have to come from elsewhere to be real, nor is it inexorably frustrated through being the compatriot of power. It exists all the more by being in the same place as power; hence, like power, resistance is multiple and can be integrated in global strategies. (1977:142)

This emphasis on the interconnectedness of power and knowledge and the importance of resistance and micro-sites of power has had an obvious appeal for many feminist theorists. A focus on the local and specific also has clear attractions for research on gender relations within institutions. It allows for a concentration on the personal and inter-relational aspects of gender at the same time as not losing sight of the wider 'global' picture. And yet, the work of Foucault is not unproblematic for feminists. These problems concern Foucault's conceptualisation of *agency, power and resistance* and they are all connected.

Foucault's focus on local sites for the operation of power does not mean that his focus is on the local operators. As Giddens puts it when discussing Foucault's work: 'Human beings do not make history, rather history makes human beings' (1987:97). Giddens goes on to state:

> Foucault's history tends to have no active subjects at all. It is history with the agency removed. The individuals who appear in Foucault's analyses seem impotent to determine their own destinies. Moreover, that reflexive appropriation of history basic to history in modern culture does not appear at the level of the agents themselves. The historian is a reflexive being, aware of the influence of the writing of history upon the determination of the present. But this quality of

self-understanding is seemingly not extended to historical agents themselves. (1987:98)

Lois McNay echoes this point when she argues that the emphasis that Foucault places on the effects of power on the body results in a reduction of social agents to passive bodies and fails to explain how individuals may act in an autonomous fashion. She goes on to make the important point that this lack of a theory of agency conflicts with a fundamental goal of the feminist project: to rediscover and re-evaluate the experiences of women (1992:3).

The issue of agency in the work of Foucault is related to his view of power. His concept of power ultimately *has no foundation* in that it is 'free-floating', all-encompassing and in a sense 'everywhere' (Walby 1992:35). A common theme throughout all of Foucault's work is its attempt to de-legitimise the priority given to the notion of social structures such as patriarchy, gender order and class, by replacing this approach with one which seeks rather to uncover the complex strategies and relations of power (Barrett 1991:151). Hoy has explained it this way: 'So without attributing power either to conscious agency or to underlying forces like the modes of production, Foucault explains contemporary society by mapping the network of power relations that have evolved historically' (Hoy 1986:128). And yet as Dews has pointed out, if the concept of power is to have any critical value, there must be some principle, force or entity which power 'crushes' or 'subdues', and whose release from this repression is considered desirable (1987:162). Foucault clearly sees power as 'rooted deep in the social nexus' but does not offer (and does not intend to offer) any account which would enable us to theorise any source or reason for power or the interests behind it. Nancy Fraser makes a similar point when she criticises Foucault for failing to develop a new, normative framework for understanding modern power. She argues:

> Only with the introduction of normative notions could he
> begin to tell us what is wrong with the modern
> power/knowledge regime and why we ought to oppose it.
> (1989:29)

Here there is a clear problem for feminist theory which is driven by a political project and a set of assumptions

concerning inequitable power relations and a vision of a possible future emancipation.

The issue of resistance in Foucault's writings is as pervasive
and as amorphous as his analysis of power. Yet he is often
quoted on resistance—'There are no relations of power without
resistances'—as though this somehow makes up for the lack of
agency inherent in his view of power. However, upon examination it is apparent that while resistance is posited as being
inextricably connected to power, the connection is a logical one
(or 'ontologically' connected: McNay 1992:39) rather than one
which is actively chosen through conscious, human practice.

So while his emphasis on power as a complex strategy
which is spread through the social system in a 'capillary
fashion' and which is manifested at local points as 'micro
powers' is a useful one for a study of power 'at the margins',
the inadequate account of subjectivity, of agency and resistance
renders his analysis of discourse and power as problematic.
Because of these and other problems, there is a spectrum of
feeling regarding the utility of Foucault's work for feminists.
Some, like Walby, argue that Foucault's dispersed view of
power, together with a de-emphasis on economic relations
makes analyses of gender overly free-floating (1990:15). Pringle
has made the point that Foucauldian and feminist approaches
sit uneasily together, and at many points contradict each other
(1988:96). And yet, as with her own study of secretaries, both
frameworks have much to offer for an analysis of nurses' and
doctors' work. Weedon is perhaps more 'permissive' (or 'inclusive') on this issue when she argues:

> If Foucault's theory of discourse and power can produce in
> feminist hands an analysis of patriarchal power relations
> which enables the development of active strategies for change,
> then it is of little importance whether his own historical
> analyses fall short of this (1987:13).

Here I follow Pringle's argument that while it may not be
possible (or desirable) to fully integrate the two frameworks,
it is advantageous to keep them in some sort of tension
(1988:96).

Essentially, Foucault's work is compelling for feminists
because of the language it provides for an analysis of power
at local and marginal sites. This is particularly so in fields

connected to bio-medicine where Foucault's work has provided a radical perspective on medical knowledge, through viewing the content of medical knowledge as being socially constructed, and contributing to the shaping of social relations such as class and gender (Bury 1986:137). This has clear relevance for an analysis of medical and nursing knowledge, which are valued and recognised very differently; indeed, very unequally. To this end, the tools of discourse analysis will be put to work in this book. By discourse analysis, I mean working with the Foucauldian concept of discourse to examine various texts and dialogue for their implications for gender inequality in the daily work of nurses and doctors. At the same time, I will attempt to link discourse analysis with a theory of structure and agency in which the sense of nurses and doctors as knowledgeable, intentional agents is also not lost. The exploration of the theoretical and practical tension between structure and agency has been somewhat surpassed in recent years by the popularity of post-structural approaches within sociology. And yet at the theoretical heart of these and other approaches concerned with social action lies the structure/agency tension, whether or not it is explicitly acknowledged or explored. The theory which has come closest to achieving a satisfactory resolution to this tension is Giddens' theory of structuration.

THEORY OF 'STRUCTURATION'

In a great number of books and articles, Giddens has attempted to develop a theory which involves 'the duality of structure' (Giddens 1973, 1977, 1979, 1987). For Giddens, this duality relates to the fundamentally recursive character of social life and also expresses the interdependence of agency and structure (1979:69). By this he means that 'social structures are both constituted by human agency, and yet at the same time are the very medium of this constitution' (Giddens 1977:121). Structure, for Giddens, is both the medium and the outcome of the human activities which it organises. He makes the point that it is an important task of social theory to 'study the conditions in the organisation of social systems that govern the interconnections between the two' (1979:70).[5] Importantly, he also rejects the identification of structure solely with constraint. He argues that structures are both constraining and enabling. (Giddens 1976:161; 1979:69)[6] Both these theoretical issues have an immediate relevance for an understanding of nursing work. For instance, structures undoubtedly prevent nurses from performing certain actions, but they also create the space in which other actions take place which over time have the potential to threaten or even change the structures. An example of this is the way in which nurses have fought over many years for tertiary based education. This has the potential to create a more articulate, informed, confident nurse who is able not only to make decisions but also to question the decisions of other health professionals, and therefore to challenge the basis for the current division of labour.

There have been a number of previous attempts to apply Giddens's theory of structuration to research contexts (Burman 1988; Dandeker 1989). One of the most interesting applications of Giddens's theory has been its application to gender relations in Connell's *Gender and Power* (1987). Connell argues that a sophisticated account of the agency/structure relation is an essential requirement for an adequate theory of gender. While he agrees that Giddens's structuration theory comes closest to this requirement, he is concerned that we place more emphasis on *human practice* in the making and unmaking of social structure. He makes the point that historical process is not simply a set of alternatives allowed by a context of given structural constraints but that this context itself *is* history. In other words, structure itself has been made by history or rather by active human agents living their history. It therefore follows that the outcomes for those structures (their 'reproduction'), is never a foregone conclusion but is contingent on the social forces unleashed through human activities or practice.

While Giddens's theory of structuration and Connell's theory of practice go far in providing concepts for a feminist perspective on the relationship between agency and structure, there is, nevertheless, a key issue that remains unresolved. This concerns the actual identification of the operation of power implicit in the concept of structure and the activity of resistance implicit in the concept of agency. How do we know that power is operating in certain social relationships? How do we know that human agents are coming up against structure at all? This is not such a problem where there is a clear and overt conflict of interest or where, in Connell's words, there is 'an awareness of inequalities and the social oppositions they define' (1987:263), but what of those situations where there is no such awareness; where domination exists in the absence of overt violence or even conflict? This is especially important when analysing relations between gendered subjects where gender relations have been 'naturalised' and where surface relations may appear complimentary and compatible. We are back to the central question which preoccupied Gramsci (1971), which was how the powerful ensure the consent of the governed without coercion. Now, however, we want to extend these notions of domination and resistance to structures which may not only include, but also go beyond, the defining parameters of class.

POWER AND INTERESTS

The concept of the sexual division of labour between doctors and nurses is based on an underlying premise concerning a tension between doctors and nurses which is based in turn on unequal power relations between the two occupations. In other words, doctors and nurses don't just do different things, nurses work within a network of power with doctors at the apex. Nursing work is limited and directed by the priorities of the more powerful occupation. This hierarchy of power, authority and status is sometimes expressed as an overt conflict of interest (for example, in an open disagreement over patient care) but at other times, indeed for most of the time, it remains invisible. The question then arises: how do we know that it exists where there is no overt conflict? Put another way, how do we know that human agents in the sexual division of labour are actually coming up against structure when there is often no overt sign of conflict? Furthermore, in the absence of overt conflict, how do we recognise resistance?

For a resolution to this seeming quandary, we need to go beyond Giddens and Connell to Lukes (1974), who points to a way out of this impasse with his 'three-dimensional' view of power. This view involves a critique of the one- and two-dimensional views as being too individualistic and of having too much of a behaviourist focus. Lukes claims that the three-dimensional view can account for the exercise of power in the absence of overt conflict. Lukes argues that this occurs when *'potential* issues' are kept out of politics, so that overt conflict is avoided but what exists is a *'latent'* conflict of interests. For Lukes, this consists in 'a contradiction between the interests of those exercising power and the *real interests* of those they exclude' (1974:25, emphasis in original). He goes on to argue that those so excluded may not even be conscious of their interests but that the identification of these interests must always rest on 'empirically supportable and refutable hypotheses'. This can be done by assuming that 'there *would be* a conflict of wants or preferences between those exercising power and those subject to it, were the latter to become aware of their interests'.[7] Such a formulation, as we shall see, is not without its problems, but it does at least go part way to solving the quandary outlined above.

The main difficulty with the Lukes formulation is the seeming paradox involved in the possibility of self-emancipation for dominated groups and a critique of the existing order which holds that the consciousness of such groups has been manipulated, distorted and rendered 'false' by the essential features of that order (Benton 1981:162). In other words, how can dominated groups know and act on the knowledge of what their real interests are when their very ability to know has been shaped and distorted by the exercise of power by the dominant class (or gender or other dominant group)? This is a problem which has surfaced again and again among socialist and Marxist theorists and also for feminists. For Leninists, the answer lay in the role of the revolutionary party which, through its scientific analysis of the balance of class forces, would develop an undistorted analysis and strategy through which the exploited working class would be able to capture power. For feminists, a solution lay in consciousness-raising groups which helped women identify and understand the nature of their oppression. In relation to nurses, it has been suggested that nurses need to recognise themselves as an oppressed group and become critical of their leaders who more often than not collude with medicine and hospital administrators (Roberts 1983). Lukes himself has been accused of holding a view of interests that is in the end 'other ascribed'; that is, it requires others apart from and outside the dominated group to ascertain what the group's real interests are. To understand Lukes's answer to this problem, we need to go back to the way that he defines power in the first place.

For Lukes, power is defined by saying that 'A exercises power over B when A affects B in a manner contrary to B's interests'. Lukes explains that to identify B's interests in a situation where there is no overt conflict we need to find the 'relevant counterfactual', or to find evidence to show that B would have acted otherwise in the absence of influence from A. Lukes goes further and argues that it is also necessary to identify the 'means or mechanism by which A has prevented, or else acted (or abstained from acting) in a manner sufficient to prevent, B from doing so'. Lukes recognises that sometimes the task of identifying the relevant counterfactual is 'extraordinarily difficult' (1974:46). Nevertheless, he holds to the position that it is still possible, even in difficult situations, to find evidence, even if indirect, to support the claim that an apparent case of consensus is not genuine but imposed. In general, Lukes's approach for adducing this evidence has not been widely accepted, and it has led to the accusation that, despite his own commitment to democracy, his method for identifying the real interests of B is in the end 'other ascribed'; in other words, that some other wiser or more knowledgeable person(s) will work out the real interests of a particular misguided group. According to these critics, it therefore falls into the trap of other socialist and radical theories that have undemocratic forms of rule as their practical effect (Benton 1981).

It is not, however, necessary to break the nexus between power and interests in order to avoid this dilemma.[8] It is indeed possible, even preferable, to maintain the connection, and to develop further a direction pointed to by Lukes which will allow us to maintain a 'three-dimensional view' of power while at the same time avoiding the trap of defining interests in a way that is 'other ascribed'. This means that we must develop a method to identify the 'relevant counterfactual' in a situation where there is an absence of overt and even covert conflict.

CONCEPT OF 'HEGEMONY'

Lukes points to a fruitful direction for the generation of such a method in the work of Gramsci. Lukes discusses the section in the *Prison Notebooks* where Gramsci makes a distinction between thought and action: 'the co-existence of two conceptions of the world, one affirmed in words and the other displayed in effective action' (Gramsci 1971:326). Gramsci goes on to argue that when this contrast occurs 'in the life of great masses',

> It signifies that the social group in question may indeed have its own conception of the world, even if only embryonic; a conception which manifests itself in action, but occasionally and in flashes—when, that is, the group is acting as an organic totality. But this same group has, for reasons of submission and intellectual subordination, adopted a conception which is not its own but is borrowed from another group; and it affirms this conception verbally and believes itself to be following it, because this is the conception it follows in 'normal times'—that is when its conduct is not independent and autonomous, but submissive and subordinate. (1971:327)

Lukes himself goes further and claims that evidence can also be sought in 'normal times' by examining how people react to opportunities, 'or more precisely, perceived opportunities', to escape from domination. He goes on to examine the Indian caste system and attempts at 'Sanskritization' as a perceived form of escape in this new light. This is a valuable contribution from Lukes and is further developed below. What Lukes does not do, however, is break with the essential dualism of Gramsci's conception of the 'man-in-the-mass' (sic) who acts and his 'theoretical consciousness', which may well be in opposition to his activity (1971:333).[9] We have here echoes of the mind/body dualism of Descartes (1595–1654). Interestingly, theory and practice, and therefore 'critical self-consciousness' (and by implication an awareness of one's own interests), are finally linked through intellectuals who are '"specialised" in conceptual and philosophical elaboration of ideas' (1971:334).[10] Here Gramsci avoids the problem of interests being 'other ascribed' by linking these intellectuals 'organically' to the group from which they emerged (1971:12).

It is feasible to retain Gramsci's very useful insight into the way individuals and 'great masses' respond to domination and reveal their real interests and aspirations (even, following Lukes, in normal times), while at the same time avoiding his conceptual dualism. We can do this by reformulating the concept of discourse so that it takes into account the Foucauldian focus on discourses as *ways of constituting* knowledge, social practice and forms of subjectivity (discourse as structure or technique of power) with a focus on discourse as *language and communication* (discourse as the medium of human agency). To do this is to reintroduce 'commonsense' meanings of discourse back into the concept (Barrett 1991:125).

With this conceptualisation, discourses are more than structures which organise thought and language, they are also the utterances, actions or social practices of individuals and groups. There is no distinction to be made between the language or 'verbal attestations' of dominated groups and the 'symbolic content of their social practices' (Benton 1981:172). We are therefore able to avoid the mind/body dualism which is inherent in the Gramscian distinction between the thoughts and the actions of subjugated groups. What we are able to do as well is to operationalise Giddens's 'duality of structure', because while discourses are constituted by agents through language and practice, they are also a structuring principle within society, and specifically within social institutions, modes of thought/knowledge and individual subjectivity (Weedon 1987:41). According to this theory, language is not an abstract system but is always socially and historically located in discourses. Discourses represent political interests, *but they are not just a structuring principle; they are also the medium for the constitution, or for resistance and challenge to those structures.* They are therefore constituting and being constituted by the historical interplay between structure and agency.

Following Gramsci, who made it clear that domination or hegemony was never totally complete, it is possible to discern indications of the real interests of dominated groups through an analysis of their discourses and discursive practices (Gramsci 1971:337). While individual subjects are constituted, manipulated and often oppressed by discourses of class and gender (and other) relations, they are capable through it all, in normal times as well as in abnormal times, of expressing their interests through the medium of language/practice. This is not to say that there will not sometimes be a disjuncture between their thoughts and actions, but it may well be (against Gramsci) that it is their *practice* which conforms to the dominant ideology (through rules, custom or habit) while their thoughts and language reveal knowledge and perspectives which have been subjugated or marginalised by the dominant power. It is also likely that in 'abnormal times' or times of crisis the discourses of dominated groups will become more direct and the political interests more clearly articulated (for example, during the Victorian nurses' strike of 1987 or more recently with the mass expression of grief at the death of Diana, Princess of Wales, and the anger at the seeming indifference or lack of expression of grief from the British Royal Family).

Ultimately, the view of power developed in this approach is one which holds that hegemony at the level of knowledge, ideology and practice is never total and that subjugated knowledges and practices survive buried, hidden or at the margins within the discourses of subordinate groups. These knowledges and practices are often revealed in disguised forms in normal times and in more direct forms in times of crises. This, then, is an approach which holds that agents are capable of knowing, of expressing and hence of working towards the clarification and identification of their own interests and of acting collectively towards self-emancipation. In this way, we are able to use the insights provided by Lukes's 'three-dimensional' view of power, while at the same time avoiding the trap of having the interests of dominated groups 'other ascribed'. It also gives us a way to view a conflict of interests in the absence of any overt or covert conflict. Through an analysis of nursing and medical discourses, we are able to view the process whereby some discourses are promoted (structure as 'enabling') and others are submerged or marginalised as inferior or dangerous (structure as repressive). This may happen in the wider society or within an organisation such as a school or hospital. We are also able to view the way that, over time, discourses attain positions of pre-eminence and work to constitute, reinforce or, paradoxically, to undermine the very power structures which facilitated their rise to dominance.

To summarise, existing approaches to nurses, nursing work and the relationship between nurses and doctors have provided valuable historical detail and, more recently, different and important analyses of the operation of class and gender relations in the formation of the occupation of nursing and of the nurse/doctor relationship. They have, however, left many questions unasked and therefore many questions unanswered. In particular, a focus on the power of patriarchal social structure has had the effect of constructing both historical and present-day nurses as either victims of, or misguided handmaidens to, the dominant medical power. Even those approaches which have attempted to acknowledge some autonomous social action on the part of nurses have invariably ended up seeing them as victims to their own ambitious and self-serving leaders. By bringing together several theoretical traditions and concepts, an approach has been developed which is capable of holding on to a sense of the power of social structure, at the same time as acknowledging that nurses also have power in their daily work, in the knowledge base that underpins their work and through their professional organisations and unions to resist, evade and confront that power. In this book we will look both historically and currently at some of the themes and discourses which have been both a structuring cause and experiential effect of the social practice of doctors and nurses living and working and making their histories.

Chapter 2

Nurses making nursing

Before looking at the work which nurses and doctors perform in a modern hospital today, I want to explore the historical background to the knowledge base, training and practice of modern medicine and modern nursing and do so within the theoretical framework set out in Chapter 1. While both medicine and nursing have their own histories, the two occupations became indelibly 'grafted' together with the rise, in the nineteenth century, of the modern teaching hospital. This provided both new opportunities and new restrictions on nursing autonomy and work. To fully understand the modern nursing profession, its realities, aspirations and restrictions, it is necessary to come to terms with its complex and multi-layered history and particularly its history with medicine. In order to understand this history, I approach it through five historical themes which have had profound and long-lasting effects on both occupations. Indeed, it will be seen in the chapters that follow that these themes continue to influence both the internal shapes of modern nursing and medicine as well as the ongoing relationship between the two occupations. Relations of gender are interwoven within each of these five themes, sometimes explicitly, and sometimes hidden from view. But it is not enough to assert that gender is at the heart of relations between doctors and nurses simply because medicine dominates nursing. It is essential that we come to terms with the complex ways that gender enters into and constitutes the attitudes, habits, knowledges and everyday practices of the private and working lives of men and women—in this case, men and women who work with and care for the sick, injured and dying. An exploration of the following themes will assist our understanding of the historical background of medicine and nursing which in turn enhances our sociological understanding of present day realities.

The **first** theme consists of discourses of domination which arose from the new knowledges and practices associated with the scientific revolution of the seventeenth century.

The **second** theme, which was made possible by the first, is the theme of bodies as machines. This theme will be examined for the impact it has had on medical knowledge and practice.

The **third** is a theme of connectedness (or organicism/holism) which has existed and continues to exist alongside and in tension with the first two. In its application to health and illness this theme can be recognised as a discourse of healing.

The **fourth** theme concerns the application of this discourse of healing inherent in a type of practice which has been called Bedside Medicine.

The **fifth** and final theme consists of an examination of the institutional arrangements which impeded the autonomy of nurses and inhibited their practice of bedside healing.

The rest of this chapter is devoted to outlining these themes and examining their expression within the knowledge and practices of nursing and medicine. It is important to understand these historical dimensions because they have shaped the knowledge base, training and work practices of the two occupations and because of their continuing effect on the direct care of patients today. While healing discourses are still evident within modern medicine, they exist at the margins rather than at the centre, made illegitimate by the dominant discourses of science and objectivism. Within nursing, however, they have flourished, protected and nourished by the imperatives of the personal contact which is at the heart of the day-to-day work of nurses. Within these five themes, each of which is made up of various discourses, there are tensions which are both historical and contemporary. In this chapter I will explore some of the historical dimensions of these discourses and the impact

that they have had and continue to have on modern nursing
and medicine and the sexual division of labour between the
two occupations.

THEME 1: DISCOURSES OF DOMINATION

The scientific revolution of the seventeenth century was to have
profound effects on every imaginable form of knowledge
including, as we shall see, knowledge concerning health and
disease. Central to the emergence of a new scientific knowledge
and scientific practice is the figure of Francis Bacon (1561–
1626), often referred to as the 'father of modern science'. In
conventional accounts of Bacon's contributions to science,
emphasis is placed on the positive effects of the Baconian
inductive method, his proposals for the prototype of the
modern research institute and his marrying of theoretical science with commerce, trade and technology (Farrington 1949;
Rossi 1968). More recently his ideas have been examined by
feminist writers from the perspective of 'nature, women, and
the lower orders of society' and this has produced a more
complex picture (Merchant 1982; Keller 1985; Lloyd 1984).

These feminist writers argue that the Baconian discourses
associated with his scientific strategies worked to produce a
new view of nature as passive and exploitable. For Bacon, an
understanding of nature became reduced to a quest for understanding the patterns in which matter is organised in
accordance with knowable, mechanical laws. For Bacon, the
greater our knowledge and understanding of these laws, the
greater the potential to control, dominate and exploit nature.
The means to knowledge and therefore power is through
scientific method which is capable of 'the restitution and
reinvesting of man to the sovereignty and power . . . which he
had in his first state of creation' (Bacon, quoted in Keller,
1985:35). For Bacon, the means to achieve this is overlain with
sexual metaphor. According to Bacon:

> The new man of science must not think that the 'inquisition
> of nature is in any part interdicted or forbidden'. Nature
> must be 'bound into service' and made a 'slave', put 'in
> constraint' and 'moulded' by the mechanical arts. The

'searchers and spies of nature' are to discover her plots and
secrets. (Merchant 1982:169)

His metaphorical style was a powerful political instrument
which served to transform the earth from 'a nurturing mother
and womb of life into a source of secrets to be extracted for
economic advance' (Merchant 1982:165). At this time, the
character of the natural philosopher changed from a person
who approached nature with respect and awe to a scientist,
whose aim was to dominate, control and manipulate nature.
For Merchant, the process of devaluing nature and women by
association meant that the old, Renaissance 'organic' philosophies were also devalued and marginalised.

Common to all the traditional organic philosophies was the
premise of a vital cosmos whose parts were connected and
inter-related as a living entity. Della Porta (1535–1615)
expressed this world view, also known as vitalism, with the
words: 'The whole world is knit and bound within itself: for
the world is a living creature, everywhere both male and
female, and the parts of it do couple together . . . by reason
of their mutual love' (quoted in Merchant 1982:104). According to this perspective, all parts of this world are imbued with
life; metals as well as plants and animals. This common bond-
ing of the world's parts also implied mutual suffering as well
as mutual nourishment and growth: 'When one part suffers,
the rest also suffer with it' (Della Porta quoted in Merchant,
1982:104). While both the nurturing and domination discourses had long co-existed in philosophy, religion and
literature, the advance of the scientific revolution facilitated the
spread of the dominion metaphor beyond religion and into the
social and political spheres.[1]

In this way, the sixteenth century concept of the cosmos as
living, sentient and organic was transmuted into a mechanistic
universe. By the seventeenth century life and vitality had been
sacrificed for a world filled with dead and passive matter. For
Merchant, who carefully chronicles and interprets the struggles
within and between these discourses, the removal of animistic,
organic assumptions about the cosmos constituted 'the most
far reaching effect of the Scientific Revolution' (1982:193).
With the ascendancy of this new world view, nature was to
become a vehicle for knowledge and a knowledge of nature

became more important than nature itself: 'Now we govern nature in opinions, but we are thrall unto her in necessities; but if we would be led by her in invention, we should command her in action.' (Bacon, 1597:242) Commanding nature 'in action' was to have effects in every field of human endeavour. From this time on, knowledge was to be gained by observation and experimentation rather than through 'inefficient' philosophical speculation and theorising. While Merchant's focus is on the implications for nature and for women, the struggle and shift between the two approaches was also to have significant and far-reaching implications for knowledges and practices surrounding health and healing.

THEME 2: THE BODY AS A MACHINE

The shift in discourses concerning nature and knowledge opened up new terrain for exploration and discovery. Themes that Bacon had applied to nature in general were picked up by like-minded philosophers and scientists and applied to the human body. Descartes (1595–1650) and later La Metrie (1709–51) are two of the better known exponents of this approach: 'I do not recognise any difference between the machines made by craftsmen and the various bodies that nature alone composes' (Descartes, quoted in Capra 1983:47). La Metrie broke with the mind/body dualism of Descartes and went further to put forward a totally materialistic view of the human body. He denied that humans were any different to animals and he compared humans and animals to intricate clockwork:

> Does one need more . . . to prove that Man is but an
> Animal, or an assemblage of springs which all wind up one
> another in such a way that one cannot say at which point of
> the human circle Nature has begun? . . . Indeed, I am not
> mistaken; the human body is a clock, but immense and
> constructed with such ingenuity and skill that if the wheel
> whose function it is to mark the seconds comes to a halt,
> that of the minutes turns and continues its course. (Capra
> 1983:100)

With these and other writings La Metrie surpassed even

Descartes' mind/body dualism, by denying for humans or animals any spirit or soul or quality of mind that differentiated them in any way from a well designed machine.

Conventional histories of medicine have documented the profound influence that this emerging scientific perspective and method eventually had on medicine (Shyrock 1936:11). The most well known of the early proponents is probably the physician, William Harvey (1578–1657), who applied the mechanistic world view to the specific problem of the circulatory system and explained the phenomenon of blood circulation in purely mechanistic terms. This approach reached a practical apogee in the work of Boerhaave, who has been called the most influential physician of the entire eighteenth century (King 1958:59). Within conventional medical histories much attention is given to Boerhaave, the professor of medicine and chemistry at Leyden University for the first part of the eighteenth century and sometimes referred to as the 'father' of modern, clinical medicine. Boerhaave pioneered what Foucault has called the 'proto-clinic' which was the forerunner to the modern teaching hospital. In this new type of institution, treatment and medical education became inseparable (Foucault 1973:58). This marked an important change from the old style of hospital or hospice which was more a place of sanctuary and care for the sick and dying. In the Boerhaavian clinic at Leyden, patients were selected from the larger hospital population in order to provide students with a representative sample of the major types of diseases for the purposes of study (Gelfand, 1981:169). The influence of the Boerhaavian method should not be underestimated. In 1720, it was pupils of Boerhaave who reformed the University of Edinburgh and set up a teaching hospital on the Leyden model; their example was later followed in London, Oxford, Cambridge and Dublin (Atkinson 1981; Foucault 1973:57). It was really the beginning of the modern teaching hospital that we know today.

In many ways, the writings and practices of Boerhaave can be seen as epitomising the Baconian/Cartesian approach within medicine. According to Boerhaave, a physician should base his knowledge on the data of anatomy, chemistry, mechanics and 'experimental Philosophy'. 'A Fact' (or experiment in the sense he uses it) 'carries conviction along with it, and is indisputable: nothing being more certain than Demonstration from experience' (quoted from King 1958:97). In an acclaimed lecture in 1702, Boerhaave set out the applicability of mechanistic reasoning in medicine. He argued that the 'clear light of truth' was shed by the use of this method and so recommended it to scholars. Nothing else that the age brought forth was so highly praised and approved. Only medicine he saw as lagging behind and needing to be further developed (cited in Rather 1965:119). It comes as little surprise to learn that one of his better known pupils was La Metrie, who was responsible for developing the metaphor of the body as a machine/clock to extremes.

While it is certainly true that the mechanistic discourse eventually permeated every academic field of endeavour, including that of medicine, it is also true that the case of the domination of this discourse is frequently overstated. Capra, for instance, argues:

> The ancient concept of the earth as nurturing mother was radically transformed in Bacon's writings, *and it disappeared completely* as the Scientific Revolution proceeded to replace the organic view of nature with the metaphor of the world as a machine (1983:41, emphasis added).

However, it is clear that no discourse ever disappears entirely. At the same time as some become established in a firm institutional base and become dominant and hegemonic, the discourses they oppose continue to exist, often in marginalised and disguised forms and sometimes for long periods in silence. Keller, for instance, has demonstrated in an applied way the co-existence of different and even opposing discourses within scientific writings (1985). In addition to documenting the strands of Baconian inspired themes of domination and control within science, she provides a fascinating account of the existence of alternative discourses such as those contained in the work of Barbara McClintock, which are based on ideas of interconnectedness and eroticism. Despite early vicissitudes, McClintock (1902–) went on to receive a Nobel prize and numerous other awards for her work on genetic transposition. According to Keller (her biographer), McClintock, however, still feels an outsider in the world of modern biology, not because she is a woman, but because she is a 'philosophical and methodological deviant' (Keller 1985:159). Despite this, her work has not been ignored and provides evidence to support the argument that neither the values nor the ideas of the dominant discourses have been uniformly embraced by the community of working scientists. In other words, the hegemony of the Baconian and Cartesian discourses within science has not been and is not in any sense absolute.

The hegemony of these traditions within medical knowledge and practice can also be seen as an ongoing process which is never finally complete or stable. While certain discourses may for a period of time be hegemonic, this form of domination is always an achievement of power, an achievement based on conflict with oppositional discourses (Macdonell 1986:34). In a period of almost complete hegemony, dominated discourses may come close to 'extinction'. They may take on forms of 'disguise' or remain active but hidden within the dominant discourse. It is also possible to find marginalised and subjugated discourses actually flourishing by remaining unrecognised and unacknowledged and by, in a sense, 'hiding' themselves within the hegemonic discourse. The examples that I examine next make up the third theme to be explored and concern the existence within medical knowledge and practice of opposing discourses which are based broadly on organicist or holistic views of nature and healing. By holistic I am referring to an approach to healing in which the practitioner attempts to work with the mental, emotional, spiritual and somatic aspects of health and illness.[2] These discourses exist alongside, sometimes hidden within and sometimes explicitly situated against, the dominant discourse which is based on principles of mechanics, atomism and images of control and domination. I demonstrate that these oppositional discourses, now marginalised, are based on concepts of holism, ecology and metaphors of nature as nurturing (and sometimes as a nurturing mother).

THEME 3: DISCOURSES OF CONNECTION, ORGANICISM AND HOLISM

Jerome Gaub and the mind/body connection

In the same way that the total dominance of Baconian and Cartesian discourses in science has never been achieved, the voices of holism and organicism and their application in relation to health and medicine have also never been completely silenced. Opposition to the dominant discourses of 'mechanical man' emerged and re-emerged throughout the seventeenth and eighteenth centuries. Opposition was not limited to the fringes of public life but emerged even within the citadels of academic science and medicine. In fact, it is another pupil, and eventual successor of Boerhaave and contemporary of La Metrie, who has left us with a set of discourses which link clearly with the Hippocratic, nature-reverent tradition of the vitalists. In these discourses there is an attempt to refute and break with the Cartesian notion of 'mechanical man' and to re-establish both the mind/body connection and the connection with the power-ful forces of nature. Unlike Boerhaave, Jerome Gaub is rarely mentioned in medical histories. His works are little known and he has become, like the ideas he articulated, marginalised and forgotten. Yet his translator and commentator, L.J. Rather, makes the point that Gaub was not a lone pioneer in the field of mind/body medicine:

> The triumph celebrated by somatic medicine—medicine
> centring almost exclusively on the body as an object of
> scientific study—in the nineteenth century, and in particular
> the importance achieved by pathological anatomy in the new
> form of cellular pathology, to a very great degree *succeeded
> in wiping out recollection of the attention traditionally
> accorded to mind-body relationships.* Hence psychosomatic
> medicine in our time has appeared to many as a new and
> almost unprecedented movement in medical thought. (Rather
> 1965:15, emphasis added)

In his time, Gaub was no isolated or fringe character. He was known throughout Britain and Europe. He belonged to numerous learned societies including the Royal Society of London and the Royal Society of Medicine at Paris and there is evidence of the frequent citation of his opinions (Rather 1965:18). Boerhaave himself invited Gaub to lecture in chemistry and, three years later in 1734, he was appointed Professor of Medicine at Leyden. From this position of authority and influence, Gaub was able to lecture and publish his quite extraordinary corpus.

Very little of Gaub's work has been translated into English. What we have are two essays which were published in the original Latin in the Netherlands in 1747 and 1763. These became available (with a commentary) in English in 1965 (Rather 1965). The essence of Gaub's approach can be appreciated from this subheading from the essay of 1747:

> xi The Physician's Duty is to Care for the Whole Man; Mind and Body are Abstractions (Rather 1965:70).

In this essay, Gaub enters into a discourse which is in opposition to the prevailing Cartesian view of the body. Instead of viewing the body as a machine, Gaub presents a detailed argument concerning the complex interaction of the mind and body in health and disease. It is also clear from the essay of 1763 that he holds to a view of nature and of healing which is firmly in the Hippocratic tradition.

> It is, then, rightly taught that nature is the physician of diseases and the physician the servant of nature (Rather 1965:168).

Elsewhere he states:

> Shall I lament the dull credulity of those who mistrust nature and the art that is her minister, but are ready to entrust life and health—which ought to be man's most precious possessions—to windy quacks, nostrum vendors and barber surgeons . . . (Rather 1965:128).

It is in the second essay that Gaub enlarges on his theme concerning the connectedness of the mind and body. Reading the subheadings in this essay is akin to skim-reading a 'new age' tome in a modern 'alternative' bookshop. A list of some of the most notable headings and subheadings will serve to illustrate the point.

> Harmful Effects of Suppressed Anger on the Body
> Harmful Effects of Grief on the Body
> Harmful Corporeal Effects of Terror
> Harmful Corporeal Effects of Unrequited Love
> Beneficial Corporeal Effects of Hope in Connection with
>   Various Ailments
> Beneficial Corporeal Effects of Joy, Faith and Love
> Corporeal Effects of Expressed and Suppressed Emotions
>   Compared
> Anger as a Therapeutic Agent

The Role of the Mind and the Emotions in the Cause and
Cure of Bodily Disease

and finally:

The Physician's Difficulties and Limitations (Rather
1965:139–196).

While we may be surprised at the existence of such a
'modern' approach within medicine as long as two centuries
ago, it is important to remember that making connections
between emotional states and bodily effects was a conventional
and indeed common approach in eighteenth century medicine
(Rather 1965:13; Duden 1991). The fact that it appears so
novel today is a testimony to the success of mechanistic discourses and the subjugation and marginalisation of alternatives.

The process of conflict between these discourses was neither
subterranean nor simply implicit. It was open and frequently
hostile. Gaub, for example, begins the second essay of 1763
with a spirited attack on the writer of *Man a Machine*, La
Metrie.

I do indeed regret bitterly that a little Frenchman—a Mimus
or Momus?—brought forth a repulsive offering, to wit, his
mechanical man, not long after sitting before this chair and
hearing me speak, and did this in such a way that it seemed
to many people that I had furnished him with, if not sparks
for his flame, at least matter for embellishing his monstrosity.
(Gaub quoted in Rather 1965:115)

It appears that La Metrie had been present during the oration
for the first essay in 1747 and had, with others, 'borrowed
certain illustrative material' from Gaub's lecture and used it to
support his own thesis (Rather 1965:117). After this attack on
La Metrie and the Cartesian perspective, Gaub proceeded to
present in detail his own alternative approach on the connection between the mind and body. It is important not to see the
conflict between Gaub and La Metrie as simply a struggle
between two 'great men'. The conflict between Gaub and La
Metrie was profoundly also a conflict between two opposing
and contradictory discourses. The anti-mechanistic approach
articulated by Gaub can be seen to have connections with the
vitalist tradition within philosophy and the organicist and
nature-reverent Hippocratic tradition within medicine. The

work of this eighteenth century medical academic is a good illustration of the way a discourse can be prominent at one time, almost disappear for a time in which it becomes invisible or exists only on the 'fringe' and then reappear as though emerging for the first time. Throughout this process, the discourse will be engaged, as we have seen, successfully or unsuccessfully in a struggle with other discourses.

In this instance, we have a picture of two professors of medicine (Boerhaave and Gaub), sequentially tenured, at Leyden University who articulate and constitute two opposing world views concerning health, nature and healing. We are witness, in a sense, to a rather long and extended turning point whereby one framework is gaining both popular and institutional primacy over another. In the process, there are many instances where the nature-reverent discourses reassert themselves and emerge within the dominant discourse or are absorbed and transmuted (see, for example, King 1974; Le Fanu 1972; Benton 1974; Brown 1974). In conventional medical histories, this is often presented as evidence of the 'chaos' of eighteenth century medicine (Shyrock, 1936:32). It is possible, however, to view this apparent disorganisation as the manifestation of discourses in struggle, a process whereby one framework becomes dominant and widely held, then becomes displaced, absorbed, marginalised and finally re-emerges to engage in struggle at another time in another form. The many forms and interpretations of vitalism in eighteenth century medical theory can be viewed in just this way (Benton 1974; Brown 1974).

Nightingale, nursing and opposing discourses

Challenges to discourses of domination and bodies as machines emerged again strongly in the nineteenth century among social reformers who believed that sanitary reforms and not morbid anatomy were the key to good health in populations. One of the most prominent of these reformers in Britain was Florence Nightingale who is frequently presented as being progressive in relation to public health while remaining deeply conservative around issues of nursing reform and the relationship between medicine and nursing. In fact she is usually presented as the handmaiden to medicine *par excellence*. In relation to nursing reform there is certainly ample evidence from her writings and actions to support a view that her vision was essentially a conservative one. Her writings can appear to be unambiguous about the hierarchical status of the social and professional relationship between the male doctor and female nurse. For instance:

> It is the duty of the Medical Officer to give what orders, in regard to the sick, he thinks fit to the Nurses. And it is unquestionably the duty of the Nurses to obey or to see his orders are carried out. (Nightingale, 1865:14)

And yet it is also possible to discern within her writings other, deeply oppositional, discourses which have remained unexplored. Of special interest is one concerned with an eco- logical or organic view of nature, health and healing. Through this theme it is possible to trace connections to Renaissance organic thought, which itself had roots in Greek concepts of the cosmos as an intelligent organism. Throughout Greek an- tiquity, healing was associated with many deities, two of the most prominent being Hygeia and her sister Panakeia: 'Hygieia ("health") was concerned with the maintenance of health, personifying the wisdom that people would be healthy if they lived wisely. Panakeia ("all healing") specialised in the knowl- edge of remedies, derived from plants or from the earth'. (Capra 1983:339) Together the two deities symbolised the balance between the environment, health and healing. At one level, Nightingale can be seen to follow firmly in this tradition. She begins her famous *Notes on Nursing* with the statement:

> Shall we begin by taking it as a general principle—that all disease, at some period or other of its course, is more or less a reparative process, not necessarily accompanied with suffering: an effort of nature to remedy a process of poisoning or of decay, which has taken place weeks, months, sometimes years beforehand, unnoticed, the termination of the disease being then, while the antecedent process was going on, determined? (Nightingale 1860:1)

With this statement, Nightingale sets the framework for a view of nursing which holds firmly and consistently to an ecological approach to health and healing. It is very much within the Hippocratic tradition, which is based on a convic- tion that disease is a natural phenomenon but one which can be influenced by gentle, therapeutic techniques and by wise management of one's life. Her entire book argues for a wide and autonomous field of practice based on principles of Hygiene (in its classical sense). On her own theoretical terrain, she writes confidently and unhesitatingly about the power of 'kindly nature'. For example, later in the same publication she comments:

> A fashionable physician has recently published in a
> government report that he always turns his patients' faces
> from the light. Yes, but nature is stronger than fashionable
> physicians, and depend upon it she turns the faces back and
> TOWARDS such light as she can get. (1860:71)

Here there is no concession to the 'knowledge and power' of the physician.

She goes on to detail the consequences of a disregard or a misunderstanding of the necessary laws of Hygiene. At the conclusion of this seminal work, she presents her finest tribute to Hygeia:

> And nothing but observation and experience will teach us the
> ways to maintain or to bring back the state of health. It is
> often thought that medicine is the curative process. It is no
> such thing; medicine is the surgery (sic) of functions, as
> surgery proper is that of limbs and organs. Neither can do
> anything but remove obstructions; neither can cure; nature
> alone cures. (1860:110)

And what of nursing? What role does the nurse have in this process? Nightingale states: 'And what nursing has to do in either case, is to put the patient in the best condition for nature to act upon him'. (1860:110) With these and other like statements, Nightingale places herself firmly in the tradition which sees nature as wise and powerful. Her words echo those of Paracelsus, the originator of vitalism, who wrote these words four centuries earlier:

> There is nothing in me except the will to discover the best
> that medicine can do, the best there is in nature, the best that
> the nature of the earth truly intends for the sick. Thus I say,
> nothing comes from me; everything comes from nature of
> which I too am part. (Paracelsus, quoted in Merchant
> 1982:120)

It is possible to see from these excerpts from the work of
Nightingale that the holistic, nature-reverent discourses continued to influence ideas on health and that these ideas were in
opposition to those which held a mechanistic view of the body.
Having examined the three major themes which are a profound
undercurrent of both medical and nursing knowledge, I want
now to explore some of the ways that these competing discourses were expressed in the practice of health care and the
organisation of health care occupations.

Tensions within medical practice

While it is true that the scientific revolution had a significant
impact on anatomical research, it had little immediate impact
on the fundamental features of medical theory and therapy.
Even Sir William Harvey who made such a momentous impact
with his discoveries concerning blood circulation left no printed
evidence of his views on medicine or of his influence on
contemporary practice. This situation continued for most of
the eighteenth century (LeFanu 1972). In fact, in eighteenth
century formal medicine there was no necessary connection
between any theory and practice at all (Shyrock 1936:94). It
was possible and indeed common for medical practitioners to
hold diverse theories concerning disease aetiology, and yet
continue to practise and rely on identical forms of treatment
(King 1958). An interesting illustration of this process is the
work of Broussais (1772–1838).

A significant figure in French post-revolutionary medicine,
Broussais made an important contribution to pathological anatomy by re-interpreting the connection between general
inflammation and local lesion (Foucault 1973:182). But while
he was involved in the key debates of his time concerning the
causes of disease and the expansion of the use of post-mortems,
his practice continued to be firmly based on the old Galenic
concept of the humours. It is an understatement to say that
Broussais was an enthusiastic practitioner of all forms of
bleeding. In her unique work, *A History of Women in Medicine*, Kate Hurd-Mead comments:

> It is said that, while he lived and taught in Paris, every
> person in the country was bled at least once; and that in
> pneumonia nothing but death stopped the work of the lancet.

His treatment for gastro-enteritis was mainly the application of leeches, and often he had the abdomen entirely covered in these creatures. (1938:515)

Broussais was typical of many who were at the forefront of new medical theories and debates, but whose actual practice was locked in the old traditions. At the risk of oversimplification, it could be said that scientific medicine needed industrial capitalism *and* the teaching hospital before it could become coherent in terms of theory and practice and also before it could attain dominance. In order to make sense of the massive re-organisation of health and medical care that resulted in the dominance of the teaching hospital in the nineteenth century, it is necessary first to understand the complexities of eighteenth century medical practice. It is in this very complexity that the seeds of many alternative and marginalised discourses are to be found.

The first thing that strikes the reader of eighteenth century English medical history is the extent of the diversity of medical and healing practices and practitioners. The variety of practitioners who worked in this area included the 'regular' practitioners, physicians, surgeons, apothecaries (it was common, especially after 1847, for practitioners to combine these last two functions and thus create the forerunner to the general practitioner) and the 'irregulars'—empirics, 'wise-women', midwives and nurses (Shyrock 1936; Hurd-Mead 1938; King 1958; Loudon 1986).[3] It is simply not possible to delineate the tasks and functions of these different groups. Nor are we able to divide regulars and irregulars along strict gender lines, although it is clear that women had been excluded from the Royal College of Physicians from the outset (Pelling & Webster 1979). Nevertheless, Hurd-Mead gives several examples of women in the eighteenth century who had practices as a 'physician-accoucheur' who may have lacked formal recognition but who were nevertheless highly regarded for their skills (1938:472). While women were formally excluded from the Company of Barber-Surgeons when it was established in 1800, Clark gives several examples of women, especially in the provinces, who continued to practise as surgeons through the eighteenth century (1919:259). There was a similar situation in regard to the Apothecaries, who were separated from the

Grocers in 1617. In this case, women were prohibited from Company examinations but were admitted to the Company by marriage or apprenticeship. This meant that in eighteenth century England there were a not insignificant number of women, especially widows, who worked as regular practitioners.

It is also not possible to say with certainty which practitioners serviced which particular classes and groups in the population. While Jewson argued that the elite physicians served the upper classes and aristocracy almost exclusively (1974), more recently this view has been challenged by research showing that it was common for physicians, especially in the provinces, to treat a wide variety of patients including housewives, domestics, labourers and shopkeepers (Loudon 1986:226). Indeed, it would seem that there was a considerable interchange of information, functions and practices across the groups. Clark, for instance, provides accounts of a number of instances where patients, including wealthy ones, turned to the services of 'wise women' after the regular practitioners had been unable to help them. At the same time, even ordinary people, who could not be considered wealthy, frequently bought treatment from regular practitioners. Loudon's examination of the diaries, case-books and ledgers of several eighteenth century practitioners suggests that regular practitioners did, in fact, treat a wide variety of patients from different levels of society (Loudon 1986:102). It is possible to imagine that sick people in eighteenth century England moved between regular and irregular practitioners and that this was likely to be dependent on such factors as their own experiences, recommendations from others, availability, cost, and reputation.

THEME 4: BEDSIDE MEDICINE

The question of *how* this range of practitioners treated people is as important as the issue of *who* treated them. In an attempt to organise the material on contrasting types of medical treatment, some writers have developed the concept of mode of production in relation to different styles and types of medical knowledge and practice (Jewson 1974; 1976; Berliner 1982).

Jewson in particular has introduced the notion of three specific modes of production of medical knowledge which he calls Bedside Medicine, Hospital Medicine and Laboratory Medicine (See also Ackerknecht 1967:15). He argues that Bedside Medicine was the dominant type of medicine in eighteenth century England and was characterised by a relationship between wealthy, powerful patients and less wealthy, lower status physicians. This relative difference in wealth and status meant that it was the patient who held the power in the consultative relationship. In this relationship the patient became, in a real sense, the patron of the physician who had to defer to the demands of his patron in order to maintain and extend his livelihood (1976:234). This in turn acted as an imperative for the practitioner to undertake 'showy', heroic remedies in order to impress the patron.

In tandem with the concept of Bedside Medicine, Jewson also developed the concept of *medical cosmology* and argued that different modes of production are associated with different medical cosmologies, which he defines as 'conceptual structures which constitute the frame of reference within which all questions are posed and all answers are offered'; he also agrees that they bear a close resemblance to Foucault's concept of a 'discursive field' (1976:225, 240). He argues that the medical cosmology associated with Bedside Medicine emphasised 'the conscious human totality of the sick person', distinguishing it as an organicist model which was 'person oriented' and therefore at odds with the mind/body dualist 'cosmology' of Descartes and the mechanicists. Further, it located illness in the context of the whole body system rather than in any particular organ or tissue. Indeed, in the period of Bedside Medicine, cosmological analogies emphasised an image of the person as a living entity which was akin to the wider living universe. In this sense, it opposed 'object oriented' medicine which is characterised by a concentration on the disease. Finally, in addition to the patient's physical disposition, all aspects of their social, emotional and spiritual life were deemed relevant to the understanding of their constitution.

I am adopting Jewson's concept of Bedside Medicine with one fundamental difference. In his work, Jewson infers that his 'deference' model of patron/physician Bedside Medicine applies generally to medical practice in England. At the same time, we have seen that there is an assumption in his work that it was only the wealthy who could afford a regular practitioner. It is therefore inferred that all other classes of people made do with irregular practitioners, and that their forms of consultation either followed the 'deference' model or some other model(s) which is not specified but is not of significance (presumably because it is the physicians who are the 'leaders' and the elite in the medical world). This is a 'top down' view of history and, while an important contribution, it ignores the fact that these other classes made up the vast majority of the population and were therefore not insignificant.

The type of medical and healing practices that took place at the other levels of society is equally interesting. It is possible to speculate that a type of medical practice—I will call it bedside healing—was characteristic of a significant proportion of *all* practitioners, formal and informal, in eighteenth century England and was not just a characteristic of the relations between the elite physicians and their upper-class clients. Used in this way, bedside healing was not inevitably marked by the use of heroic remedies. Rather, bedside healing included an organicist medical cosmology and the knowledge and practice of both formal medicine and informal healers, especially herbalists (Shyrock 1936:74). This resulted in healing practices that were sometimes heroic, sometimes gentle and caring and frequently contradictory. They were, in essence, the embodiment and expression of cosmologies or discourses in struggle. This is important in that it demonstrates that there were conflicting tendencies, discourses and practices both *within* medicine as well as *between* medicine and other healing modalities such as those offered by the women healers.

This view opposes others which hold that it was only the wealthy, upper classes who could afford health care from regular practitioners, while the bulk of the population received health care from informal, women healers. It has been argued that it was the 'male professionals who clung to untested doctrines and ritualistic practices' while the women healers adopted 'a more humane, empirical approach to healing' (Ehrenreich & English 1973:4). While this may well have been true in many instances, it is something of a romanticised over-generalisation of the whole picture, which is more complex. People at all levels of society, including the very poor, did at times receive health and medical care from the regular, male practitioners (Loudon 1986:242). At the same time, there were many instances of upper-class patients receiving medical care from women healers and other irregulars (Clark 1919:257–8). As to the type of care delivered, it is true that while the women healers appear to have commonly adopted an approach to health care that was both 'empirical' and holistic, male empirics were also a significant group within medicine (Shyrock 1936:74). There also existed within the formal, male medicine of the apothecaries in particular, tendencies toward a holistic medical cosmology and a caring practice.

Bedside healing: published evidence

The evidence to support the view outlined above is harder to find than that concerning the use of heroic remedies for the upper classes (on these remedies, see, for example, King 1958). Nevertheless, there have been in recent years several publications based on diaries, correspondence and journals which provide rich and valuable insights into different aspects of eighteenth century life, including sickness and health care. While some of these are from medical practitioners, others are from patients and their family members. There is also evidence to be found in medical texts and commentaries. One of them is a significant work by James Makittrick (1728–1802) in *Commentaries on the Principle and Practice of Physick*. Here, he sets out the responsibilities of the Master who takes on an apprentice in surgery or apothecary. Makittrick recommended a proper syllabus of training for the apprentice. Through these recommendations, it is possible to view a holistic medical cosmology in action. He recommends that in his third year, the apprentice should attend his master to the patient's bedside where he should make notes of:

> the patients mode of life, his profession, the situation of his dwelling, the season of the year and preceding and present state of the weather; together with an accurate account of his former state of health, the probable cause of the disease, and his habit of body. He should then enter into an inquiry on the symptoms, and this he ought to do with some regularity, beginning generally with the vital functions, proceeding to the

natural, and from thence to the animal functions and
qualities. (Makittrick, quoted in Loudon 1986:45)

He goes on to advise that the apprentice must also be
taught to have humanity towards his patients and look after
the poor. In terms of personal qualities, the apprentice should
cultivate 'prudence, decency of manners, candour and circum-
spection' (Loudon 1986:45). As this was a widely used text, it
is possible to see that an approach based on bedside healing
was a significant influence on the lower orders of practitioner
and not one exclusive to either the wise women or the physicians.

There is other evidence concerning the existence of a healing cosmology within formal, male medicine which is contained
in the self-help and advice books which were popular in the
eighteenth century. Some of these early works dealt with pre-
ventive medicine, in particular the practice of 'regimen'.
Regimen consisted of a system of living and illness prevention
based on the 'non-naturals' of air, diet, sleep, exercise, evacu-
ations and passions of the mind, as originally laid down in
orthodox Greek hygiene (Smith 1985:257). While a good proportion of these works were written by lay people and informal
healers, many more arose within formal medicine from groups
of practitioners, especially general practitioners, who were critical of professional monopoly and excessive drugging practices.
Interestingly, many writers referred to regimen as 'nursing', as
with Hugh Smith who wrote in 1770: '[G]ood nursing is a part
which has either been too much neglected, or mistaken; nevertheless it is of first consequence in the cure of diseases, and
the preserving of delicate and feeble constitutions'. (H. Smith
1770, quoted in G. Smith 1985:275)

A year earlier, William Buchan had mounted a rigorous and
successful attack on the dangers of professional monopoly and
the need for a fundamental change in therapy. In his *Domestic
Medicine*, he attempted to give professional credibility to
hygienic prophylaxis, or *nursing*, which he considered to be a
neglected area of therapeutics. It was an attempt to re-focus
both patients and practitioners towards hygiene and illness
prevention:

In the treatment of disease, I have been particularly attentive
to regimen. The generality of people lay too much stress upon

Medicine, and trust too little to their own endeavours . . . physicians, as well as other people, are too little attentive to this matter. This part of Medicine is evidently found in Nature, and is in every way consistent with Reason and common sense. Had men been more attentive to it, and less solicitous in hunting after secret remedies, Medicine had never become an object of ridicule. (Buchan 1769, quoted in Smith 1985:276)

While still a significant thread within formal medicine, these nature-reverent discourses were increasingly being relegated to the margins, and Buchan was frequently attacked by fellow practitioners on both academic and scientific grounds and for revealing 'trade secrets' with insufficient cautions.

Bedside healing in practice

It is also possible to view holistic and caring tendencies in the actions and attitudes of practising apothecaries and apothecary/surgeons of the eighteenth century. Many comments from the diaries and correspondence of eighteenth century patients indicate that the care these people received from regular male practitioners could be humane and caring and was not necessarily based on a self-serving desire to impress. For instance, one diarist noted that despite the fact that her sister had died, 'The Doctor's kindness and attention ought never to be forgotten'. Another diarist, Judith Milbanke, wrote in 1782 of an attentive though unnamed apothecary whose efforts 'certainly saved Sophy's life and he sat up with her all night and nursed her as if she had been his own Child' (Lane 1985, p. 232).

From the diary of Richard Kay, an eighteenth century apothecary/surgeon, we get a picture of a hard-working and compassionate man (Loudon 1986:116). Kay makes many references to dividing the day with his father, a fellow practitioner who usually saw patients at home while Kay 'rode abroad' to visit patients in their homes. Kay often returned late from such rounds only to be called out again, as on 24 April 1746 when having

returned home this Evening betwixt 10 and 11 o' th' clock and not many Minutes afterwards [I] was sent for to visit a Person who was seized very bad this Evening in his Belly, waited on him till three o' th' clock this morning.

Kay frequently travelled many miles on horseback to visit patients in the night, sometimes to stay for hours and sometimes until the next morning, not leaving until he was sure that the patient was either improving or that there was nothing more he could do. His own comments indicate that he felt and cared for the people he saw:

> [I]n the course of my business [I] have frequently to deal with Persons where their disorders are attended with favourable and many Times with unhappy Circumstances; I am not an idle Spectator, an unconcerned Visitor, when I see the Afflictions and Distresses of my Neighbours and fellow Creatures; yet the Lord hath hitherto in some good Measure helped me; by his Grace I am what I am. (Quoted in Loudon 1986:117)

The point of this evidence is not to show that these attitudes and this type of practice was typical of eighteenth century male, formal practitioners. There is ample evidence to show that treatment from male practitioners could be uncomfortable, painful, useless and seemingly heartless (King 1958:297; Clark 1919:258; Lane 1985:219, 221, 237). The point is to dispute accounts which argue that male medical practice was *necessarily* inhumane and uncaring. It is clear that a healing cosmology, and a 'person oriented' and caring practice, was a significant if not a dominant trend in eighteenth century male medical practice. It is as essential to understand these contradictory tendencies in the constitution of modern medicine as it is to understand the tensions implicit in the foundation of modern nursing. It is the antecedents of modern nursing that I now explore.

Nurses and bedside healing

The first point to be made in relation to nursing is that nursing did exist as a paid occupation prior to its supposed 'invention' in the nineteenth century. From the ledger of William Pulsford, a provincial surgeon from Somerset, we have an account of routine daily practice from 1757 to the early 1760s. It is apparent from the ledger that much of the work of the practice revolves around the treatment of chronic problems such as leg ulcers and chronic infections. It is also apparent that from time to time, the surgeon employed a nurse to assist with the treatments (Loudon 1986:77). This is not to say that nurses only existed in paid employment to doctors. Clark provides several accounts of women, some of them nurses, who provided independent services earlier in the century (1919, p. 256). In rural districts, where there were few hospitals, fairly regular entries can be found in the parish account books of payments made to women for nursing the poor. For instance, from the account book of Cowden, 1704:

> To Goody Halliday, for nursing him and his family 5 weeks £1.5; to Goody Nye, for assisting in nursing, 2s. 6d . . . to Goody Peckham for nursing a beggar, 5s. For nursing Wickham's boy with the small pocks 12s. (Clark 1919:251)

There are numerous other examples of well-to-do people engaging the services of nurses for themselves, for their servants and for the needy poor (1919:251).

Clark also provides accounts of upper-class women who engaged in activities which were identified as nursing. For instance, a diary entry from the Rev. R. Josselin on 27 January 1672 states:

> My L. Honeywood sent her coach for me: I stayd to March 10, in which time my Lady was my nurse and Phisitian and I hope for much good: . . . they considered scurvy. I tooke purge and other things for it (1919:257).

From a history of the Verney family published in 1647, Clark quotes Sir Ralph Verney who writes to his wife and advises her: '[to] give the child no phisick but such as midwives and old women, with the doctors approbation, doe prescribe; for assure yourselfe that by experience know better than any phisition how to treat such infants' (1919:258).

Any mention of sick babies and children in the records of regular practitioners was relatively rare and this suggests the treatment and care of this group was likely to have been in the hands of women 'local irregulars'. This impression is reinforced by the virtual exclusion of children from the care of hospitals and dispensaries of the eighteenth century (Loudon 1986:15). It is interesting to note that in both these quotes there is a description which involves more than one single category, that is, nurse/physician and midwives/old women. There is other evidence to suggest that the women irregulars moved across the different health care categories. Loudon, for instance, cites a source that supports the view that midwives in the early part of the eighteenth century were seldom fully employed in midwifery alone. He concludes that it was indeed probable that women combined the roles of healer (especially of babies and children), nurse, midwife and layer-out of the dead (1986:16). Other evidence to support the view that nurses both co-existed with and worked as healers and/or midwives is provided by the regulars, with their written admonitions against the irregulars. The surgeon, Coltheart, was one of many early eighteenth century practitioners who wrote with venom against the 'Coal-Porter, Tinker, Taylor, Midwife, Nurse, etc. [who] spring up like Mushrooms in a night to be Physicians and Surgeons' (quoted in Loudon 1986:14).

While there is a paucity of material on the actual practice of healing and nursing by women, there is evidence that it was marked by a cautious and conservative approach to therapeutics and one which relied on regimen, herbs and basic physical care where this was necessary (Hurd-Mead 1938:513; Lane 1985:219). While we have seen that bedside healing was not exclusive to women healers and midwives, there is evidence that it was a major part of their overall approach (Hurd-Mead 1938:473; Hughes 1943:61). There is extensive evidence of and references to the connection between wise women and the use of herbs and other natural products for the treatment of illness (Hurd-Mead 1938; Clark 1919; Hughes 1943; Porter 1987; Shyrock 1936). There is also evidence to support the view that many of these herbal remedies were taken up and included into the *materia medica* of formal medicine. Digitalis and cinchona bark (later known as 'quinine') are two of many possible examples. However, there are often artificial categories established for supposed different types of women healers. Hughes, for instance, in *Women Healers in Medieval Life and Literature*, has separate categories for 'Medieval Nurses' and 'Lay Women Healers'. However, when we read in detail what women from both these categories actually did, we see that the only basis for such a distinction is the fact that one group belonged to a religious order and the other group did not. Yet the popular (and academic) view is that women healers were the unofficial, unsung, autonomous health workers who provided health care for the majority of the population well into

the eighteenth century, while nurses were little more than
domestic servants or hospital workers of the 'lowest class'
(Versluysen 1980:185; Clark 1919:249).

In order to counter this view, it is worth looking in some
detail at the work of medieval religious nurses. From accounts
of the treasurer of Abingdon Abbey, we find that the infirmar-
ian secured from an apothecary, through one of the lay sisters,
'the oils, vinegars, wines, and drugs with which she mixed
medicaments' (quoted in Hughes 1943:127). Physicians were
to be summoned only for a very serious case—and sometimes
not at all. Hughes comments that: 'Since the lay sisters were
free to extend their services beyond the nunnery, some of them
won reputations as healers among the villagers near the con-
vent' (1943:130).

It is also apparent that the skills of these religious nurses
were not limited to treating the body as against the whole
person. The 'calming of Bertrand' (a hysterical child, brought
to the sisters for treatment) is a graphic example of the way
psychodynamic techniques were incorporated into their healing
repertoire at a time when there was no separate language to
describe such actions (1943:130).

Hughes's remarks at the end of her section on lay women
healers could equally apply to the nurses of the religious orders:

> Evidently these medieval women had acquired a good deal of
> sound elementary knowledge as to the treatment of wounds
> and sores, based on experience. They knew the importance of
> rest and sleep, the efficacy of hot baths and herbal
> concoctions. Some of them could treat a dislocated shoulder
> or a broken bone. And most of them were not bothered by
> the erudite hocuspocus which was the stock-in-trade of their
> professional brethren. (1943: 130)

The archives of both St Thomas's and St Bartholomew's
hospitals (London) also contain rich material on women and
healing work. At St Bartholomew's, the Minutes of the Board
of Governors contain references to payments made to women
who were either employed on a regular basis or paid to effect
particular cures. The Minute Book for 1549–61 contains references to payments for four women, Elizabeth Hall, Frances
Holcombe (later Worth), Katherine Elsum and Anne Harris,
who were appointed to treat skin conditions, in particular,

'scald heads' (apparently a type of ringworm). The amounts paid to these women surely reflect a high regard for the efficacy of their treatments. For instance, Francis Worth held office in 1635 and was paid £125 while Katherine Elsum held office in 1642 and received £126 (Minutes of the Board of Governors, 1549–61, St Bartholomew's Hospital). At St Thomas's there are frequent references to payments for treatments from 'outsiders'. A woman mentioned more than once was Mother Edwin, who, in the year 1561–62 was paid to treat 'a boye that is burstin' (a boy with a hernia). She was to receive 13/4 and 'when the child is whole and perfectly cured' another 6/8. She undertook to restore the money if 'she did not cure the boy of his disease'. There is no record of a refund but a year later there is a record of further funds paid to her for the making of a truss (Minutes of the Court of Governors, St Thomas's Hospital, 1561–62).

On the basis of this and other evidence, it is really not possible to strictly delineate different categories of female carers and healers. There is simply no consistency of usage or description in the literature concerning different categories of nurses, midwives and women healers. It is entirely possible that women themselves used different titles depending on market advantage, legal restrictions and personal preference and identification. There is, however, evidence of some consistency in their mode of operation. On the whole, these nurses, carers, healers and midwives worked or lived in the homes of the people they were treating. The evidence we have points to the fact they worked within a framework or cosmology which took into account the person in the context of their physical environment and lived experience. They did not treat the sick person in a way that was consistent with a view of the body as a machine but used herbs extensively to aid and abet the healing powers of nature. Where necessary and appropriate they sat by the sick person's bed to watch and wait and to provide essential, basic care. Like some of the formal and informal male practitioners of the period, they practised bedside healing. This type of practice and its associated cosmology was the result of both the personal agency of the practitioner (as we saw with Richard Kay) and structural constraints and freedoms including the fact that, as a general rule, the care was practised in the sick person's own home.

Hospital nurses

At the same time, it is clear that there were also nurses working in hospitals during the sixteenth, seventeenth and eighteenth centuries. Alice Clark provides much interesting documentation concerning nurses who worked in hospitals in the seventeenth century. In relation to hospital nursing as an occupation, she argues that nursing 'appeared as a sordid duty, only fit for the lowest class in the community' (1919:249). The evidence she provides certainly shows that these nurses were poorly paid and highly regulated. At the Savoy in London there were numerous regulations concerning the personal and professional behaviour of nurses. For instance:

> If any of the nurses . . . shalbee negligent in their duties or in giving due attendance to the . . . sicke souldiers by daye or night or shall by scoulding, bawlinge or chidinge make any disturbance in the said hospital, she shall forfeite 12d. for first offence, week's pay for second, be dismissed for the third. (1919:249)

At St Bartholomew's during the reign of Edward VI there were at least as many regulations, including one which stated: '. . . and so much as in you shall lie, ye shall avoid and shun the Conversation and Company of all Men' (1919:244). It is clear that an emphasis on personal qualities and regulations concerning the nurse's personal life were not invented by the Nightingale system! However, the view that hospital nursing was work 'only fit for the lowest class' is countered by other evidence. In his fine history of St Bartholomew's, Moore quotes Sir James Paget who gave an address to the Abernethian Society at St Bartholomew's in 1885. In his address, Paget reflects on the improvements in nursing that he has witnessed in his time. It is a passage worth quoting:

> It is true, that even fifty years ago there were some excellent nurses, especially among the sisters in the medical wards, where everything was more gentle and orderly than in the surgical. They had none of the modern art; they could not have kept a chart or skilfully taken a temperature, but they had an admirable sagacity and a sort of rough practical knowledge which were nearly as good as any acquired skill. An old Sister Rahere was the chief among them, stout, ruddy, positive, very watchful. She once taught an erring house

surgeon where and how to compress a posterior tibial artery;
she could always report correctly the progress of a case; and
from her wages she saved all she could and left it in legacy
to the hospital. (Paget quoted in Moore 1918, vol. II:775)

In this same address, Paget calls on another description of
a hospital nurse written some sixty years earlier than the one
above (taking us back to around 1775). He quotes his source
as saying that the nurse:

had scarce given herself time to tell me, 'she would be my
nurse' when she hastily turned about to begin the office of
one, and prepare something for me; and in a short time,
though I thought it a long one, she came back with flannels,
etc etc. and having fomented my knee soundly for a couple of
hours etc, and made me a basin of thin gruel for my supper,
she wished me rest, and promised to be with me early in the
morning. (Paget quoted in Moore 1918, vol. II:776)

These are hardly descriptions of the drunken slatterns commonly believed to inhabit the 'dark ages' of nursing. Indeed,
what we have here are several very different pictures of pre-
Nightingale nurses. As with the regular male practitioners, one
is struck by the degree of the diversity of their backgrounds,
level of skill, level of autonomy and reputations. It is fair to
say that, in general, nursing/medical histories present one or
other of these 'pictures' depending on the perspective they wish
to develop (Williams 1980). The radical history of women
healers developed by Ehrenreich and English takes the position
that nursing was 'invented' in the nineteenth century and that
before that a nurse was 'simply a women who happened to be
nursing someone—a sick child or an aging relative' (1973:35).
This is part of their general argument that nursing emerged as
the expression of the defeat of the 'wise women'. Yet we have
seen that nurses co-existed with the wise women and indeed
were sometimes interchangeable with them. We have also seen
that women called themselves nurses and were called and
documented as nurses by others who paid them for their work.
More conventional histories, on the other hand, frequently
acknowledge the existence of nurses before Nightingale, but
present them only as lower-class servants or slatterns who
worked in the hospitals of the period (Clark, 1919; Abel-Smith
1975). In these accounts the emphasis is on the positive trans-

formation wrought by Nightingale and a comparison of 'before' and 'after'.

Is there a 'real' story of the origins of nursing? Which one of these 'pictures' of nursing is the true one? Each is partially true as a reconstruction of pre-nineteenth century nursing. Each portrayal—nurse as a skilled wise woman and healer, nurse as doctor's assistant, nurse as a poorly paid and regarded hospital worker—was a reality for the nurses working in these capacities with their different sets of freedoms and restrictions, and each became embedded in the 'reformed' occupation of nursing and the reorganised division of labour with doctors. In the same way, pre-nineteenth century medicine was neither uniformly callous and heroic nor effective and caring. It was a series of knowledges and practices imbued with conflict and contradiction. Not the least of these was the tension between healing models and practices, on the one hand, and the momentum towards mechanistic models and technocratic, scientific medicine on the other. The practical expression of these two traditions becomes apparent when we see how they became incorporated into aspects of the work processes of nursing and medicine within the modern teaching hospital.

Conflicting discourses and conflicting practices: challenges to bedside medicine

The concept and practice of 'observation' of the sick is a good example of the tensions involved in the practical expression of the different traditions. From the perspective of a healing model, Nightingale is quite clear about why observation is necessary. She is also clear on the dangers involved when an activity becomes an end in itself or 'fodder' for the scientific process. She details her approach in a chapter from *Notes on Nursing* titled 'Observation of the sick':

> In dwelling upon the vital importance of sound observation, it must never be lost sight of what observation is for. It is not for the sake of piling up miscellaneous or curious facts, but for the sake of saving life and increasing health and comfort. The caution may seem useless, but it is quite surprising how many men (some women too), practically behave as if the scientific end were the only one in view, or as if the sick body were but a reservoir for stowing medicines into, and the

surgical disease only a curious case the sufferer has made for
the attendant's special information. (Nightingale 1860:103)

For Nightingale, observation involved watching and waiting for the cues of nature, so that healing and patient comfort
could be achieved through a co-operative effort. Contrast this
with the almost joyous anticipation of Pinel, best known as a
reformer of Bicetre mental asylum but also an important figure
in the 'new', post-revolutionary medicine of France:

> What a source of instruction is provided by two infirmaries
> of 100 to 150 patients! . . . What a varied spectacle of fevers
> or phlegmasias, malign or benign, sometimes highly developed
> in strong constitutions, sometimes in a slight, almost latent,
> condition, together with all the forms and modifications that
> age, mode of life, seasons, and more or less energetic moral
> affections can offer! (Pinel 1815, quoted in Foucault 1973:109)

Foucault has examined the way that the 'birth' of the
clinic—the teaching hospital—allowed the medical 'gaze' to see
in a way that was not possible under the old codes of knowledge (1973:196). In France, centralised state control and
ownership made possible a rapid and dramatic expansion of
the teaching hospital (Waddington 1973:212). By 1830, Paris
possessed 30 hospitals which housed approximately 20 000
patients and which gave instruction to the 5000 medical students in the city. The Hotel Dieu alone possessed 1000 beds
(Shyrock 1936:153). Under these circumstances, a shift
occurred from the notion of the patient as an object of charity
to that of the patient as a body to be observed, known and
treated. With this shift, the expression of the Baconian language
of domination and control in science became evident in the
discourses of medicine. One member of the medical profession
in Victorian England praised the resources of a teaching hospital in a way that is reminiscent of the earlier quote from
Pinel:

> The clinical material is simply overflowing, especially in the
> surgical and gynaecological departments, and there is any
> amount of opportunity for men to work clinically at
> dresserships and clerkships, if they will only come and finger
> the material for themselves. It is a perfect paradise for every
> kind of tumour known, and the accidents are numerous.
> (Keetley 1885, quoted in Peterson 1978:174)

Keller (1985) has examined the way that the Baconian tradition has invited a form of 'objectivism' in science, whereby the subject totally severs any connection with the 'thing' under study. To achieve this 'severing', it is necessary to deny the 'experiential realization of the kinship between oneself and the other' (quoted in Keller, p. 121). In modern, scientific medicine, the process of observation also involves a detachment from the suffering and pain of the patient so that knowledge in the form of 'information' may be gleaned from the situation. Foucault quotes Amard (1821) who succinctly summed up the position: 'The art of describing facts is the supreme art in medicine: everything pales before it' (1973:146).

Noske (1989) has explored the process of severing the bond of kinship between oneself and 'the other' in relation to animals and its apotheosis in vivisection. There are disturbing parallels in the history of scientific medicine, where observation becomes the first stage in a process of objectification which *can* lead to cruelty and sadism. Waddington describes one such instance among many which occurred at the Hôpital de la Charité in Paris in 1828. Here, an otherwise healthy young woman was operated on to close a vaginal fistula. Observed by up to 250 students, this woman suffered nearly an hour of unspeakable agony while the surgeon 'boldly' sought the miscreant opening in her abdominal cavity. The witness who recorded this event noted that the 'patient' died shortly after. This same witness, himself a doctor, was torn between his admiration for the 'coolness and presence of mind' of the surgeon and the admission that it was 'next to impossible' that the woman could survive such an ordeal (Waddington 1973:218). This same witness recorded similar events at the (also ironically named) Hôpital de la Pitié.

In England, the letters of the Weekes family (1801–1802) are similarly revealing for the process of 'severing the bond of kinship' between the doctor and the patient. Much of this correspondence consists of letters from the eldest son, Hampton, a medical student in London who writes to his father, a surgeon/apothecary, and his younger brother Richard, who is apprenticed to the father. Hampton Weekes describes the way the students harden themselves against the sights and sounds of the hospital. At first, Hampton 'fainted away' at the horrors he witnessed (24 September 1881, correspondence of

Richard Weekes and Hampton Weekes (1801–1802), Greater London Record Office, St Thomas's Hospital Archivist Papers). In a short time, however, pride at being associated with the top surgeons of the day (Cline, Chandler and Cooper) and an academic fascination with the observations of the operating theatre and dissecting room soon took over any initial delicacy of feeling: 'as to fainting away, I have entirely done that away, I take no Brandy now'. By 8 October he was able to write:

> I have seen several operations since I last wrote and mind *nothing* about it, the more the poor devils cry the more I laugh with the rest of them,—two amputations of the leg one after the other by Chandler (he is in a hurry) a scirrhus breast that had ulcerated in a woman, operation for a hydrocele both by Cooper (a neat operator). (St Thomas's Hospital Archivist Papers)

He also reports that on several occasions autopsies were carried out on patients when their relatives had specifically asked that this not occur. The strategy in these cases was to claim that they had begun the examination before any message had reached them. In one instance, he reports on the death of a woman who had died under the 'care' of Cooper at 1 o'clock in the afternoon:

> At 4 o'clock Mr. Cooper came up into the little dissecting room, and dispatched some one after her pretty soon. He laughed with us and said, that Mr. Polhill a great Tobacconist at St. Margates Hill had sent word that she should not be inspected (Mr. P was also a governor of this hospital) but the answer should be to him that she had been opened before his message had arrived but which was not the case! so we were very merry about it. (St Thomas's Hospital Archivist Papers)

In these cases he writes pages of anatomical details to his father and brother. It is apparent that a focus on the details of the procedures, the speed at which they are performed and the prestige of the operatives has taken over from any connecting human pity that he may ever have felt for the patients under-going these ordeals. In the case quoted above and in others (as discussed in correspondence of 3 July 1802) there are strong insinuations from the writer that the surgical interventions are implicated in the deaths of the patients. And yet at no point does the writer express any critical attitude to the great surgeons. It appears that this form of apprenticeship was not simply an arrangement for instruction in the technical knowledge and practice of surgery. It was, importantly an induction into the masculine culture of hospital medicine which was based on the imperatives of observation, technique and discovery rather than the ease and comfort of the sick and injured. It is important, however, not to see this trend away from bedside healing as an *inevitable* feature of medicine within the modern hospital. It is clear that the individual experience and agency of the practitioner also played a vital part. An alternative approach is exemplified in the work of Dr Richard Bright (1789–1858), physician at Guy's Hospital who is most famous for his discovery of the disease which bears his name (Bright's disease, now more commonly known as glomerulonephritis). With his colleague Dr Addison, Bright co-authored a textbook for medical students titled *The Elements of the Practice of Medicine* (1839), to inform and advise students in their practical work. This text is a testament to the attempts of some doctors to maintain features of bedside healing within the environment of a teaching hospital. According to his biographer, Pamela Bright, Bright himself had always been concerned about patient care, learning of its importance to recovery during his own convalescence from typhus fever. 'Doctoring', he says in his textbook, 'did not only mean learning diagnosis, observing the signs and symptoms of disease and recognising complications; it included treatment and care, learning how to give comfort, anticipate wants, urge recovery or render peace at the end' (quoted in Bright 1983:193). When describing his own experience of illness and recovery, Pamela Bright wrote:

> He never forgot those things—which were not mentioned in medical books until he himself wrote about them some years later. It was largely because of these experiences that he was to become so beloved as a physician. Patients were always to say they preferred Dr. Bright to other doctors because he understood exactly how they felt. (Bright 1983:110)

It is clear, however, from the Weekes letters and other sources that bedside healing came under strong challenge with the growing ascendancy of hospital medicine throughout the nineteenth century. As well as seeing the discourses of bedside healing in conflict with those of hospital medicine, it is important to make the connections between the discourses and the wider knowledge frame of which they are part. The discourses of hospital medicine can be seen to be associated with Baconian objectivism and Cartesian mechanism and dualism (Merchant 1982:268; Capra 1983:138). Within these knowledge traditions, nature is perceived as something to be known and mastered. Descartes added a new dimension with his concept of the separation of the mind and body and the notion of the body as a machine. This helped to create the rationale within hospital medicine for any number of interventions, including surgery without anaesthetic. It also allowed for the almost total neglect of the role of psychological and emotional factors in illness and healing.

On the other hand, the discourses associated with Gaub, Nightingale and the practitioners of bedside medicine can be situated broadly in the organicist tradition, with close connections to the vitalists. We have seen that, within this tradition, nature is regarded as living, 'vital' and powerful. For Nightingale, even the 'bad' side of nature was powerful—effluvia, miasmas and noxious smells were all full of dangerous life. This tradition also placed emphasis on the interconnectedness of all living things. Within this tradition, discourses which promoted the cool, distant observation of suffering would simply not be possible. Subject and object are one and the same: 'When one part suffers, the rest also suffer with it' (Della Porta, cited above). It is clear that, throughout the eighteenth century, the Baconian and Cartesian traditions were extended, consolidated and finally became dominant in a wide range of intellectual disciplines including, with the advent of the teaching hospital, scientific medicine (Capra 1983; Merchant, 1982:268). It is therefore not surprising that nineteenth century medical discourses should contain vivid and crude illustrations of the hegemonic knowledge becoming grounded in medical practice. What is noteworthy is the fact that the defeated knowledges surface so clearly in Nightingale's work, and continue to thread their way into the work practices of modern nursing itself, as modelled on the Nightingale vision. The notion that these marginalised knowledges may also be present within modern medical practice will be explored in later chapters.

THEME 5: STRUCTURAL CONSTRAINTS ON NURSING AND BEDSIDE HEALING

While it is important to understand the connections between the history of nursing and holistic philosophies and practices, it is also important not to idealise nurses and nursing. Nursing discourses were not uniformly holistic nor were they unproblematically translated into institutions and practices. There was concern about the status, authority and proper place and role for nursing among doctors and among nurse leaders. In particular, nurse leaders were 'caught' and divided between, on the one hand, claims and beliefs about what made nursing practice unique, and on the other, the imperatives of public and professional recognition which necessitated acceptance of a medical/scientific model and the hierarchical authority of the medical profession. This dilemma was reflected in the divided vision of the future of nursing and the different discursive constructions of nursing developed by opposing nurse leaders. The issue of nurse registration neatly encapsulates this dilemma and it is commonplace in histories of nursing to focus on the conflicting positions surrounding this issue. While Brian Abel-Smith (1975) saw this 'battle' as one which reflected different class positions and aspirations (elite, status-conscious leaders versus lower-class, working nurses), Gamarnikow emphasised the common assumptions underlying both camps (an acceptance of subordination to medicine, 1978). Certainly there were important areas of agreement between the two sides, but there were also significant differences in the way the protagonists saw the future of nursing. The two camps were represented on the one hand by the larger London hospitals, their training schools and matrons along with Florence Nightingale who opposed registration and on the other by Ethel Gordon Manson (Mrs Bedford-Fenwick), some other matrons from London teaching hospitals and some doctors (including the 1895 British Medical Association), who passionately supported it.

The pro-registrationists looked to state registration of nurses as the key to the establishment of nursing as a profession which could control its own fees and conditions of work. It was a vision of nursing as a high status occupation which would have financial contractual relationships with patients along the same lines as doctors'. Over more than two decades

Mrs Bedford-Fenwick pursued the cause both as a political lobbyist and as editor of the *British Journal of Nursing*. While some commentators have dismissed the struggle for registration as 'a battle for status conducted against a background of rampant snobbery and militant feminism' (Abel-Smith 1975:67), others have argued that Bedford-Fenwick's support for registration was not just snobbery but was part of a coherent and far-sighted 'professional project' for nursing which would place the organisational control of nursing out of the hands of the administrators of the voluntary hospitals and within an autonomous professional body (Witz 1992:141).

In professional terms, the registrationist strategy made good sense and was based on a coherent and long-term plan. While the reasons for opposition from the voluntary hospitals are understandable, the question arises: why did Nightingale, leading matrons and nurses also oppose state registration? The answer usually given is that Nightingale and her supporters were primarily concerned with the character of the nurse, something which could not be guaranteed by a register (see Witz 1992:142). This is only partly true. The answer is to be found in the different conceptions of the future of nursing. While Bedford-Fenwick and her followers looked toward a professional model of home-based private nurses, Nightingale and her supporters saw that the future for the vast majority of nurses in the foreseeable future was within the ever-expanding hospital sector (Nightingale 1863). For this reason, Nightingale's focus was on the workplace, on its architecture, accommodation and, crucially, on the internal arrangements for nursing administration. From the beginning of the Nightingale School at St Thomas's Hospital in 1860, Nightingale insisted on nurses being managed by nurses:

> The whole reform in nursing both at home and abroad has consisted in this; to take all power over the Nursing out of the hands of the men, and put it in the hands of *one female trained* head and make her responsible for everything (regarding internal management and discipline) being carried out. Usually it is the medical staff who have injudiciously interfered as 'Master'. How much worse when it is the Chaplain. Don't let the Chaplain want to make himself matron. Don't let the Doctor make himself Head Nurse.

(Letter from Nightingale to Mary Jones 1867, cited in
Abel-Smith 1960:25)

There is still much over-simplification concerning the role
and motives of Nightingale. For instance, there is undoubtedly
an abundance of evidence from Nightingale's writings concerning desirable character traits for the nurse. But the point that
is overlooked in this analysis is that these desirable qualities
and attitudes were not seen by Nightingale as ends in themselves. Rather they were viewed as attributes which allowed
the nurse to care for the patient *in a way which put the
interests of the sick person before the interests of the practitioner.* Certainly these qualities for Nightingale were gendered,
but this was because, as a proto-feminist, she believed men
incapable of them! In this concentration on her supposed
preoccupation with character for character's sake, her whole
corpus on the practicalities of nursing the sick is overlooked.
The point is that she believed that a certain character was
required in order *to do* nursing in a way which promoted
healing and patient well-being.

For this reason her reforms focused on the internal
organisation of the hospital rather than on the concern with a
professional organisation for nursing. In a modern sense, her
focus was on the workplace rather than on professional power.
She was concerned to establish a separate nursing department
within the hospital where there would be a nursing chain of
command, a nursing culture and a repository for nursing
practice based on the priority of patient well-being over professional imperatives for knowledge and status. While it has
also been argued that it was primarily the matron and not the
ordinary nurse who benefited from the Nightingale reforms, it
is difficult to argue for or against this proposition given the
fact that we have very little historical material on the day-to-
day actual work of nurses. While nursing texts are sometimes
used as a guide for past activities (see Armstrong 1983b), in
reality they give very little insight into the daily compromises,
subterfuges and independent decision-making that nurses act
out in a hospital ward. Of course nurses themselves could not
and did not make claims about what a separate line of authority would enable them to do. They were keen to do the
opposite, that is, to pacify the doctors and reassure them that

the Nightingale reforms would *not* affect nursing and medical practice and the relationships between the two. The doctors, however, thought otherwise and it is from their statements concerning their fears and misgivings and the occasional provoked responses from nurses that a clearer picture emerges concerning the full implications of the Nightingale system.

Nurses and doctors under the Nightingale system

When the Nightingale School was established at St Thomas's Hospital in 1860, it was through negotiations with the treasurer and the lay governors. The medical staff were not consulted (Peterson 1978:179). Some sections of the medical staff were immediately hostile. Most vocal was a Mr J.F. South, Senior Consulting Surgeon of St Thomas's, who published a small book, *Facts relating to Hospital Nurses Also Observations on Training Establishments for Hospitals*, at around the same time as Nightingale released her *Notes on Nursing*. In it, he made disparaging remarks about the idea that nurses needed training, claiming that all doctors needed were efficient housemaids. The whole idea of training for nurses was ridiculous and its purpose was, he claimed, to place the whole nursing establishment 'in the hands of persons who will never be content till *they* become the executive of the hospitals and, as they have in the military hospitals, a constant source of annoyance to the medical and surgical officers' (South, quoted in Forster 1986:114).

It is possible that the issues were defined even more sharply when attempts were made to introduce Nightingale-style nursing reforms at Guy's Hospital in London in 1879. Included in the reforms were changes to the system of ward service, which meant that sisters would no longer be attached to a single ward but rotated from ward to ward in order to assist their training. This was perceived by the doctors as a direct threat to medical authority, as the nursing sisters would now be responsible to the matron and therefore not be required to study and follow the ways of individual medical men. The system of rotation was part of a total reform package which would establish Guy's as an institution for the training of 'lady nurses' (Peterson 1978:181). The combination of these reforms, which had the ability to combine training, autonomy and social rank in nursing, was clearly a significant threat to the doctors, who responded negatively through professional publications and in the general press. The nurse leaders responded in kind. Margaret Lonsdale, a former lady pupil and supporter of the reforms, made some very specific accusations, which were published in the *British Medical Journal*:

> [T]he honorary staff of Guy's and other hospitals prefer this class of woman to the highly trained lady-nurse, for three reasons. Firstly, because they are able to indulge in obscene language before the patients without let or hindrance; secondly because the afore-described 'old style' of nurse is no restraint upon the students coming in and examining the patients at any hour; and thirdly, because the staff can prosecute experiments upon the bodies of their patients of such a nature that they dare not perform in the presence of a trained lady-nurse. (Lonsdale 1880, quoted in Abel-Smith 1975:28)

With this statement, Lonsdale quite explicitly sets out (i) a distinction between nursing and medical priorities and (ii) the increased authority of the trained nurse. On the issue of training, some doctors viewed even brief training as a possible excuse for unauthorised treatment and to a 'supposed supreme knowledge of lady-nurses for nursing' and 'the fancied independence of their position and work' (Peterson 1978, p. 182). Despite the attempts of prominent nurse leaders to reassure doctors that they had no wish to interfere in medical matters, the doctors viewed the reforms as a direct threat to medical supremacy. Sir William Gull, Consulting Physician to Guy's Hospital, summed up the medical position when he wrote: 'The profession can never sanction a nursing system which claims for itself not to be under their control and direction . . . There must be no "divine right" assumed for nurses' (Gull 1880, quoted in Peterson 1978:182).

While the modern reader is struck by the baldness of these statements, the truly interesting comments from members of the medical profession concern their opposition to any notion of a separate knowledge for nurses. In defending the superior knowledge of doctors, a senior physician at Guy's argued that the proper (hierarchical) order of care would show that 'long experience and professional science are of more value than sentimental theories' (Peterson 1978:183). Gull agreed with this and enlarged on the theme in what must have been, for the nurses, insulting detail:

> In fact, there is no proper duty which the nurse has to perform, even to the placing of a pillow, which does not or may not involve a principle, and a principle which can only properly be met by one who has had the advantage of medical instruction. *It is a fundamental and dangerous error to maintain that any system of nursing has sources of knowledge not derived from the profession* . . . (Gull 1880, quoted in Peterson 1978:183, emphasis added)

It is possible to see from the recorded responses from some of the prominent nurses that they fought hard against these attempts by the medical profession to deny them anything but the status of medical servants. Lonsdale, for instance, had this to say: 'A doctor is no more necessarily a judge of the details of nursing than a nurse is acquainted with the properties and effects of the administration of certain drugs' (quoted in Peterson, 1978:182).

From statements like these, it can be seen that nurse leaders like Lonsdale, Nightingale and Burt (then matron at Guy's) were attempting to justify a separate territory and discourse for nurses, while at the same time pacifying medical concerns about possible interference in medical matters and prerogatives. However, it was an impossibly fine line to draw, since virtually any claim for an autonomous area of knowledge not under the direct authority of the medical profession constituted a potential threat to medicine.

This inherent conflict was also played out with great drama when Lucy Osburn attempted to introduce Nightingale style reforms into the Sydney Infirmary in Australia (Wicks 1995). In this instance, the conflicts became so entrenched and the working relationships so hostile that the colonial parliament eventually approved a Royal Commission to be conducted to investigate and recommend on the situation. The transcripts of the Commission provide a fascinating window into the internal arrangements and work practices within the hospital. In particular, it provides a window into the fears of the doctors concerning the perceived threat to their practice posed by a separate authority structure under the direction of a nurse. This one example illustrates their concern. The Commissioners are questioning a Dr Renwick on his views of the Nightingale system in Britain. When asked 'Is that a good system?', he replied:

> It is a very bad system: but supposing that the lady superintendent were allowed to order (these) tents and so on, and the general management were under her control, then the system would be very much like the Nightingale system, and it would not work satisfactorily. (Royal Commission [RC]:175)[4]

When asked why, he answered with disarming openness:

> Because their interests would clash. If you clothed the lady superintendent with that authority, her duties would still clash with those of the house surgeon and physician. I have no doubt of that. (RC:176)

The Commissioner sought clarification: 'How will they clash, if it is part of the system that the lady superintendent and her nurses, as far as the doctoring of the patients is concerned, have to obey the orders of the medical men?' Renwick (R) replied with a hypothetical example which gets to the heart of the matter:

> (R) Supposing a man came in, and the medical man ordered him to have ice applied, and the lady superintendent, in her nursing experience, did not think that ice was necessary –
> (C) But she could not have an opinion?
> (R) But allow me to say that people do have opinions of that kind, and I am satisfied that in working the system you would find it so—you would find that the authorities would clash. I have not the slightest doubt of it. (RC:176)

In these transcripts there are numerous examples of doctors referring to how work is organised in practice between doctors and nurses in the real world of the hospital ward. These doctors saw quite clearly that there was the potential for the Nightingale reforms to affect nursing practice and by implication medical practice at ward level. What actually happened on a day-to-day basis in British and Australian hospital wards has largely been inferred from official writings and texts. What is needed is detailed, historical research into the actual practices within hospital wards in relation to patient care. While we have only limited historical information concerning the day-to-day realities of nurses' work, Nightingale's *intentions* regarding nurses and their work were clear. They have, however, been historically misjudged and oversimplified. She believed that certain individual qualities were essential to enable a nurse to undertake good healing practice. She also believed that a good nurse was in a superior position to make certain judgements about patients and their conditions. When writing on the spread of fever in hospitals, for example, she had this to say:

> But I would go further and state that to the experienced eye
> of a careful observing nurse, the daily, I had almost said
> hourly, changes which take place in patients and which
> changes rarely come under the cognisance of the periodical
> medical visitor, afford a still more important class of data
> from which to judge of the general adaption of a hospital for
> the reception and treatment of the sick. (Nightingale 1863:6)

Nightingale also believed that certain physical and architectural qualities were necessary to maximise the healing qualities of an environment. While Nightingale and her supporters focused on the need for a separate nursing department within the hospital in order to maximise the influence nurses had over patient care, Mrs Bedford-Fenwick and her followers were concerned with the professional and status issues surrounding nursing in the employment and education fields. They advocated different strategies with different emphases, one with the emphasis on patient care and the other with the emphasis on the professional aspirations of nurses. (I will return to this theme in the concluding remarks to this book, but suffice to say here that there is now an attempt to unite these strategies in the rhetoric underpinning the 'New Nursing'). From a nursing standpoint the element that united these approaches to the future of nursing was a desire to enhance the authority and reputation of nursing as an occupation, a system of knowledge and set of practices in the face of ferocious medical opposition and pragmatic political accommodation on the part of the state. Nurses certainly did not passively accept domination from the medical profession or the hospital governors. However, their plans, visions and expectations were shaped and constrained by the limits being established in the developing structures of the class and gender orders of the late nineteenth century. Put another way, these nurse leaders occupied subject positions which in large part had been constructed for them by the influence of powerful discourses in society. In concentrating on the initial failure to attain state registration (finally attained in 1919), it is easy to overlook the significant concessions wrested from the patriarchal gender order of the time. In particular, what has been overlooked is the defining feature of the Nightingale system: an autonomous nursing hierarchy, located in a separate department of the hospital. This provided an autonomous area of accountability, which had, and continues to have, potential as a 'protectorate' for marginalised nursing discourses and the practice of bedside healing.

DISCOURSES AND POWER

The organic/holistic discourses, which are apparent in the work of Nightingale, exist in a state of inherent tension with other nursing discourses that acknowledge and accept the superiority of the mechanistic and nature-controlling discourses of modern, scientific medicine. Because of this 'duality of focus', modern nursing was constituted as an occupation with an inherent tension which has been expressed in the lived experience of nursing work. This tension also exists, though to a lesser extent, within scientific medicine itself where the holistic discourses have been marginalised far more completely.

The main expression of the 'clash' of these discourses exists between nursing and medicine, especially in situations where nurses are torn between obedience to doctors and their view of what is necessary to ensure 'ease and comfort' for patients. So while the occupations of modern medicine and modern nursing were formed in a hierarchical and gendered division of labour which makes overt conflict difficult for nurses, the survival within nursing of antagonistic discourses means that the tension between the two occupations is never finally settled. It also means that power must operate at different levels and in different ways. For medicine the most successful operation of power occurs when doctors successfully present the imperatives of Hospital Medicine as the imperatives for both medicine and nursing (and for the patient). It is only when the power of the medical profession is under a real or apparent threat that sanctions regarding the operation of power are made overt. In these circumstances, the most common responses of the medical profession and/or individual doctors are either to reassert the authority relationship between the two groups (based on the superiority of medical expertise), or to deny that nursing has an alternative or autonomous knowledge base.

In this chapter, I have explored five key themes in the history of medicine and nursing. In particular, I have situated an analysis of historical aspects of the nurse/doctor relationship within an account of the subordination and marginalisation of certain forms of knowledge and discourse. In doing this, I have also put to work Giddens's notion of the 'duality of structure' and so presented a dynamic account of the interplay between agency and structure in the making of the sexual division of labour. Nursing was not 'made' solely by Florence Nightingale. It was 'made' by all the nurses who have looked after the sick as either family members, friends or paid workers. Nevertheless, they made it within the constrictions and freedoms of their class and the gender order at specific times and in places and institutions not necessarily of their own choosing.

Nightingale was important as one of several influential Victorian women who fought to have the issues of public health, paid work for women and standards of care for the sick, placed at the centre of the political agenda. In addition, her copious writings reveal the contradictions and tensions inherent in the potentially dangerous and destabilising formulation of an occupation for women in the public domain, which had its own 'memory' of autonomy, skill and a contrasting cosmology of healing. The occupation that resulted was both needed and feared by the medical profession. It was also an occupation that had to be constantly re-made within the institutional constraints and freedoms of the sexual division of labour. In the following chapters I take up the theme of the survival of marginalised discourses and examine their expression within the work practices of modern nursing and medicine. In particular, discourses of healing will be examined to provide a bridge between the historical work of nurses and other healers and the work of nurses and doctors in hospitals today.

Chapter 3

Pleasure

How is the sexual division of labour 'made' each day in hospital wards and other work settings? Are nurses powerless victims of patriarchal medicine or are they implicated in the very foundations of work arrangements which bring both pleasure and pain? To what extent and in what ways do nurses resist the power of doctors? Is there a nursing knowledge and practice, a nursing way of doing things, which is independent from and different to medical care and the work of doctors? What happens if medical and nursing priorities clash? These are some of the questions which I explore in this and subsequent chapters. I am particularly interested to examine the possibility that the space made by the Nightingale reforms (a separate nursing department) constitutes a 'sanctuary', albeit a precarious and contradictory one, where the marginalised organicist discourses of 'bedside healing' have been able to survive. Implicit in this investigation are questions concerning the processes and structures through which the sexual division of labour is actively made and challenged on a daily basis in a hospital ward. I undertake this investigation through an analysis of the discourses of nurses and doctors (which includes language *and* practice) enacted within work settings and in follow-up interviews. With this procedure I also put to work Giddens's concept of the duality of structure (1979, 1984).

There have been other attempts to examine nursing discourses as part of an analysis of power relations between doctors and nurses. In particular, the work of Turner is relevant here, given that he writes of a split in the occupational culture of nursing into discourses of 'compliance' and 'complaint' (1986:375; 1987:152).[1] For Turner, this is part of a sophisticated argument concerning 'the acquisition of and socialisation into a sub-cultural occupational ideology which describes and specifies what the job is "really" about' (1986:357). However, Turner tends to focus on the 'safety valve' function of complaints, rather than on another aspect of this vocabulary, which is the way it points to 'an underworld or sub-cultural occupational structure where there is much conflict and animosity between doctors, nurses and other para-medicals' (1986:382). In this section of the book, I extend the schema developed by Turner which I consider underestimates the complexity of nursing discourse. I reveal that nurses have a significantly wider range of discourses. While discourses of compliance and complaint may be present, they may be interpreted not as static categories but as dynamic stages in a process whereby nurses are constantly re-making, transforming or even challenging the sexual division of labour. For example, in some cases, discourses which began as a complaint gained momentum and support and ultimately became what I shall call a discourse of conflict. It is then a matter of tracing the process whereby this conflict goes on to become expressed in individual or collective action (for example, referral to a hospital nursing committee with a recommendation for changes to hospital policy).[2]

As well as compliance, complaint and conflict, nurses also articulated other discourses with which they attempted to constitute the sexual division of labour in terms more favourable to themselves. In other words, they constructed their subjectivity as nurses and as individuals in ways which were more comfortable and more positive for themselves. In certain circumstances, this meant defining their knowledge and practice in a way that emphasised its value to medicine but which also emphasised its autonomy, uniqueness and, in some cases, its superiority. These discourses are not necessarily a component of complaint (Turner 1986:378). For many of the nurses in my study they were an accurate description of their work from their *standpoint* (Smith 1984). Based on the interviews and periods of observation, I have categorised nursing and medical discourses into the following 'semantic domains' (Johnston 1987):

* Discourses of pleasure[3]
* Discourses of power
* Discourses of conflict
* Discourses of skill
* Discourses of healing.

In order to deal adequately with each of these categories, I organise the material in the following way. Discourses of healing are central to the struggle between holistic and mechanistic knowledges both in relation to the underlying opposition between nursing and medicine and to the tensions *within* these two occupations. I therefore analyse these in considerable detail, and the findings from this domain are presented in the final chapter. Discourses of power, conflict and skill can be seen as discourses concerned with territory and autonomy and will also be dealt with in separate chapters. However, I begin on a somewhat contrary note by exploring the discourses of pleasure that emerged from the research.

PLEASURE

It is common for a fairly gloomy picture to emerge whenever nursing work is discussed. In the standard literature, much emphasis is placed on 'burnout' and 'role conflict' while the radical and critical literature tends to concentrate on the ways that nurses are oppressed by both class and gender. In Britain, an important book on the issues of professionalisation for nurses, begins with a chapter titled 'Introduction: the discontents of nurses' (Davies 1995). In a recent Australian text designed for use by undergraduate nursing students, the chapter headings for 'Nurses at Work' consist of: Bureaucracy, Reality Shock and Occupational Stress and Burnout (Short, Sharman & Speedy 1993). Added to the miserable picture presented in the literature are the statistics which show a high attrition rate for nurses (Mackay 1989). Yet what struck me during my observations of nurses at work was the fact that for much of the time, the nurses in the ward under study actually seemed to be enjoying themselves![4] How could this be? Was the literature wrong? Or were these nurses so dominated that they did not even know that they were oppressed and miserable? Was this an example *non pareil* of false consciousness? I decided to listen to and to take these nurses seriously, but to do so within the context of their overall work and (where possible) life context. In this way I was, once again, attempting to use the concepts of discourse, agency and structure in order to understand nursing work and the sexual division of labour.

Through a process of listening and observing on the wards, and then following up with specific questions during interviews and conversation, I was able to conclude that these nurses knew very well about their own oppression. They did, of course, know much more than any sociologist. Oppression was part of their daily experience and, when they did experience it, they recognised it and they did not like it. But they also experienced aspects to the work which gave them real pleasure. This seemed to me to be worth pursuing, for it indicated, once again, that nurses had 'made' and continued to 'make' nursing in ways which gave them the space for satisfaction and pleasure. Certainly, they also gave voice to the fact that they frequently came up against restrictions and limitations (as we shall see in the following chapter), but an analysis of the discourse of pleasure seemed to be a useful antidote to the common image of the nurse as a passive, complaining or even colluding victim.

Pleasure in collegiate relationships

One of the nurses[5] confirmed my own observation that nurses were genuinely cheerful and happy for a significant part of the working day:

> (Denise) Happy, yeah. There are times when you're happy when, well that's obvious, that's a lot of the time.

I asked the nurses what it was that gave them pleasure. Many spoke about how they enjoyed 'the people aspect' of their work. This included contact with both patients and other staff. While several told 'horror stories' about fierce, old sisters from the past who had filled them with terror, most appeared to regard their fellow nurses, especially the ones on their ward, with affection and loyalty. This was apparent in the jovial atmosphere which prevailed for much of the time in the ward.

This was especially so on weekends, when 'there were no doctors to trip over' and when a more relaxed and informal environment was enjoyed by both nurses and patients. There also appeared to be a lot of support for each other through difficult times. This became especially clear through an incident which I observed involving two experienced nurses, one of whom had picked up a serious mistake made by the other (an overdose of an anti-coagulant drug). The nurse who had picked up the mistake simply showed her colleague the completed incident form (the incident had to be reported) to make sure it was accurate and then turned to her and said: 'And listen, remember we all make mistakes. It's happened, it's finished, don't worry about it. I made one twice as bad as this so don't stew on it!' She was supportive without being patronising and both worked well together for the rest of the shift through what could have been a tense and difficult situation. While several nurses told stories about frightening, punishing, authoritarian ward sisters remembered from their training, the behaviour I grew accustomed to seeing on this ward was a far cry from those 'bad old days'. There are many factors responsible for these changes, a pivotal one being the fact that all nurses now working in Australian hospitals are fully qualified (many with university degrees) when they begin work. They see themselves as competent professionals and expect to be treated that way, especially by their peers.

Pleasure in collegiate relationships also appeared in nurse/doctor encounters. In one situation, a doctor (Senior Resident/Senior House Officer/SRMO) was sitting at the desk with two of the ward nurses. He began to tell a story about how he had forgotten to inform his Visiting Medical Officer/Consultant (VMO) that one of his patients had died and how the VMO was displeased about this. The nurses immediately began to advise him on what he should say to this particular VMO to keep out of trouble. They spent quite some time embellishing how he should look, what he should say, in a lighthearted but empathetic way which the hapless doctor clearly appreciated and enjoyed. I also witnessed an interaction between a Senior Staff Specialist/Consultant and a very senior nurse which demonstrated an affable familiarity between the two. The two were leading a large and very formal ward round which had reached the bed of an elderly, unconscious patient.

There was a rather sombre report from one of the junior doctors outlining the results from several blood tests. In the pause after this report, the senior doctor turned to the nurse and inquired: 'You still smoking?' Quick as a flash she responded: 'Shut your face'. At this he grinned broadly as though this was exactly the response he had hoped for. In its own way it was an intimate encounter, one which excluded everybody else as it further emphasised the closeness and familiarity of the two involved.

Nurses and sexuality

This is a complex area to write about. For so long nurses have been represented in the popular media as either (i) sex objects (the gorgeous, sexy young nurse in the tight uniform or (ii) anti-sex objects (the fat, old, battleaxe matron). In a recent film on nursing (*Handmaidens and Battleaxes*, Roslyn Gillespie, Silver Films, 1991), a young, tertiary-educated ward sister explained the outrage that had greeted a television program in Britain which specialised in granting the realisation of fantasies for successful candidates in a televised game. In this program, a young man was provided with his fantasy which was a beautiful sexy young woman dressed up as a nurse to cater to his 'every need'. Apparently the switchboard of the television station was inundated with protest calls and the national nursing organisation requested and received a formal apology on behalf of British nurses. Nurses have consciously rejected the image of themselves as personifications of male fantasy. Yet the issue of nurses, doctors and sexuality is not as straightforward as a simple denial and rejection of nurses as sexual objects. For instance, it is certainly true that nurses have campaigned and worked towards removing sexual harassment from the workplace. Yet it seems that even this seemingly straightforward issue gets caught up and is complicated by their 'duty of care'.

This was brought home to me one morning during a discussion over morning tea with three of the nurses from the ward. They had been attending an in-service education course provided by the hospital but run by a nurse academic from the local university. The topic was sexuality. The three nurses were discussing some of the issues raised at the in-service and it was apparent that they were both dissatisfied and annoyed at the underlying assumptions of the lecturer. They felt that the presentation had emphasised the male patients' rights to fantasise and masturbate at the expense of nurses as the objects of fantasy. They felt that the stress had been on the 'overwhelming power' of male sexuality and its need for expression in the hospital setting. They were made to feel that it was their 'duty' to accommodate and be tolerant of their male patients' sexual needs and to overcome their own discomfort. The issues were raised in a context of professionalism and the need for them to have a sophisticated understanding of the sexual needs of their patients. This was something of a dilemma for these nurses given that they were being situated as sexual 'objects' through a discourse of professionalism! While this was an example of sexuality experienced as oppressive, there was also a subtle undercurrent of erotic sexuality which would occasionally surface and in which nurses would actively participate.

There are analogies here with Pringle's (1988) work on secretaries. In her book, Pringle makes the point that feminists have essentially regarded sexuality in the workplace solely in terms of sexual harassment, that is, its unpleasant and coercive dimensions. Yet we know that viewing sexuality exclusively in this way situates women as passive and as victims while men are constructed as active and all-powerful. Pringle makes the point that the reality is more complicated, for 'it is not clear where "male power" begins and ends, whether women are in all cases "victims" or whether they too can exercise sexual power'. She goes on to argue that any analysis of sexuality in the workplace needs to include analyses of the ways that sexual pleasure may be used to disrupt male rationality and to empower women (1988:96).

Most people are familiar with the romantic sub-themes of 'hospital' television programs. The reality is that there are aspects of truth to these over-embellished fictions. Lots of nurses do end up marrying doctors and sometimes patients whom they have met on the job and got to know and like. A hospital is not just a repository for the sick. It is also a workplace and it is one where physicality is at the heart of the actual process of labour (Lawler 1991). People are constantly moving, bodies are constantly brushing up against each other and the atmosphere is often charged with intense emotion. In such an environment, an experience of the erotic and the sexual can be a pleasant distraction from a stressful and highly instrumental work situation. This will often amount to a kind of flirting. I saw numerous examples of this, often in relation to nurses and doctors making requests from each other which involved going beyond what might have been considered normal expectations. Mackay (1993) has reported similar findings. There were other, more subtle expressions of reciprocal, eroticised encounters.

One of these involved a very senior ward nurse and a senior and respected VMO.[6] The VMO arrived with an RMO (Resident Medical Officer/Senior House Officer) to visit his patients on a ward round. The nurse and VMO greeted each other warmly and seemed pleased with the opportunity to visit the patients together. What struck me was the hierarchical arrangement in this instance. The RMO exhibited quite deferential behaviour toward the VMO in both verbal language and body language (bending forward, stepping back). The nurse appeared much more the equal of the senior doctor; for instance, they walked together talking and laughing, while the RMO trailed behind carrying the patient's notes. When they reached the patient's bedside, the nurse and doctor took up positions at either side of the bed while the RMO stood in the background and took notes or provided information when requested by the VMO. The patients also benefited from the relaxed casualness of the visit. Both doctor and nurse sat on either side of the bed and chatted and joked with the patients. I saw none of the mystified, intimidated apprehension on the faces of patients—a common feature of the more usual ward rounds. They (the nurse and doctor) would unselfconsciously touch each other on the arm or hand to make a point or draw each other's attention to something. It struck me that the doctor and nurse were enjoying temporarily playing 'a couple'. The patients seemed to unconsciously pick this up as well, as more than one asked: 'What do you both think . . .' It occurred to me that this was a reversal of that commonplace in Western culture—boys and girls 'playing' at doctors and nurses. In this case, the doctor and nurse were, at some level, playing with the idea and actions of 'being together'.

Another incident involved a young RMO whom just about every nurse on the ward had referred to as being rude and uncommunicative. The nurses expect the RMOs to be friendly. They put up with many of the more senior doctors being aloof and non-communicative but they know that the junior doctors need them and most junior doctors have the sense to develop good relationships with the nurses. This one was, however, an exception. As one enrolled nurse put it:

> (Ellen) We have one particularly arrogant Resident at the moment. My natural inclination I'm ashamed to say is to not greet him, is to try and be arrogant with him, to pretend I don't see that he's struggling with something where I would naturally help somebody I could see in the same situation. Several of the nurses have told me, well they've just made the decision, they're going to ignore and not speak to him at all. I've really had to pull myself up and say, Ellen, you're acting in the same way he does. Where's that going to get us?

It was evident from the interviews that many of the nurses struggled over this issue. Some reported him to the hospital administration for his attitude to them and the patients, some tried to talk to him directly, another described to me her way of dealing with this man.

> (Meg) There has been a doctor who has been rather cranky. I don't know whether he's disillusioned with medicine or his wife's giving him a hard time but everyone's been picking up on his aloofness and reacting the same way whereas I've sat back and thought, why, he must be feeling so awful and so lonely. So one day he was sitting there and I stood up and started to massage his head and neck. He sat me down and put his head on my shoulder, I keep rubbing his head and he looked up and said, keep going so I said okay, so I keep going and he says, what's your name and I told him.

She goes on to describe how she used this intimate opportunity to say to him: 'I understand your difficulties, but it's not our fault, don't take it out on us. We have bad days too but we try to help each other'. She went on to tell me that 'Since that day every time he's gone in to a patient he's brought an extra chair and sat down with the patient and called me over'. She also attempted to mediate with the other nurses: 'I said to them, he's having a bad day and he's got some problems, after that he'd smile and they'd say I wonder why he's smiling now and I'd say why don't you just be nicer to him'.

In this instance, the nurse clearly enjoyed an encounter where she felt that at last she was the one in control of the communication. She was not responding or on the defensive but was initiating the contact in a way with which she felt comfortable. Yet there are obviously many ways to understand this encounter. Is it once again women (nurses) doing 'emotional work' and mediating social relations? Certainly this is going on. Is it to be understood as a type of mothering/nurturing behaviour? Perhaps, yes, this too. At the same time though, it seems that this very direct physical and emotional approach undercut his 'mystique' as the angry, young doctor and took the poor patterns of communication onto another plane. On the plane of aloofness and arrogance he would win every time because of the structural location of doctors *vis à vis* nurses. Everyone could be aloof and unfriendly but in the end he would get done what he wanted because of the reflected power of the senior medical officers above him. This nurse introduced eroticism into the contact and watched him melt beneath her fingertips. She simply ignored the instrumental and the rational and moved the encounter on to a plane where she felt both comfortable and in control. I am not advocating this as an ideal strategy for nurses to use with difficult doctors. However it indicates that nurses actively use eroticism and sexuality to construct their work environment in ways in which they feel comfortable and that are more likely to give them pleasure.

Pleasure at skilled work

A strong theme which emerged concerned the pleasure which nurses felt through using their skills. Once again this echoes Pringle's work with secretaries who also made a strong connection between exercising skills and pleasure at work (1988:189).

Lisa was one of the nurses who spoke with great animation about the pleasure she took from using her skills. After her interview we talked casually for a while about the skills involved in doing a 'pill round'—on the surface a fairly simple, straightforward task consisting of giving out medications to patients. She described this seemingly simple job from her standpoint, by listing all the components that had to be balanced at the same time. These included concentrating on drugs and dosages, noting any changes or possible side effects in the patient, dealing with patient requests while on the round, dealing with other nurses—answering questions, giving advice, and all the while keeping in mind that a seriously ill patient could deteriorate or arrest. Lisa described it as a process of 'juggling demands, remembering facts and requests, constantly setting and re-setting priorities'. She concluded by trying to explain to me that: 'Somehow, all of this is addictive. Imagine trying to do another job—it would be so boring.'

Others described the pleasure they got from ward work and bedside care—often considered a mundane area of nursing work.

> (Julie) Well, ward work is interesting. You get a variety of people and even, you look after two people with the same disease or whatever and they can be two completely different cases. I like, I suppose one of the nicest things about nursing is the contact with the patient. I mean it's not a job where you're mindlessly doing something. You're thinking all the time about what you're doing but you can also relate to the patient, so you're meeting new people and that's one thing that I really like, and I like the work. I think it's interesting. What we do is interesting.

> (Denise) You actually get something achieved during the course of the day. You can view something in a day that you know you've done. You can see results for your work although some days are better than others that way. It's interesting and you get to meet a whole range of characters, the oldies in particular, if you can sit down and have a talk to them you get heaps of good old yarns from them. That's what I like about it.

There was also great pleasure derived from successful out-comes.

> (Lisa) Well you are doing for people what they can't do for themselves so you're achieving in that sense. I mean obviously you want someone to be comfortable, clean, dry, well fed, happy . . . they've had their pills, you see it's just that sort of motherly instinct again . . . I think it gives you a sense of satisfaction seeing somebody sitting up there being comfortable and heading on the track. I mean if they've been particularly sick and you see them looking better three or

four days later then you can say, wow, we've sort of done that, you know, we've sort of helped to get them back and that's the satisfaction you get out of it.

(Bev) It's very satisfying when you see someone walk out the door who has been 'touch and go' and you know that it has been good nursing care that made the difference. A couple of years ago there was one lady in particular who was a CVA (cerebral vascular accident or 'stroke') patient and when she finally walked out the door I knew it was through us busting our guts and her really trying and that was one of the happiest days of my life and I still remember her.

These sentiments are echoed in Jill Ker-Conway's wonderful Australian memoir when she describes her mother's reactions to the experience of nurse training at a general hospital between the wars. Ker-Conway says of her mother:

She was never homesick for a moment. She loved the order and discipline of hospital life, the starched and shining order of the hospital world, and the chance to be in charge. She was a natural healer. No effort was too great to make a patient comfortable. No reward was sweeter than the total dependence of the very sick or the helplessness of an infant. She revelled in blessed independence: money to invest in clothes and outings, a chance to explore the world. (Ker-Conway 1993:22)

They also resonate with many of the statements recorded by the huge study of American nurses undertaken by Everett Hughes and his team in the 1950s. The following exchange occurred between an interviewer and a nurse:

Question: You enjoy taking care of patients?
Answer: I do. I do; especially when they're real, real sick. You go in and give them their baths and fix them all up, and . . . oh, you know how they're rested after that and how they feel . . . I really like to do it.

Hughes quotes one study where 2425 nurses in Pennsylvania were asked: 'What is the single best thing about being a nurse?' Two-thirds of these nurses gave 'altruistic' reasons such as 'opportunities to help others' and 'seeing patients recover' (Hughes et al. 1958:214). However, nurses in this study made it clear that a successful outcome did not necessarily mean a full recovery from illness. Time and again nurses made the point that they accepted that some people would not get better, some would die and that this could be a good outcome if the death was peaceful and dignified. Conflict could (and did) arise in situations where the nursing goal for a 'good death' was interrupted, usually by medical imperatives involving further investigations or interventions. (See chapter on Healing for details.)

Pleasure in intimacy

In further exploring the dimension of pleasure in nursing work it seemed that it was, for many nurses, explicitly the close contact with patients that they enjoyed:

> (Ellen) I just love the close contact with the patient. I love the chance to sort of be involved in their lives. It's just amazing what someone can kind of tell you about themselves when you're sponging them or making their bed or giving them that back rub. I think we're really trusted in most cases. I think that if a patient can see that we want to deliver some comfort and bring them some care, they really trust us with their lives from what they tell us and from the fears they tell us about. I just really think I'm privileged to be at that stage of a person's life. So D, I love that actual hands on the patient, not just touching them physically but in touch with what's going on in their lives and that mostly involves their whole family or lack of family and really it's the non-bedside things that I don't enjoy.

> (Julie) Well one of the most worthwhile things in life for me is people and that, the people side of work is the most satisfying, and I think when a person's sick you probably get to know, they're probably a bit more honest about themselves . . . You're doing something that at the end of the day may count. You hope you make a difference.

One nurse was surprised at her own reaction upon returning to nursing after five years in a health-related but non-nursing job:

> (Denise) Coming back, it was like coming home. It really was. After about a week, you stand back and think, yeh, I've come home . . . that sort of thing. It was sort of second nature, you know.

While there has been some recent, overdue attention to the

concept of 'emotional work' and nursing, it needs to be balanced by a perspective which allows nurses the pleasure they
speak of concerning emotional involvement and closeness to
their patients (Hochschild 1983; Smith 1992). While this closeness can also bring considerable emotional pain (there were,
for instance, several instances in the interviews where nurses
began to weep as they recalled a sad or painful incident), none
of the nurses interviewed mentioned this as a negative feature
in nursing. Invariably, their identification of negatives revolved
around situations where their goal of caring for a patient was
impinged upon by other factors.[7] The closeness to patients was
expressed wholly in positive terms; the pain and sadness when
it came was accepted as an inevitable part of the job.

Discourses of pleasure were revealing of at least two important aspects about nursing and its relationship with medicine.
The first concerns the way that the domain of pleasure was
primarily *relational* in character. By this I mean that nurses
gained pleasure from the skills of initiating and maintaining
relationships and from their own emotional responses to the
needs of patients. This would seem to support Chodorow's
argument that the primary attachment to the mother results in
'blurred boundaries' for girls who grow up with a strong need
for 'completion' in other close relationships (1978:92). If correct, it indicates that the roots of the sexual division of labour
go far into the unconscious and to the early construction of
femininity and masculinity. In terms of Chodorow's analysis,
changes to the division of labour would need to go beyond
organisational change—such changes would also need to go to
the heart of the process of the construction of gendered subjectivity.

The second aspect revealed by these discourses concerns the
way that the relational character of this domain is anathema
to the dominant, distancing, objectifying discourses of scientific
medicine. It is an approach which celebrates closeness and
connectedness (Keller 1985). It is an approach which links
physical and emotional care. It occurred to me that it could
be for this reason that it has in the past received such a low
profile in the nursing literature and in common perceptions of
nursing. It is, in a sense, illegitimate. While in medicine
'involvement' is a by-product of the quest for knowledge, for
nurses it is a central and pleasurable part of their work. In this

sense, discourses of pleasure are in themselves oppositional. They claim legitimacy for a more holistic model of healing which is enjoyable because it does not do violence to human experience. While this means that it can also be painful, it is ultimately more comfortable (' . . . it was like coming home'). It is about real, fully rounded human contact (see also Davies 1995: chapter 7).

This is not to say that it therefore cannot be abused or turn into something else. The feminist writer Rosalind Coward (1992) discusses both the pleasures and the dangers for women as mothers in taking care of others. 'Burying yourself in the neediness of others is not quite the same as an altruistic concern for them. Our culture has difficulty separating the two, and mothering is an activity which hovers above the narrow dividing line' (Coward 1992:52).

The connection between mothering and nursing has been made from the time of Nightingale onwards.[8] In this context Gamarnikow was right to point out that historically the subordination of nursing to medicine was made analogous (and therefore 'natural') to that of the wife/mother to the husband and child (1978:111). A critique of the social relationships between nurses, doctors and patients being 'naturalised' into gendered relationships has been a recurrent and useful contribution to the sociological literature on nursing. As a sociologist and feminist, I felt uneasy when, on several occasions, nurses in this study referred to their feelings about their work as 'maternal'. However, I had heard it; I could not ignore it and I had to try to understand it. It seemed to me that when they talked about their work in this way, it was to do with the deep satisfaction they got in transforming an environment where someone was uncomfortable, soiled, and in pain, to one where they could be comfortable, clean and 'on the track' to recovery again. Perhaps this is a real human pleasure (as well as being 'work') that men rarely experience, although it is becoming more common for men to enjoy these pleasures in relation to their own children. (See the comments from a doctor on this in chapter 6.) Rather than ignoring or denying it as a pleasure for women in general and nurses in particular, perhaps it would be more useful to further explore this dimension of pleasure and to analyse just why so many men see it as an illegitimate pleasure for their gender.

Hilary Rose has recently discussed this issue in relation to 'alienated' and 'non-alienated' caring. Firstly, she establishes that there is a 'real', non-alienated caring that occurs in certain situations between human beings.[9] She says:

> It is possible to feel or recollect the satisfaction of caring for someone, of finding all the little pieces of comfort that were important to that small child, that very elderly person—a mixture of words and silences, of favourite food and drink, of hard work in cleaning up a wet or dirty bed, of special ways of doing things. All the senses were involved; the cared-for looked good, smelled sweet. Yet the pleasure did not just belong to the carer; it belonged also to the cared-for; at best it was mutual. (Rose 1994:39)

The problem is, as Rose goes on to argue, that this pleasurable caring has in so many instances been alienated through either crass commercialisation—the invitation through television commercials to feel that love *is* white shirts for husbands and children—or the 'compulsory altruism' of low paid service work available to women in the sexual division of labour (1994:39). And yet it is important, indeed crucial, not to downgrade or lose sight of the real, sometimes only 'glimpsed moments' of the un-alienated form of caring within the other type. She concludes:

> But this does not mean that the pleasure of caring for someone is unreal, nor that it involves no work, nor that taking part in the relations of caring labour does not yield understanding. Indeed both feminist psychologists and philosophers have proposed that the scrutiny of women's caring could yield an ethic of care, even to a theory of citizenship in which caring like other duties, becomes a citizen's public obligation. (Rose 1994:39)

Writing from a post-structuralist perspective, Fox points to the ever-present danger of 'healthy' and generous care permutating into a relation of possession, in which the cared-for becomes the property of the carer, becomes the bearer of their desire for a particular outcome and upon whom the carer 'does' a care which both smothers and envelops (1993:95). This of course is a particular danger in a system where relationships are sharply hierarchical with a corresponding lack of reciprocity and equality. It seemed to me that in this hospital ward, the pleasures of closeness experienced by the nurses were, as far as I could tell, also experienced by the patients. At the same time, it appeared that it was this very lack of closeness and relatedness which caused patients to experience anxiety. This was especially apparent during very formal ward rounds. Nevertheless, the potential dangers of an 'excess of care' cannot be ignored. On the other hand, an absence of care and a lack of human empathy has costs for both the recipient and provider of 'professional care'. It would be an intriguing area for further research to examine the possibility that this is one of the costs that doctors pay for practising scientific 'hospital medicine'. Certainly, the ability of doctors to avoid care was made possible by nurses' care 'overtime.'

All of this begs questions about male nurses. They are conspicuously absent from this study simply because there were none on this particular ward during the time I was there. This in itself is interesting as this was a 'high care', 'low tech' work area for nurses. When I commented on the lack of men working in the ward, I was told: 'You'll find them in OT (operating theatre), A and E (accident and emergency), Intensive Care and making careers in Administration'. This certainly appeared to confirm Christine Williams's study where she found that: 'Male nurses go to great lengths to carve for themselves a special niche within nursing that they define as masculine' (1989:14). However, there are certainly male nurses who are working in areas other than those listed and a study of these men and their work areas will be an essential area for future research.

In this chapter I have examined a dimension of nursing work—that of pleasure—which has been largely ignored in the sociological and feminist literature. In doing this it is not my intention to romanticise nursing or to gloss over the many and deep problems that nurses face in their day-to-day work and over their working lifetimes. But it seemed to me important to allow nurses a voice about what they actually enjoyed about their work and how they experienced pleasure in what they do. To do otherwise is to regard them as powerless or misguided or both, and to see them as caught within structures over which they have no control. To be so caught would be to be unaware of the restrictions that inhibit those very aspects that do give pleasure and satisfaction. In fact, nurses' experience of their work includes a well developed sense that they are constantly coming up against something in relation to their potential as professional practitioners. A sense of restriction, limitation and redirection was revealed in particular in their discourses on power, conflict and skill. In spite of this, however, nurses find ways of going about their work in ways that provide immense satisfaction and ongoing pleasure.

Chapter 4

Power

Power is ever-present within health care settings. It is evident in the way people walk, in the way they communicate, in who gets recognised as having a presence and who gets ignored. It is evident in the tone people use when they speak, whether loudly or softly, and whether or not their words receive answers. I found on entering the hospital ward as an observer that many of the rules of ordinary behaviour were, to a large extent, suspended. For instance, people working in close proximity to each other would simply not recognise each other's presence. In other work situations there would be at least a head nod or a few words exchanged but in the hospital ward, contact between individuals and groups was highly structured and often highly ritualised. Over a five month period, I never saw, for instance, any contact between a cleaner and a doctor. They simply did not recognise each other. This was also sometimes the case between doctors and nurses, especially if the nurse was very junior. In these situations the doctors (usually in a group) would seem to sail in like a ship of state, walk up to the patient's bed and proceed to talk to or examine the patient as though the nurse was simply not there. They would then walk out of the ward, after scribbling a few (often illegible) notes in the patient's report, leaving the nurse to decipher what they had written (often a request for the nurse to follow up) after they had gone. Nurses would sometimes do a similar thing in a different way. They would sometimes congregate together around the ward desk and laugh and talk together as though an Intern (Resident Medical Officer/Junior House Officer) sitting and writing notes was not there at all. To an observer used to a more informal work environment, this could all appear quite strange.

It certainly stimulated me to ask, what was actually being worked out here? What were these patterns of behaviour achieving or preventing? I came to think that, in a silent sort of way, it was about claiming ownership of the ward. The doctors acted as though it was their ward and the nurses were there to provide the necessary but secondary services. The nurses on the other hand attempted to constitute the ward as belonging to themselves and the patients, with the doctors being regarded as a necessary but disruptive and distracting presence. I was frequently advised by different nurses to 'come in on the weekend; it's a different place altogether, no doctors to get in the way' or 'no doctors to trip over and interrupt the work'. While both nurses and doctors constituted the reality of 'ownership' in different ways, according to their standpoints, there were definite occasions and definite issues when it became very clear that power was operating in ways that advantaged doctors and their approach to illness and therapeutics.

MEDICAL POWER IMPOSED ON NURSES

This was brought home in a vivid way during the course of an evening shift. After a busy day, the nursing priorities revolve around giving evening medications, taking observations and, in general, settling patients, rubbing their backs, making them comfortable and readying them for sleep. Unless it is urgent, they prefer medical procedures to be undertaken during the day when the ward is full of activity. This particular evening was rolling along in a quietly busy way when a newly admitted patient walked up to the desk at 7.00 p.m. and informed the nurses that the RMO had told him he may be back later to perform a chest aspiration (a fairly major procedure). The nurses checked the notes, found nothing documented and so told the patient they doubted that it would be done that night as they had been told nothing about it. At 8.40 p.m. the patient, now agitated and anxious, approached the nurses again and stated that he wanted to know one way or another about the procedure. He needed to ring his wife at home to let her know what was happening. The charge nurse for the evening (a nurse with about five years experience) checked the time and told him: 'No, he won't do it now because we haven't got the equipment up here'. The more junior nurse (a recent graduate) went further and added: 'He will not be doing it because we won't be doing it with him. We have no equipment and it's too late.' The patient then asked to use the phone to let his wife know, which he did. At this point, I found myself being rather impressed with the assertive and definite way in which these nurses set the boundaries for medical activities.

At 8.50 p.m. (ten minutes later), the RMO (the same one discussed in the previous chapter as being rude and non-communicative) arrived on the ward and asked calmly: 'Sister, have you a chest pack?' Both nurses looked at him in a startled way but simply replied, 'No'. He then said: 'Well I want to do a chest aspiration, so get one up.' To this very direct command the more senior nurse replied: 'I don't know if we can get one at this hour of night, I'll have to check.' But if this RMO detected any subtle resistance in this comment, he certainly did not acknowledge it. He replied: 'Yes, do that please. You can always get one from casualty.' At no point did he offer them any explanation or apology for his total lack of courtesy and the absence of even a rudimentary level of communication concerning his plans. At the same time, at no point did the nurses confront him with his rudeness or the fact that he was seriously inconveniencing them, not to mention the patient. The more junior nurse then began ringing round to other wards after which she went off to borrow the necessary equipment. The other nurse also had to stop what she was doing to set up the trolley for the procedure.

This story has a further twist. After returning with the borrowed equipment, the nurses were preparing the trolley and setting up for the procedure. At this point the Registrar (Senior House Officer) arrived on the ward. I heard the Registrar diplomatically mention that chest aspirations are usually done first thing in the morning so any complications occur during the day rather than in the night. They discussed this for a few minutes and then 'together' decided that the procedure could be postponed until the morning. The RMO then looked around for a nurse and called out: 'Nurse, we won't be doing that aspiration now.' Again, no apology, no explanation. This was too much for the recent graduate. She asked incredulously 'What?' He repeated the message. She then simply walked over to him, placed her hands around his neck and proceeded to pretend to choke him. There was a sort of half-embarrassed humour about this, but the Registrar made an effort at conciliation by offering an explanation as to why the procedure had been postponed.

This unusual incident raises some interesting issues. It was, firstly, a rather naked demonstration of power. As such it was not typical of the more usual interactions between nurses and doctors on this ward. But the exercise of power in this instance was not just blatant. It also had an impersonal, almost mechanical quality to it that was only finally broken by a physical, directly confrontationist (if playful) act. The work of Jessica Benjamin is useful to help understand an incident such as this (1990). Benjamin discusses rationalisation, which as Weber conceived it, defines the process in which abstract, calculable and depersonalised types of interaction replace those founded on personal relations and traditional beliefs and authority. She makes the important point that the 'missing piece' in the analysis of Western rationality and individualism is the structure of gender domination (1990:188). Benjamin describes the way that male individuality dovetails with what has been defined as 'rationality' in Western culture. This is largely achieved through seemingly genderless and objective processes. As Benjamin puts it:

> The public institutions and the relations of production display
> an apparent genderlessness, so impersonal do they seem. Yet
> it is precisely this objective character, with its indifference to
> personal need, that is recognized as the hallmark of masculine
> power. It is precisely the pervasive depersonalisation, the
> banishment of nurturance to the private sphere, that reveal
> the logic of male dominance, of female denigration and
> exclusion. (1990:187)

As a result, we are dominated by impersonal forms of social relations and a 'rationality' which attempts to objectify and control everything. In this way, 'the man can remain in rational control, maintaining his separateness, denying his dependence and enjoying a sense of omnipotence' (Pringle 1988:53). This enjoyment, however, comes at a price for the person being controlled, who is in this process denied recognition. It may be that it was this aspect of the transaction which so infuriated the nurse. Pringle makes the point that, 'Violence, whether actual, ritualised or fantasised, is an attempt to break out of the numbing barriers of self, to experience intensity and to come up against the boundaries of the other' (1988:53). Perhaps we can view the nurse's actions in this light. In an earlier interview with this nurse, she had gone out of her way to tell me that she 'did not play the doctor/nurse game'.[1] Yet it seems that endless permutations of this game are inevitable in a situation which is not based on mutual respect and recognition.

A second issue concerns the fact that the individual players in this situation were significant. This particular RMO was known to be abrupt and rude. He had in fact been reported by other nurses for unacceptable behaviour. Indeed, many of the nurses referred to him specifically during interviews to illustrate unpleasant and unsatisfactory nurse/doctor contact. In retrospect, it was apparent that the Registrar had attempted to ameliorate and defuse the situation, as though he too understood that the RMO lacked 'interpersonal skills'. The nurses, too, lacked the experience and the confidence of some of the other nurses on the ward. But while the starkness of the interaction was unusual, it did nevertheless demonstrate the power that was there to be called on behind the more polite culture that was usual for this hospital. It also demonstrated the implicit devaluing of nursing work that underpinned this interaction and may well underpin other more polite transactions. In this case, there was no recognition or acknowledgment that these nurses were being called away from anything of any importance at all. In this situation the medical agenda was *the* agenda and the nurses were there to serve it.

Power was also imposed on nurses in a way that could be described as chronic rather than acute. This concerned the constant, 'sleeping' issue of the doctors' indecipherable handwriting. This is sometimes presented as a sympathetic joke about doctors in terms of everyday folklore. 'Everybody knows that doctors have the worst handwriting'. And yet at the same time, it seemed to me to have a very serious dimension, a dimension which very much expressed a relationship of power and dominance. I came to this observation after about the sixth or seventh time that I watched two or more nurses struggling to work out what orders a doctor had written in a patient's notes which the nurses were expected to follow up. I asked the nurses about my observations when I interviewed them individually. They all confirmed that this was a nuisance and sometimes a real problem but it was also something to which they had become accustomed. When I asked (Lisa) if she had trouble sometimes reading the doctors' writing, she replied:

> (Lisa) Oh yeh, oh yeh.
> (Interviewer) What do you do about it?
> (Lisa) Use a bit of nous I guess . . . if you know what the patient's in for, you sort of know logically what tests they might be going to have or what medications they might be going to have or if it's a change of dosage you just grab the medication chart and there are various little ways you can use to sort of figure it out . . . Yeh, usually it's just because you know what the disease is, the disease process, and you can sort of figure it out.

This is a wasteful and inefficient use of nursing skills and one for which there clearly seems to be no justification. Another nurse also described the issue as 'a big problem'. She went on to say:

> (Bev) It's their scrawl that is the problem and all of us have problems reading it and we're often giving a report (to the other nurses at change of shift) and it is hard to tell what they (the doctors) want and what they've said. So you usually have to put two or three heads together and then we can work out word by word, you know.

It appeared that this subtle exercise of power worked all the way up and down the medical hierarchy. I asked:

> (Interviewer) Is it a problem for other doctors to read the scrawl?
> (Bev) I think they, a lot of the Residents, have problems too. Dr C (names a VMO), he's the worst. I'll show you his when we go back, he's the worst one I've ever seen. It's just so, you know, like a line.
> (I) Have you ever heard the Residents complaining that they can't understand the writing?
> (Bev) Yes, they've asked us sometimes.

(I) Have you thought how the situation might be made better?
(Bev) If they printed.
(I) Printing?
(Bev) But I mean how could you get them to print?
(I) Do people ever say anything to them?
(Bev) I don't think they do, no. I don't think they're game
enough.

In this exchange the nature of a seemingly technical problem
was revealed very clearly as one which had power relations at
its heart. This nurse knew immediately how the problem could
be simply and promptly remedied, but the question, '*how could
you get them to print?*' revealed her understanding of the issues
of power and status which underpinned the problem. It seemed
to be a clear example of the operation of 'micropower' while
at the same time it carried both a heavy symbolism and strong
structural connections to explicit, hierarchical, power structures. The symbolism of illegible writing says so many things.
It says: I'm too busy and too important to bother about writing
more slowly or carefully. It says: Your time is less important
(you are less important) and therefore you can keep trying until
you work it out. It says: You should be able to work this out
and if you can't then you are inadequate (this introduces an
element of shame and so therefore reinforces the relationship
of dominance and subservience). It also very successfully under-
cuts the ability of nurses to construct any sort of professional
mystique around their access to esoteric medical knowledge. It
was not uncommon for the nurses, in desperation, to ask the
patient what the doctor had said to them. In the same interview
(above), Bev explained to me when I asked:

(I) Do you ever have to go to the patients and check with
them?
(Bev) Well actually there was something that come up today,
. . . that lady that went for the angiogram . . . no one could
understand what she was to have, there was just one word,
no hints . . . someone said, perhaps if we ask the patient, she
might know . . . In the end we did find out, it was in a
previous report written by a nurse, on a previous page in one
of the nurse's reports she said 'going for an angiogram', so
we knew then that's what it was but we were just about, I
was just about to go down and ask the patient.

This appeared to be a 'sleeping' issue, one which caused

annoyance and inconvenience and perhaps one which had (but for the extra work of the nurses) the potential to be dangerous to the patient. It has probably existed since doctors' 'orders' have been written and was probably worse when doctors wrote in Latin (although it occurs to me that perhaps the handwriting has got worse to compensate for the lack of mystique associated with the demise of Latin!). Theoretically, it probably most closely corresponds with Lukes's 'three-dimensional view of power' which, he argues:

> allows for consideration of the many ways in which *potential issues* are kept out of politics, whether through the operation of social forces and institutional practices or through individuals' decisions. This, moreover, can occur in the absence of actual, observable conflict, which may have been successfully averted—though there remains here an implicit reference to potential conflict. This potential, however, may never in fact be actualised. What one may have here is a *latent conflict*, which consists in a contradiction between the interests of those exercising power and the *real interests* of those they exclude. (Lukes 1974:24)

Practically, it is an implicit exercise of power which goes against the grain of modern management theory with its emphasis on efficiency and teamwork. It also appears to be a practice which has survived the reforms of 'the new managerialism' in health care settings (Nettleton 1995:219).

MEDICAL POWER IMPOSED ON PATIENTS

In the sociological literature there have been a variety of ways that the doctor/patient relationship has been conceptualised. Parsons (1951) saw the relationship as reciprocal, if unequal. For him the inequality of the relationship was not a problem given the prescribed rights and duties of the physician which are underpinned by social norms and values (1951:435). This view has faced considerable challenge over the last two decades from several quarters, including from the influential work by Freidson, who has argued that reciprocity ought not be assumed; indeed, he maintains that the doctor/patient relationship is more accurately characterised as one based on implicit conflict (1975:286). At the heart of this conflict is the necessity (from the doctor's point of view) for the patient to 'give over' authority and control of his or her body to the doctor. Both the doctor and the patient may recognise that the patient has 'rights' in the transaction but the 'good patient' will ultimately trust the doctor's expert knowledge to advise and act on what is in the patient's best interests. Fagerhaugh and Strauss (1977) have observed that different organisational settings profoundly influence the nature of patient/doctor interactions. The formality of the VMO's (Visiting Medical Officer/Consultant) visit in a teaching hospital appeared to be a situation which required more submissiveness than reciprocity on the part of the patient. This may very well be quite different from other organisational settings such as the Specialist's consulting rooms where the patients appear in their own clothes, with their own identity much more intact and where they are in a much better position to negotiate and bargain. I saw several instances of medical power unambiguously imposed on patients.

In the first instance, a senior and junior RMO (Senior House Officers) arrived at the patient's bedside at 9.00 p.m., after she had been 'settled' for the night and announced: 'We will just examine your back passage to see if you have been bleeding from there'. I could not catch the exact words of the patient but it was apparent that she was shocked and that she raised some objection to this. The doctor then replied 'Yes, I'm sorry but this is very important. Just turn onto your side please'. While I was prepared for an expression of medical authority, it struck me as quite unacceptable that the doctor had not asked permission for this most intimate and invasive procedure. The doctor had announced his intention in a loud, clear voice which would surely embarrass the patient in front of other patients and staff. (Was this a strategy to ensure co-operation?) When the patient objected, the objection was treated not as a real objection which required negotiation, but a small protest which required another instruction even more firmly put and which was clearly to be obeyed.

In the second instance, the VMO went with a nurse to visit an elderly woman who had been suffering from angina (chest pain) and who was hopeful that she would be allowed to go home. When we arrived, she was sitting on her bed and looking expectantly at the doctor. He pulled the curtains around her bed and said: 'Let's have a look at you'. She was wearing a 'nightie' which conveniently had a button open at the front and without further ado he slipped his hand down the front of her 'nightie' and over her breast. I shall never forget the look on her face. To say she looked shocked would be an understatement. Her face flushed and he instructed, 'Relax, your heart is pounding away'. Little wonder. I assumed that he placed his hand directly over her heart in order to feel the rate and strength of the heart but it obviously had not occurred to him to explain to her what he was about to do and why. It seemed not to occur to him that the very act of examination was influencing what he was finding in his examination, and so seriously interfering with medical 'best practice'.

Both of these incidents raised the issue of the normal expectations of citizens living in civil society. If either of these incidents had occurred outside the hospital, the perpetrators would have been liable for state-sanctioned legal action. In his book on modernity and self-identity, Giddens discusses the way that in the transition to the modern state local communities were largely autonomous in terms of traditions and modes of life (1991:151). He argues that: 'In the modern social forms, state and civil society develop together as linked processes of transformation. The condition for the process, paradoxically, is the capacity of the state to influence many aspects of day to day behaviour' (1991:151).

It is almost as though a 'modern' teaching hospital is a pre-modern remnant of a remote community, which remains aloof and to some extent unincorporated into the purview of the state, 'since the state also helps define private rights and prerogatives in a positive fashion' (1991:151). At a very basic level, the obligation to show good manners to a fellow citizen was missing here.

Power also operated in subtle ways and without any obvious conflict. In the incident I am about to relate, power worked to define a situation in a way that, once again, advantaged doctors. In this case it concerned a patient's perception of her own illness and recovery. The following conversation took place between a VMO and his patient on a medical round in the presence of other medical staff, the NUM (Nurse Unit Manager/Senior Sister) and myself. This patient had been suffering from severe head and neck pain and had undergone investigations which had produced a diagnosis. The VMO explained that she (the patient) would need to have a biopsy taken just to make certain that they were correct.

> (VMO) Well, the good news is that this condition is treatable. So there is no reason why we shouldn't be able to give you considerable relief.
> (Patient) Well it won't be for want of trying!
> (VMO) (laughs) We haven't started yet.
> (Patient) I've never been so well treated in my life. I just feel so much better.
> (VMO) You have six or seven doctors to see yet.
> (Patient) Oh, I see.

It was apparent that, in this conversation, the patient's perception was that her treatment had already begun and that she did indeed feel better. For the last week she had been on bed-rest, a good diet, symptomatic pain relief and had been receiving plenty of 'TLC' from the nurses. The VMO, on the other hand, did not consider that treatment would begin until a definite diagnosis (including biopsy) had taken place, a formal treatment regimen of medication had begun and the required number of doctors had been seen. Then the patient was free to start feeling better. There are at least three points of interest here. The first concerns the fact that we are witness to two different paradigms of illness and recovery, one the subjective experience of the patient (and presumably the nurses) and the other the objective assessment by the most powerful of the expert professionals. Nicholas Fox quotes a study by Tuckett et al. which documented an effort to introduce British doctors to the possibility that patients' own beliefs and values could contribute to their care (1993:96). The research team found that doctors saw lay beliefs in a narrow and ultimately instrumental way. These beliefs were construed as: 'a useful way of "getting the whole picture", so as to discover the real problem; to avoid appearing superior and as an aid in communication; to provide clues so that doctors could give appropriate reassurance; or as a waste of time, and only worth listening to on grounds of courtesy' (Tuckett et al., quoted in Fox 1993:96). The study concluded that the 'medico-centrism' of doctors' behaviour was a consequence of the urge to make a diagnosis and the urge to stay in charge. This incident appeared to be consistent with these observations.

The second point concerns the fact that a real and conscious effort had to be made by the VMO to redefine the situation in the eyes of the patient. In other words, the power to define the situation as a medical success had to be worked for and an appropriate and individual effort had to be made. While the second point can be seen to be about agency, the third concerns the structural location of the VMO in relation to the patient and the nurses.

A medical round is a highly structured and ritualised activity (Atkinson 1981). It is led by the VMO (who carries no paper) and is made up of the registrar, the NUM who carries the nursing notes, the Intern or RMO who carries the medical notes and various request forms, other health professionals—occupational therapist, physiotherapist, social worker—and frequently some medical students. As a ritual it is both the exemplar and the symbol of medical power in the hospital. It also openly represents the hidden face of hierarchy to the patient. It is a formal occasion and one in which the right to speak is constrained by the formality and hierarchy. The patient is permitted to speak but not to say too much. In line with Foucault, it can be said that the patient is there to reveal, not to claim subjectivity. The other staff are there primarily to answer any questions the VMO may put to them. The third point then, is that while the VMO had to make an effort to reclaim ascendancy, he had the structural location from which to do it. Finally, through the action of reclaiming it, he reinforced the structure.

Another incident highlighted a slightly different aspect of the power of the doctor *vis à vis* the patient to be 'in charge' of the patient's body and illness. In this case there was a young (19-year-old) cardiac patient in the ward who was suffering from a severe congenital disorder which had resulted in a lifetime of illness and disability. Like many others with a long-term health problem, this young woman had an extensive and expert knowledge of her condition and its treatment (MacIntyre & Oldman 1985). On this particular day she had made quite a fuss when handed her medication. She thought she recognised one of the tablets as a drug which had caused her a previous bad reaction. She asked the nurse the name of the drug and confirmed that, yes, it was the drug which had caused a problem on a previous occasion and, yes, her specialist had prescribed it for her. She then point blank refused to take the drug and asked to see her doctor when he came in. The next day her Specialist (VMO) arrived to visit her along with his Registrar. After the charge nurse explained what had happened the day before, the doctors walked over to her bed and pulled the curtains for privacy. This patient was confident, knowledgeable and quite assertive regarding her treatment and the nurses listened with great interest to see how the doctor would react to a situation where his authority had been challenged on apparently quite firm grounds.

After greeting her, the doctor adopted a tone which was both authoritative and patronising. He patiently explained (as though to a child) that he had not intended for her to be on the drug long-term but because she had that previous bad reaction, he wanted her to have it again so that they could see in more detail just what was going wrong with it. He successfully presented this in such a way as to make her appear at fault in doubting his judgement. She became very quiet and appeared to accept what he had to say. In the end she apologised for the inconvenience she had caused! The nurses commented that really, he ought to have discussed all of this with the patient and themselves beforehand and the patient would not have been put through this unnecessary upset. He however appeared to have no such doubts about his actions and he and the registrar sailed out of the ward, power intact and probably *enhanced* by what had occurred.

POWER TO RESTRICT

There were at least two issues which emerged during the period of this study which concerned the power of the medical profession to restrict the work of nurses. One concerned the restriction on nurses to 'put up' blood. The other related to the restriction on nurses to site and re-site intravenous cannulas. The blood issue was one which several nurses at one of the hospitals complained about. It was explained to me that even when a patient had an intravenous line *in situ*, a nurse was not permitted to replace the intravenous fluid with the blood, when it became available. The nurse had to 'page' the

Resident to come to the ward and perform this simple task. Many nurses saw this as an imputation that they could not be trusted to correctly read a label:

> (Julie) . . . and the reason they give you is that a nurse might grab the wrong bag out of the fridge, but, then in another instant you'll hear that a nurse can go and get blood but still has to check it before it goes up. I don't know, I suppose different hospitals are different but in . . . (another city), the pathologist, when you wanted blood, the pathologist in office hours checked the blood with you, in the ward you got another nurse and checked it again and put it up and out of hours, the nursing supervisor got the blood, so I mean it's just a checking game. I mean the most important thing about the blood issue is that it's cross-matched correctly and labelled correctly. So you see what I'm saying? It's so silly.

Another nurse talked about the way that this restriction worked against patient comfort as well as causing frustration to the nursing staff:

> (Bev) Just a classic example, you know, the patient has anaemia and they are waiting on blood and you want to get the blood up and running. We can't do that.
> (I) Right.
> (Bev) And the Resident knows dammed well that the patient's got to have observations with the blood and he knows he's gotta come and do it and you sit there, half the morning's gone so then the blood's running all night keeping the patient awake and creating the extra work for people.

A similar set of circumstances pertained to the issue of inserting intravenous cannulas and re-siting cannulas that had slipped from the vein and become embedded in the surrounding tissues. One nurse in particular, who had worked in pathology and had skills in venipuncture, found this restriction frustrating and annoying:

> (Denise) I just get really frustrated at the way they collect (blood). No one ever, ever collects off a supported arm. That was one of the basic rules in pathology.

She went on:

> The other thing we learnt, was always to be sure of what you feel before inserting the needle. You never push the needle in

until you have felt exactly where you are going. I've never seen that done here yet. They just come in and . . . oh, no . . . sorry, I'll go over here and try and the more they miss the crankier they get, the more frustrated, the less time they spend on looking where they're going. Our limit was two tries. I don't care now, I just get up and say, 'I'm sorry, but it's someone else's turn now'—I've just seen too many bruises and I won't let them keep going.

This particular nurse took the issue further. It was a procedure in this hospital to hold a monthly, hospital-wide nursing meeting. At this meeting, information was disseminated 'from the top down' but it was also an opportunity for nursing staff to raise and discuss issues among themselves and with the nursing hierarchy. At the next meeting, this nurse put forward the idea that there be certain nurses from each ward who are nominated to perform venipuncture when they decided it was necessary, for instance, when a Resident was unavailable or to resite a 'tissued' intravenous. There were two reactions from nursing administration.[2] The first concerned the need to set up a training program for these designated nurses. The second illustrated the caution exhibited by sections of nursing administration over issues of territoriality. One senior administrator put forward the view that if nurses took over this job, it would take away training opportunities for Interns and Junior Residents. How else would they practise their skills? The majority of the nurses considered this argument but were ultimately unmoved by it. The nurse who initiated the discussion later recalled the meeting in this way.

> (Denise) You know, and at the meeting, I just said: 'I don't mean to be rude, but will someone tell me what sort of training the Residents had for taking blood or for doing cannulas?' and they weren't able to come up with anything apart from that little bit they get at the beginning of their training, nothing . . . that and so they virtually said that if we take that job off the Residents they won't get any good at it, but I really think they should have a training program because you should see the bruises. I mean the big bruises you see around the wards and I'm sure not just here, you would have been sacked in pathology.

There was quite a lot of support for her proposal from other nurses so this nurse then prepared a more formal proposal to the nursing medical/surgical committee for consideration. This committee (made up of senior nursing practitioners) agreed in principle with the proposal, refined it and then made a request to another committee to set up an in-service training course for the nurses who would participate in the scheme. It was then given approval by the hospital management committee. One senior NUM remarked to me in passing: 'I wonder what will happen when we try to take something off them that they don't want to give up. That's when it will really get interesting'.

This note of scepticism notwithstanding, the issue and its outcome have much to say about the operation of power between doctors and nurses. Firstly, they demonstrate very clearly that nurses can be acutely aware of the effects of power especially in relation to restrictions on their ability to care for patients. It can also be seen that this awareness is expressed in discourses and discursive practices relating to a particular issue. Secondly, they demonstrate that, given the right structures, nurses will not just hang around the pan room and complain about these restrictions. If they see that there is a way to do it, they will identify and articulate an issue from their standpoint, and take action for change. This raises a third point which concerns the ambiguous and sometimes contradictory role of nursing administration. It can be seen from this incident that nursing administration acted to both retard and advance nursing action over this issue. In the first instance, there was an attempt to deflect action by emphasising the need for junior doctors to get practice at venipuncture. At one level, it could be argued that nursing administration was policing the sexual division of labour. But at the same time, it was nursing administration which initiated the setting up of the structures (hospital-wide expert nursing committees) which permitted the issue and the nursing proposal to gain institutional support. In relation to this issue, I gained the impression that senior nurse administrators were prepared to support nursing demands if they were thoroughly prepared, were based on sound nursing principles and supported by a significant proportion of nurses.

This impression was later confirmed at an interview when I spoke to the Director of Nursing. I asked her if she saw support of staff as a central part of her role. She replied:

> Yes, exactly. First of all encourage them to have the courage
> to come forward with what it is that they really believe,
> based on sound professional interpretation of the situation,
> but then promoting what it is they believe at the level it
> needs to be promoted in order to have, you know, the total
> outcome.

She went on:

> I attempt to take every opportunity to get people to go away
> and think, to gather together and talk together and resolve
> together and then to come back and then for me to promote
> whatever the group thinks . . . I might need to offer guidance
> as to pitfalls they're going to face if they don't perhaps
> consider something, but I mean, that's got to be my role, to
> offer that advice, that recommendation, 'have you looked at
> this and that and the other?'

And finally:

> So I believe I share full responsibility for making sure that the
> structure is available for them and the processes are available
> for them to facilitate what has to happen.

She made it clear, however, that the pressure for change
had to come from the nurses themselves. This was a telling
illustration of the interrelationship between agency and structure in the making and the possibility of the unmaking of the
nurse/doctor division of labour. On the one hand, it was
nursing agency in the form of individual and collective dissatisfaction with existing practices which led to a more formal
proposal for a change which resulted in an extension of nursing
jurisdiction. At the same time, these actions would not have
been effective or even possible without the setting up and the
gaining of legitimacy for structures which facilitated agency.
This agency in turn strengthens the structures and enhances
their legitimacy in the eyes of the nursing staff. In this way, it
is possible to see the 'duality of structure' discussed in chapter
2. These discourses and practices are also far removed from
'the doctor–nurse game' (Stein 1967). They are also more
complex and more sophisticated than the typology of discourses proposed by Turner as 'compliance' and 'complaint'
(1986, 1987).

POWER AND MOVEMENT

These stories also demonstrate the relational nature of power and the fact that dominance has to be continually worked at and reinforced. The fact that it also had to be learnt was revealed to me in an unexpected way. It was my habit during the research for this book to spend some time during the day sitting at the nurses' station reading and writing up my notes. I had learnt that this was guaranteed to make me 'invisible'. People, especially medical staff, would conduct conversations as though I was not there. One particular day, a new patient was admitted and a VMO and a Registrar arrived to examine and admit him. After the examination they returned to the station to discuss the case. It was apparent that the VMO was using the situation to test the Registrar's knowledge and technique and rehearse him for his Fellowship exams. (These exams are the final hurdle to becoming a Specialist.) The Registrar ran through his observations and differential diagnosis, and then the VMO tested him further with more detailed questions and comments on his knowledge and technique. I became interested in the amount of time being spent on the details of the *method* of examination. It became apparent that the technique of the Registrar was being discussed not in terms of its effectiveness, *but on how it looked*. The VMO commented:

> I always sit my cardiac patients up for an examination. That way you don't have to move from their front around to their back. It just looks more professional if you don't move around too much. It just works out that way . . . the less movement you make, the slicker it looks.

The Registrar was being prepared for admittance to the elite club of the Specialists/Consultants and it was clear from this conversation that techniques which enhanced the prestige and power of the doctor were an important part of this preparation. This is especially interesting in light of the emphasis traditionally placed on movement and speed in nursing. One nurse recalled her first job as a nurse in a small country hospital where the matron was her aunt:

> (Gail) And my mother (also a nurse) said to me before I went, she said for God's sake around Thelma if you've got

nothing to do I don't care what you do but walk fast because
if she catches you walking slow you'll be for it . . .

In a hospital ward, the nurses are rarely still. The doctors,
however, moved in and out of the ward but very rarely around
(unless they were conducting a formal 'round'). It was surprising, but not greatly so, to find that movement, its range and
pace, both expressed and constituted power in the hospital
ward. It seemed that the right to be still and have others move
around you was expressive of power and gender relations.

POWER REVERSED

While power can be, and frequently is, challenged in subtle
and sometimes more obvious ways, it is rare to find it completely reversed. However, this was the case in an incident
described to me by one of the interviewees, (a senior, very
experienced nurse who was involved with 'in-service' education). I asked about the new, university-educated graduate
nurses and whether she could distinguish any significant difference in their attitudes with patients or other staff. She
replied:

> (Gail) Well actually they have less fear. I'll give you an
> example, this was a classic. You know Dr T (names a VMO),
> you know what he's like. Well he's a 'gynie' [gynaecologist]
> and if you lived in England you would call him Mr, he is
> that type of 'where's my nurse' sort of doctor. Well he was a
> patient in the ward here and was being nursed by one of the
> college people and it was beautiful because she knew nothing
> about him except that he was a doctor and on her first
> morning she walked straight up to him and said, 'All right
> Allen, up you get, off to the shower'. And it was gorgeous.
> And there was this rather straight, old-style registered nurse
> nearby and she told me, 'my teeth almost hit the floor and I
> didn't know where to look but all I knew was that I bloody
> loved it'. And he was treated just like any other patient. He
> was asked, mind if I call you Allen, not given the chance to
> answer of course, and I think in that regard even when they
> know a little bit about it, they're sort of not so intimidated.

This was interesting as well as amusing. In the long term
this incident did not represent any lasting challenge to the

existing power structure. It did, however, demonstrate the interdependency of agency and structure to power relations. When a particular agent (Dr T) was separated from the hospital power structure, the relationship of power was completely changed, even reversed. This was a rare treat for the older nurse who could not have conceived of treating the doctor in this casual, offhand way. It also demonstrated the mixture of attitudes with which the older style nurses regard the new, university-educated nurses. On the one hand, many are critical of the new graduates' 'time management skills'. On the other, they admire their courage and their sense of professional confidence. I had a strong sense that the older nurses held out great hopes for the changes that now seemed possible in a future when these more assertive and formally educated nurses would be in charge. In this regard, Australia is somewhat ahead of Great Britain where the Project 2000 reforms are being implemented more slowly.

Discourses of power were instructive and sometimes surprising in that they revealed some of the many dimensions of the way power operated in the sexual division of labour. They also revealed that nurses themselves were aware of both the restrictions and opportunities connected with these dimensions. This supports the proposition that all social actors, no matter how oppressed, have some degree of insight into the social processes which oppress them. In addition, they demonstrated the relational nature of power and the fact that while medical power was dominant, it had to be continuously worked at and reinforced. Related to this is the observation that power could be challenged over certain issues in ways that enhanced the power of the subordinate group and which had the potential to destabilise the power of the dominant group. Discourses of power also pointed to the possibility that power may well be operating in other situations where no *overt* discourses of either power or conflict were evident. I shall explore some indications of this in the following chapter and return to it again in the concluding chapter of the book.

Chapter 5

Conflict

Discourses of conflict were of particular interest in the research reported in this book for three main reasons: first, because they illustrate a clash of interest in what is supposed, in the functionalist literature, to be a 'natural' harmonious relationship based on the complementary roles of doctor and nurse. The second reason was because the existence of such discourses calls into question the widely accepted truism which casts nurses as passive or at best manipulative in their relations with doctors. Third, discourses of conflict more generally problematise the notion of the 'team' in health care with its associated assumptions concerning common goals and a community of interest. In this chapter I explore some of the many dimensions of conflict among the different health occupations within the ward under study, but in particular, that between nurses and doctors. Before moving on to an analysis of inter- and intra-group conflict, however, I will begin on an area which emerged very strongly during the interviews with the nurses—conflict with self.

CONFLICT WITH SELF

Issues around internal conflict appeared most commonly to be the result of a clash of expectations between an individual nurse's own values and expectations of self and institutional and peer priorities. Meg, a recent graduate, spoke about some of the conflicts that she experienced as a working nurse as opposed to being a student nurse on placement for clinical experience.

> (Meg) I don't think the university prepares you for the problems you have to deal with. For instance, there are many times in the day where I have time to psychologically nurse a patient and listen to their worries and try and reassure them and get them relaxed . . . but it's mainly done either when I'm feeding them breakfast or giving them a shower. I don't actually have the time to sit with them while they're relaxed and totally concentrate on them to nurse them the way I was encouraged to do as a student . . .

While Meg acknowledged that her time management skills were improving and that this was allowing her more flexibility in the time that she spent with patients, it was clear that this was an ongoing problem for even the most experienced of nurses. During an interview with an older nurse who had clocked up years of experience, Julie made what appeared to be a contradictory and somewhat mystifying statement. After describing in enthusiastic detail the things that she loved about direct patient care, she responded to my question on what she didn't like about bedside care by saying; 'I suppose the only thing that I really don't like is, I don't like the ward care'. When pressed to enlarge on this she explained:

> (Julie) Because the things that we do on the ward are serious and it doesn't really give you enough time to think about what you're doing. I mean, there are always, you know, little mistakes made and occasionally, very occasionally there are big mistakes made but it just doesn't sit well. You go home and you think, I've forgotten to do something, and I mean okay, someone else might have forgotten to type a letter, you may have forgotten to give an important medication to someone and that worries me.
> (Interviewer) Do you think that's more likely to happen when things are busy?
> (Julie) I think you'll find if you look at any hospital statistics, if they keep any records on mistakes made in nursing care, that the ward was, you know, very understaffed and busy and that's when things are more likely to go wrong.

It was apparent that what Julie did not like was the *context* in which the bedside care took place. The fact that 'it doesn't really give you enough time to think about what you are doing' creates a conflict between what had to be done and what might have been forgotten. The personal and folk knowledge of past serious mistakes only serves to heighten the tension and apprehension around issues of responsibility and their consequences. Perhaps most eloquent on this issue was Ellen, a mature-aged, enrolled nurse who had trained for nursing about five years earlier. Enrolled nurses do much of the direct patient care in a ward and it might have been expected that this would allow more time for counselling and discussion with patients, but it seemed that this heightened rather than reduced the inner conflict around time management.

> (Ellen) I suppose the whole pace of working in an acute
> hospital goes against some of the things that you've been
> taught and that really stays in your gut. You find basic types
> of things like infection control . . . you find yourself
> throwing a pillow case onto the locker because the poor, old,
> fat lady's nearly rolled off the bed and the other little nurse
> is, you know, gonna drop her any minute and every time I do
> that I can hear the lectures that we've been given. There are
> times when I'm torn when a patient asks me something and
> you know you could spend fifteen, twenty minutes . . .
> they're really just wanting you for a while and there are
> seventeen other blood pressures, temps to be taken and you've
> only just come on and they've got to be done by two-thirty. I
> find those sort of conflicts, in the acute situation, where there
> is not much time to play with, that everything is so tightly
> scheduled that if that sponge doesn't go perfectly, then yes,
> you're throwing linen onto the floor, you're using the same
> water when you know really you should have changed it,
> when your whole person is saying, look they just want you
> there, the question was just an end-in but you find yourself
> racing off.
> (I) And do you think, well this is what you're telling me . . .
> oh look, those observations aren't as important at this
> moment, but within the organisation they're the things that
> are documented and they're the things that are judged, the
> conversation is not?
> (Ellen) That's right. And I feel myself constantly torn between
> those two and compromising, staying for five minutes and
> perhaps then racing through the observations and not asking
> the next lady how she is for fear that she'll tell me. Knowing

that I've done my dash, I've spent ten minutes with bed two
and you can see the next lady sitting up ready to have a bit
of a yarn. Yeh, I find myself constantly torn.

We came back to this issue from another angle later in the
interview where she once again enlarged on what was clearly
a central and significant problem in her work as a nurse. I
include these comments as I believe they express in an honest
and clear way the sorts of feelings with which many, many
nurses would be able to identify.

(Ellen) The most frustrating thing for me is the time thing.
The tension between the time allocated for duties and the
time to offer comfort in doing those duties. So I imagine my
perfect situation as not having those time constraints because
that is where my greatest satisfaction lies, in being able to
bring comfort to someone, having time to play around with
what is going to be the best for them. Time to experiment
. . . does a rub help, does a little walk help? Deidre, we
don't have time. We end up leaving them sitting up in a chair
for two hours instead of trying that.
(I) It seems to me that you're saying that this is the central
part of how you think, of what you see as nursing, rather
than the tasks. Is that right?
(Ellen) Yes exactly. And then that carries itself over to the
task. If a lady finds a bath really much more comforting than
a shower or just having the hot water run on her back for
ten minutes. We don't seem to have the time to try that, to
be comfortable doing that, to be happy doing that. It's racing
those showers through so that they're all washed and sat up
by such and such a time and, you know, often if I'd taken
the ten minutes to have the bath or run the water, then she's
just so much more at ease for the whole morning and she
ends up not calling you back. Also, just being able to take
the time to talk to them about what they like to eat. I know
there are diet people but they're so intent on ticking and
crossing the menu . . . just to talk about nice little extra
things that they like that I know the kitchen would do if we
asked.

Of course, it was just these sort of time constraints that
primary nursing was supposed to supersede.[1] Yet it seems that
a combination of budget constraints, institutional culture, individual ward arrangements and entrenched attitudes are still
able to dominate the routines of even the most forward think-

ing of teaching hospitals. Is there some sort of 'proud house-keeping' ideology operating here? Would a nurse be embarrassed if 'her' patients were the only ones not washed and ready when doctor arrived to do a 'round'? Would visible disorder appear as some sort of outward symbol of inefficiency and inability to manage? These conflicting ideologies are powerful and inevitably put conscientious nurses in a highly uncomfortable position. They result in the nurse experiencing feelings of inner conflict and of guilt. As Coward has pointed out when speaking of women more generally: 'Nowhere is women's complicity clearer than in the way they take personal responsibility for issues which should have social and political solutions' (Coward 1992:108). In this particular case it would require a powerful and unequivocal policy from nursing administration to positively encourage a change in care priorities if any real and lasting change were to occur. It would mean ending the complicity which is built on the assumption that visibly well ordered wards and patients are the first order priority for healing the sick. It would also require nurses to acknowledge their own feelings of exposure and inadequacy if their patients do not look 'perfect'. It would mean not working towards an outer show of housekeeping competence for a real or imagined medical audience. It was these sorts of changes that were implemented in the Nursing Development Units which were established both here and in the UK. However, these units attracted medical opposition in Britain and were eventually closed (Pearson 1988; Salvage 1992). There has been renewed pressure in Britain for more NDUs and in Australia there are several in the early stages of operation.

CONFLICT BETWEEN NURSES

Despite the emphasis in nursing literature on 'horizontal violence' (Roberts 1983), during the period of observation in this hospital, I encountered little overt conflict between nurses in the ward under observation. The examples of open or acknowledged conflict which I witnessed occurred between doctors from different specialist areas and between nurses and other health professionals (occupational therapist and social worker) and, in some specific instances, between nurses and doctors. However, while conflict between nurses was not observed in person, there were reports of it which emerged during interviews. It is important not to ignore nurse/nurse conflict because in its latent and overt forms it is germane to how gender 'works' in hospitals and other health care settings (Roberts 1983). Gail talked about her feelings when, as a student nurse, she was sent to theatre. Theatre could always be a scary place for new nurses. It was (and probably still is) very much a closed world where the surgeons and anaesthetists are able to wield enormous power and where strange personalities and relationships are able to flourish.

> (Gail) Everyone was shit-scared of theatre.
> (Interviewer) Was it as bad as you thought it would be when you got there?
> (Gail) No, it was fine, I survived. They had one savage, mean, nasty, horrible, strange theatre sister in there that would pick out a person on the roster and that person would be her whipping post for the whole roster and if you were unlucky enough to score that, I mean you copped it sweet because this is theatre and you can't do much about it, but then you copped it sweet but you had the others around sort of saying, you poor bastard . . .
> (I) Do you think that there are still characters around like that?
> (Gail) Depends on the hospital administration. Depends on how much they're willing to tolerate. It depends on the position of the person. I think there's one particular hospital in this region that is an absolute haven for misfits. I was hit as a student nurse during training and that person's still employed and I wasn't the only one.

While today's student nurses are unlikely to have to put up with physical abuse, it is still clearly a vulnerable time. Meg talked about her feelings when verbally 'put down' by the registered nurses in the hospitals where she was doing her student placements:

> (Meg) The major thing that stuck in my head was not to ask another registered nurse a question while on clinical, always find the supervisor because the reaction has been, 'typical university nurse' . . . and that made you feel so degraded. Okay, the hospital, the sisters were cranky because they were

understaffed and overworked and we were the next generation of nurses and when we decided to go nursing this was the only choice we had to become a nurse and here we were on the job trying to train to become the sisters, to help out these sisters in the next couple of years and they were putting us down. It used to make me feel so depressed.

There were also instances where nurses felt let down by their peers in matters involving emotional work and emotional pain. Julie talked about an episode which still causes her pain:

(Julie) That was probably one of the things that I really hated about nursing was the fact that years ago when I trained, the emotional part of it for us, you know, we may have covered emotional care of the patient but not emotional care of ourselves, and well, it just wasn't an issue, and we certainly weren't taught anything to do with dealing with grieving relatives or dying patients. I mean I really had no idea. I remember one night, I was on night duty and a casual and I was asked to go to coronary care and do a layout on a patient which I did. It was a young person, forty-three, who had a massive heart attack and died and then they asked me to go over to another ward and 'special' a seventeen-year-old boy who was dying, he had leukaemia and he had a massive pulmonary haemorrhage and he was just bleeding to death with his mother and father sitting beside the bed. I was a mess, I was a mess, and I had to go in and out of the room trying to hold back my tears.
(Interviewer) Because in those days you weren't encouraged to show any feeling?
(Julie) What I should have done was stand there and just cry and say, oh isn't this terrible, but, and I was such a mess by the end of the night, well I went home and I sobbed all day, I just sobbed, and I thought it was a terrible thing to do because this boy had been on this particular ward on and off for the two year course of his illness and they had brought me in. I should have been out helping in the ward with a permanent member of staff in with the parents but it obviously wasn't looked at as being an important issue. I sort of went out at one stage and said, look, this is terrible, I'm not coping at all. Can't I come out and you come in? The sister went away and did something and anyway the boy died before she came back to me but I mean that was just horrendous.

She went on to say that she had changed a lot since then, had voluntarily attended grief counselling courses and now felt that this was one of her strengths. She told me: 'I feel that I do handle, oh handle's the wrong word, I'm probably a good person to have around if there's a death on the ward and I can deal with the relatives and I mean, if I cry then it doesn't worry me'.

I include this story because it is typical of the experience of countless other nurses who have endured the seemingly callous and cavalier attitude to their emotional and psychological well-being. There is also a complicity operating here. It is a complicity with scientific medicine which is focused on the illness and treatment and which values and rewards scientific detachment and finds the expression of emotion 'unprofessional' and embarrassing. There have been huge changes in the nursing literature and in nursing practice in this area, however medicine has such a long way to go. I wonder how many male doctors would be prepared to sit and weep with a patient or their relatives? I suspect it would be few indeed. Nevertheless, this research demonstrates that it is also important not to idealise nursing in this area. Caring is not something that happens automatically because most nurses happen to be women. Care is also a form of work (James 1992) and it is work that requires education, an encouraging and accepting environment and active peer support. These insights into nurse/nurse conflict are important because they show that the sexual division of labour, like gender relations, more generally is not simply imposed from above. It is also in the attitudes of nurses and nurse administrators whose daily practice may discipline junior nurses' attitudes and their expression while reinforcing medical power and authority. It has taken the courageous actions of nurses like Julie who have broken through those numbing barriers and worked for the right to share and express emotional pain with their patients and with each other.

DOCTOR/DOCTOR CONFLICT

It became apparent during the course of this research that there was also the potential for conflict to emerge in interactions between doctors. For most of the time there were subtle conflict avoidance rules at play which militated against the expression of overt conflict. Underlying these rules was a strict adherence to authority marked out by seniority and territory. Junior doctors obeyed the instructions of senior doctors even when they did not agree with them (see below). All doctors respected the territory of other doctors; that is, patients were owned ('came in under') a specific doctor or team and no 'outside' doctor would ever give an opinion on that patient unless specifically asked to do so. Even when asked to give an opinion (as we shall see), the potential was there for misunderstandings and the breakdown of the collegiate veneer.

The first incident began with an altercation between a junior Resident Medical Officer/Senior House Officer (RMO) and a patient's daughter. The daughter wanted her father, who was in great pain, to be given a dose of morphine immediately. The RMO was not prepared to do this. He stated that he wanted time to properly read the patient's notes and to thoroughly assess him. The situation was also complicated by the fact that the patient was known to be a morphine addict (the original cause of his addiction was treatment for his arthritis by a GP). The daughter then took matters into her own hands by firstly, going down to Intensive Care (ICU) (where her father had been a patient) and demanding that the Registrar come up to the ward immediately, and secondly, requesting that the VMO/Consultant (whom she met on the stairs) come up and tell the other junior doctors what was to be done. She walked back into the ward with the VMO who looked uncomfortable but who then instructed the RMO to order some morphine. As he and the daughter went into the patient's room, the RMO turned to me, visibly angry, and said: 'This is the fourth addict I've had this week. I'm sick of it'. Just then the Registrar from ICU, who had agreed with the RMO that a full assessment was needed before the 'old bloke' could have his morphine, arrived breathless and nervous. He asked: 'Is he still in there? Is it safe to go in?' His position was probably the most difficult of all. On the one hand he was required to support the junior RMO who had asked his advice, on the other he needed to be 'on-side' with the VMO who was his superior and who could be important for his career advancement. As it was, the VMO was the height of diplomacy. When he emerged from the patient's room he quietly detailed his instructions and then ended up by apologising to the two more junior doctors. He was clearly aware that while he had the authority to do what he did because of his position in the hierarchy, he had over-stepped the bounds of territory. He said: 'I couldn't avoid coming up here because she approached me directly'. This mollified the anger and anxiety of the other doctors and in this instance overt conflict was avoided.

The second incident was much more dramatic because of ambiguities to do with status and gender. It occurred while I was observing a medical round with a VMO (Dr B) and his entourage. We were leaving one patient and had just entered the main corridor of the ward when Dr B was approached by a female geriatrician (a fellow Specialist/Consultant and so his equal). She had been asked earlier by Dr B to provide a geriatric consultation on one of his patients and wanted to give him her views on this. She began with 'Hello Mark' and then went on in a somewhat jocular vein; 'what that man needs is a "happy pill"'. Dr B stiffened and said; 'No, I don't agree with that'. She appeared to be taken aback but continued in a good natured way: 'Well Mark, you won't get him home without it'. There followed a tense and increasingly hostile discussion which culminated in Dr B saying: 'Well apart from sedating this patient . . . do you have any other suggestion'? The female geriatrician replied:

> I was not suggesting you sedate this patient. I was suggesting
> that he have an interim mood stabiliser so that he can make
> some decisions about his life. Look Mark, I am not joking
> now, you have made clear your view of my clinical
> judgement. I will simply write it up and then you can do
> with it what you like!

She was furious. He appeared annoyed and sullen. We continued the ward round as though it had not happened. The charge nurse discussed the incident with me later. She agreed that she had never seen two Specialists behave to each other in such a way. She told me that the geriatrician was widely respected and an excellent doctor and would be the last person to jump to sedation as a solution to a behavioural problem. Dr B could not have put a worse interpretation on her advice nor offered her a worse insult. It was a difficult one to fathom. What had gone wrong here? It seemed that somehow the action of the geriatrician in confronting him in public with her advice broke some unspoken rule and put him on his guard. Her approach was one with which women are perhaps more comfortable. It was a more informal, slightly jocular way of approaching the subject with the expectation that the other person would respond in the same tone. It was clearly an 'opener' which she expected would be followed by some discussion between equals. However, Dr B responded in a way which was designed to put her down in front of the other staff. He could easily have deferred a discussion of the issue in any number of ways that would have avoided strong, open conflict. Yet it was as though once she had approached him publicly, there had to be a winner and a loser.

The final area of conflict between doctors, and perhaps the most significant, concerned the potential treatment of dying patients, which was also a highly contentious area between doctors and nurses. This was revealed to me during an interview with one of the doctors from the palliative care team. In this interview she talked about the underlying tension between her area and that of oncology (a medical speciality which is concerned with cancer and its treatments). In palliative care the focus is on patient comfort and quality of life. She talked about some of the difficulties which arose when one of their patients needed to be re-admitted to hospital to have a specific problem corrected. In this situation, difficulties could arise if the patient was admitted under an oncology specialist. The 'danger' as she perceived it was that it was then 'open slather' for more tests and investigations, thus putting a dying patient through additional pain and discomfort. In this situation it was a fine line between what was necessary for the patient and what was useful for medical knowledge. If the patient arrived in casualty, sometimes there would be an informal phone call made by one of the nurses (or sometimes a relative) so that steps could be taken to have the patient admitted under the remit of palliative care. While I discuss this in more detail in chapter 7, it is important to note the significance of this conflict in medical philosophy and practice. It indicates that doctors are not always a coherent, unified bloc, either in principle or in practice. A flaw in much of the sociological literature pertaining to the issue of medical dominance and the sociology of professions is that the medical profession is almost invariably presented as a powerful and unified bulwark against other health occupations. While I do not wish to underestimate the power and authority of medicine, it is also vital to see it as riven with internal conflicts and contradictions with an authority that has to be constantly worked at to be maintained. It is also important to recognise and make visible instances and opportunities where members and sections of the medical profession turn against their peers and make alliances with other health occupations. This is precisely what this palliative care Registrar described to me and we shall see other instances of it in coming chapters.

CONFLICT BETWEEN NURSES AND DOCTORS

The most significant instances of obvious conflict between nurses and doctors related, as discussed above, to appropriate levels of intervention for the dying patient. While these instances are discussed in detail below, it is worthwhile to discuss here some possible explanations for this. In relation to patients who are dying, the holistic perspective of many nurses puts them in opposition to doctors when the case for medical intervention is on less secure ground. It seems also that in this area the medical profession is less unified amongst themselves. This was one key area where overt conflict was expressed and played out. It was also an area where conflict was played out in ways which did not always reflect medical dominance.

However, it does not follow that there was no conflict between doctors and nurses over other issues. There were several instances where a surface calm and apparent consensus gave way upon probing to comments which revealed a conflict of perspective or approach. For instance, at no point in the course of the study, did any of the nurses articulate any fundamental disagreement over the division of labour with doctors. And yet, when questioned over particular issues, many revealed deep dissatisfaction and anger with medical attitudes and practices. Bev, for instance, was a very senior nurse with whom I had covered many shifts. I saw her deal with difficult situations with skill and an attitude best described as sanguine. She appeared to adapt easily to new and changed situations and I saw her more than once apologise to a VMO for something that had actually been quite out of her control. She appeared to be a classic example of a woman in a woman's job who constantly 'mediated social relations' (Smith 1984:83). I was interested to explore her ideas and feelings about her work from her standpoint. On the surface it appeared that she completely accepted the division of labour and all its ramifications. And yet at interview, when asked to talk about and give instances of relations with doctors she had this to say:

> (Bev) Well you just have to communicate with them. I can't stand it when the Residents won't co-operate. You know how it is, you can help them to do things and when you just can't get them to do their bit it just holds everything up.
> (Interviewer) What sort of things? Like writing up scripts and that sort of thing?
> (Bev) Yeh, or if a patient needs to be seen and you page the Resident and you just get totally ignored . . .
> (I) Because there is nothing that you can do beyond what you've done?
> (Bev) It's out of my control.
> (I) Yes.
> (Bev) And you just, . . . you can't get them to co-operate. Well they're holding us up so the patient suffers because we can't do what we should be doing.
> (I) Does that happen very often?
> (Bev) Yeh, it can. I mean it depends on who you work with . . . there's only one at the moment who takes his time and he's a bit slow but I can eventually get him moving. In the last lot we had one who would just please himself and it just makes it so frustrating and the patient suffers.

And:

> (Bev) I mean we can get cranky and we let off our steam and we can go out the door but it's the patient in the long run who suffers because you can't get any cooperation and that's the thing that frustrates me . . . you can't get co-operation.

This nurse had shown herself to take very assertive action over specific issues (see chapter 6) and yet there is a strong sense of general frustration at the way things happen in the ward by comparison with the way she would like them to happen. Her discourses revolve around the idea of co-operation, of health professions facilitating the work of each other in the interests of the patient. And yet the reality is a situation where one occupational group has the power (and uses it) to 'hold up the work' of another group to the detriment of patient care. The question arises: What processes are at work to prevent this general level of frustration from being expressed as open conflict? I will return to this question after describing two other incidents involving conflict which was not immediately obvious or accessible.

The first incident involved an elderly (94-year-old) patient whose condition had deteriorated after an adverse reaction to the administration of a certain drug. It was clear (from rounds and medical notes and comments) that the doctors in charge of her case felt bad about this, and were making 'heroic' attempts to 'stabilise' her. The nurses, on the other hand, considered that this patient had 'given up' and should be allowed to die in peace. This particular afternoon, the RMO arrived with a laboratory assistant and announced briefly to the nurses: 'I'm going to do a bone marrow aspiration on Mrs T'. He walked away towards the patient as both nurses said 'Oh no'. One made the additional comment: 'I've never heard of anything so cruel'. I couldn't help wondering if the Nurse Unit Manager (NUM) would have taken further action to delay the procedure. As it was, the Resident and the lab assistant returned laughing after a couple of minutes with the patient. The nurse asked what the patient had thought about a bone marrow aspiration. The Resident replied:

> (RMO) Wouldn't have a bar of it. Boy, is she confused. Wouldn't even let me roll her over onto her back. She tried to hit me and said: 'Men and women are equal now you know'. She was still going as I walked away.

The RMO then rang his Registrar to let him know that he was unable to perform the procedure because of the patient's 'confusion'. When he hung up, one of the nurses said to him: 'You can't blame her, can you?' The RMO then looked a little shamefaced and said quietly:

> (RMO) When I saw it [the order] I thought, oh, here's another general physician getting carried away . . . why can't she just die?

As he left, one nurse made the comment:

> (Nurse) Why couldn't he have said that before he tried to do it?

Another made the comment some time later:

> (Nurse) The doctors seem to want to save her for their sakes, not hers.

The second incident concerns a visit to a patient by a specialist oncologist to deliver some test results. I was out of the ward at the time, but on my return the NUM described the event to me: 'His manner of communicating the results left something to be desired. In fact, what he told her was: "You will be dead in six weeks".' According to the NUM, this had left the patient devastated, her husband in 'total denial' and the rest of the family 'disturbed and chaotic'. As a result of this incident, the nurses had to 'pick up the pieces' which they were still doing when I arrived back. This involved nurses counselling the patient, her husband and other family members and arranging a visit from one of the pastoral care people. They also arranged for the oncologist to come back to speak to the family. The last thing I heard before leaving the ward for the day was an incredulous comment from the NUM: that the oncologist had returned to speak to the family, but this time had talked about the patient's diabetes, without mentioning her impending death at all. Apparently, none of the family members were comfortable enough to raise the subject. By the end of the day, the whole family was upset and confused and all the nurses were involved in counselling the patient, the relatives and by now many of the other patients in the ward who had also become upset. One of the nurses made the comment to me: 'It's bad enough that someone is dying, they shouldn't have to go through all this as well'.

Both these incidents are notable for the way that latent conflict can be seen to lie just below the surface of the transactions between the nurses and doctors. While there was no obvious or overt conflict, there remains a strong sense that there is a quite profound difference in approach and practice that constitutes, in these instances, a contradiction between the goals and work practices of the doctors and those of the nurses. There is also a sense of the way in which the efforts of the nurses 'mediated' the emotions of the patients in ways which spared the doctors from involvement. In this case, as in countless others, the work of nurses spared the doctor from having to deal, over an extended period, with the pain, fear and anguish of the patient and relatives. In a very real sense, the doctor's ineptness and avoidance was only possible because of the emotional 'overtime' performed by the nurses. This provides a telling illustration of the sexual division of labour in action. But it is also important that this instance be seen as expressing something more than the socially constituted gendered behaviour of men and women. It was also expressive of the underlying knowledge base and framework of the two occupations. As I stated in an earlier chapter, the dominant discourse of the bio-medical model is both mechanistic and reductionist. Through its concentration on more and more detailed aspects of physical 'malfunction', it is not only easy for a practitioner to lose sight of the patient, it is almost essential that this happens. In this way the focus is kept clear and 'objectivity' is maintained. Nursing, on the other hand, has retained important aspects of other forms of knowledge which place as much emphasis on thought and feeling as on physical processes (see chapter 3). This is not to say that objectivity in itself is a bad thing. Keller makes a useful distinction between what she calls dynamic and static objectivity. She defines static objectivity as 'the pursuit of knowledge that begins with the severance of subject from object' (1985:117). This, she argues is what characterises masculinist science. A de-gendered science would, however, aim for and work towards dynamic objectivity. 'Dynamic objectivity aims at a form of knowledge that grants to the world around us its independent integrity but does so in a way that remains cognizant of, indeed relies on, our connectivity with that world' (1985:117). It is clear that many of the encounters described above are marked by static objectivity and that this diminishes both the practitioner and the patient.

GENDER AND KNOWLEDGE

What then is the connection between gender and these different models of knowledge? Feminist theorists such as Harding and Keller argue that the connection is more than coincidental. Keller, for instance, argues that the scientific approach of objectifying the subject under study is inherently gendered; that it bears the 'imprint' of masculinity (1985:78). The essence of such an interpretation, however, is at base essentialist or what

Connell has termed 'categorical', meaning that it is based on a view of masculinity which holds that it is *essentially* distancing, objectifying and controlling (1987:54). The implications of this view are that there are essential and therefore immutable characteristics of men and women which give them 'in-built' tendencies towards different attitudes and ways of being and acting. The problem with this interpretation is that it is then but a small step to arguing that men and women have inherent strengths and weaknesses which make them more suited to some jobs than others. We are then back to the ideology of 'naturalism' which was criticised at the outset of this book.

How then might we explain the evidence just presented at the same time as rejecting an essentialist or naturalist explanation? In other words, if it is not 'natural', how is it that men and medicine fit together so well? Keller points us in a useful direction when she discusses the psychoanalytic theories of Freud, Winnicott and Chodorow in relation to the development of masculinity. Chodorow (1978) is especially interesting in that she provides a social explanation for seemingly inherent masculine or feminine characteristics and behaviours. In essence, Chodorow argues that the process of primary attachment to the mother results in boy children having to repudiate their mother both as a separate person and as *female* in order to establish an independent identity which is at once separate and *male*. This results in boys growing up with a need for more clear-cut ego boundaries, a fear about the dangers of emotional merging (for fear of losing their hard won, distinct male identity) and a consequent greater need for separateness.

> Boys and men come to deny the feminine identification within themselves and those feelings they experience as feminine: feelings of dependence, relational needs, emotions generally. They come to emphasise differences, not commonalities or continuities, between themselves and women, especially in situations that evoke anxiety, because these commonalities and continuities threaten to challenge gender difference or to remind boys and men consciously of their potentially feminine attributes. (Chodorow, 1994, p. 45)

Because of early developed insecurities about core gender identity, it becomes important for boys and men to have a clear sense of gender difference and to have clear boundaries between what is feminine and what is masculine. Object relations theory has been applied to research on nurses by Williams, who found that: 'Male nurses go to great lengths to carve for themselves a special niche within nursing that they then define as masculine' (1989:14). She found that male nurses gravitated towards 'action' and high-tech areas such as Accident and Emergency and Intensive Care which became identified as male nurse territory. She concludes her study with the observation:

> The achievement of masculinity is today intertwined with
> demonstrating superiority and essential difference from
> females. It is this meaning of masculinity—deeply rooted as it
> is in personality and, ultimately family structure—that must
> be challenged if any real inroads toward sexual integration
> and, ultimately, sexual equality can be attained. (Williams
> 1989:143)

Because it underpins an explanation of masculinity which is at once social and historical, this approach also allows for connections to be made between the micro worlds of home and hospital with other manifestations of patriarchy in the wider society. In particular, it points to the fact that the degree of change possible in the sexual division of labour will, to a significant degree, be dependent on changes in the acquisition of masculine (and feminine) identities within individuals.

As well as looking at the 'fit' between medicine and masculinity, we also need to examine the attraction that nursing has historically held for women. While interviewing the nurses for this research, I frequently found that when I asked them for their reasons for choosing nursing, they could not say that it actually involved a conscious decision. Instead, they spoke of their attraction or drift into nursing as either an unconscious 'pull', or in some cases in a language which was close to a kind of longing. A few examples follow:

> (Leonie) For as long as I could remember as a child I wanted
> to be a nurse. I mean, I can remember saying 'Oh I'm going
> to be a nurse when I grow up' when I was four years old
> and the desire to be a nurse probably didn't go away.

> (Bev) As far as I can remember I'd always wanted to be a
> nurse or work in a hospital but when I left school I wasn't
> ready to commit myself to shift work.

(Denise) I guess I always did want to nurse. I went through stages when I was at school where I wanted to nurse, I wanted to teach and couldn't decide. When I was thirteen I came in here to have my appendix out and that was basically what decided it. You know, I just sort of watched what the nurses did and I knew there was no other choice for me and for a while I dipped into other things but nursing won out in the end.

(Susan) Why I decided and how long ago are probably both difficult (to answer) in the sense that for a very long time I knew I was going to be a nurse. Now exactly when that decision was made in my thinking I really couldn't say. It's sort of one of those things that I was always going to go nursing but I was never going straight from school.

There is clearly a deep, strong attraction operating here and one which the nurses, even now, could not explain. In some cases the desire for nursing had to be postponed for practical reasons. For instance, Susan (above) determined that she would not begin nursing until she had bought her own car and had enough money behind her so that she would not have to live-in at the nurses' home. She qualified as a shorthand typist and then got a job with a city council. She was promoted several times and appeared to be on a career roll. But the idea that she would eventually turn to nursing was 'always in the back of my mind'. She went on to say that her friends would tease her by saying:

Oh, you're obviously not going to go nursing, you're loving it too much . . . and, sure, I did love it. I had a great life, it was great money, it was easy street, I had a great social life, the whole bit, and people always told me, you know, you won't go nursing. But I knew I would.

In the event she applied for nursing before reaching her financial goals because she felt so 'frustrated' (her word) that she could wait no longer. She has now been in nursing for over twenty years. This suggests we need to look beyond purely conscious and rational explanations to fully understand such a strong attraction to an occupation. A crucial point here is that this is not simply about what these women were going 'to do' but more fundamentally, what they were going 'to be'. Tong describes this well when she states: '. . . femininity is not a way of being that a girl deliberately decides to assume; rather, it is a slow gradual process that seizes the psyche of a girl before she is self-consciously aware of herself as a girl' (Tong 1994:153). While this is to some extent true of many occupations, it seems that with nursing the connections between identity and occupation go deeper than most. I well remember myself the deep thrill involved in putting on that heavily starched uniform for the first time. The striped dress with detachable buttons, the starched white pinafore, the black stockings, the starched cap . . . you felt as though you were meeting a part of yourself which was at the same time completely new, and yet one with which you were thoroughly at home. I remember that we all paraded around for hours, admiring ourselves and each other in a kind of gender euphoria at having merged childhood fantasies with adult realities.

The connections between individual identity and nursing are clearly inextricably tied up with gender identity. It is women, not men, who are attracted to nursing in droves. Can object relations theorists help our understanding of 'the fit' between femininity and nursing as well as that between masculinity and medicine? You will recall that Chodorow argued that the process of primary attachment to and separation from the mother is different for female children. Unlike boy children, who must repudiate the femaleness of their mother in order to establish their own separate, masculine identity, girl children have only to undergo a single separation from their mother which does not entail a rejection and repudiation of female characteristics and identity. According to Chodorow, this results in girls growing up with less sharply defined boundaries of the self and a greater need for finding emotional completeness in relationships. Indeed, while the capacity for relatedness is underdeveloped in men, in women it is overdeveloped. Because of this, girls, and later women, look for closeness with others, take pleasure in intimacy and feel bereft if is not an ongoing part of their lives.

This does not mean that the process of acquiring and maintaining a gendered self is unproblematical or without conflict for girls. Chodorow herself sees an important source of conflict in the devaluing of so much of what is 'female' in our society.

The difficulties that girls have in establishing a 'feminine' identity do not stem from the inaccessible and negative definition of this identity, or its assumption by denial (as in the case of boys). They arise from identification with a negatively valued gender category, and an ambivalently experienced maternal figure, whose mothering and femininity, often conflictual for the mother herself, are accessible, but devalued. Conflicts here arise from questions of relative power, and social and cultural value. (Chodorow 1994:46)

These conflicts can be expressed at many levels. They are expressed when women and men devalue ideas, actions and occupations that are seen as feminine. They are expressed when nurses have to struggle in all sorts of devious ways to have patients' needs met because the male doctors have immense difficulty in dealing with the emotional dimension of sickness and death. They are expressed when individual men have to fight against their own desires to nurture because of societal discomfort with challenging images of masculinity. They are certainly expressed at every level in the sexual division of labour. The point is that men have the social power to institutionalise their unconscious defences against repressed yet strongly experienced developmental conflicts (Chodorow 1994:47). In other words, they have the social power to avoid or at least minimise their involvement with situations which they find emotionally confronting or uncomfortable. The work of Chodorow and other object relations theorists points to the crucial fact that the sexual division of labour is permeated from within by the deepest psychic desires, fears and insecurities.

There have been important criticisms of the work of Chodorow and other object relations theorists. In particular, there have been criticisms concerning both the ahistorical and uni-cultural underpinnings of her work. It has been argued that Chodorow failed to take into account the diverse cultural forms taken by the family in different cultures and at different times (Lorber et al. 1981). Others have criticised the prescription of dual parenting as the solution to complex problems of gender and identity (Jaggar 1983; Raymond 1986). Certainly, to view primary attachment and differentiation from the mother as *the* cause of gender polarities and dual parenting as *the* solution to the sexual division of labour is both overstating the case and seriously underestimating the complexity of the issue. Such a blueprint for action also has serious political limitations. If gender polarities are constructed in the psyche in early childhood, what is the point of working against them elsewhere? Clearly the sexual division of labour operates at every level, in the psyche, in the family, in organisations as well as in and through the institutions of the state. Attempts to break it down will also have to be worked through at each of these sites, across different events and times. What object relations theory is able to do is not so much provide a cause and solution for gender inequality; rather it reveals important aspects of the inner workings of gender construction and the splitting of emotional life. It reveals the way that men, and to a certain extent women, have investments in the sexual division of labour despite its (sometimes terrible) effects and consequences. It indicates that the construction of a gendered identity goes to the heart of the sexual division of labour and that the polarisation of emotional impulses goes to the source of human unease with current work arrangements, especially those which involve caregiving and close human contact. It is in work environments such as the hospital ward that supposedly functional work arrangements can be seen to be conflictual at their very core. In such an environment deeply felt latent and overt tensions are unavoidable and inevitably the care of patients is affected and not infrequently diminished.

Chapter 6

Skill

The concept of skill—how it is defined, recognised and rewarded—is fundamental to the sexual division of labour between doctors and nurses. Its importance was underlined for Australian nurses when the Australian Council of Trade Unions (ACTU) failed to win a wage increase for nurses in 1986 through the application of the principle of 'comparable worth'. Comparable worth is a method of job evaluation where the pay rates for male and female workers are evaluated in order to bring female pay rates up to the level of those of men doing work of equal value in the same or different occupations (Dickenson 1993:281). The ACTU had asked the commission to compare nurses with ambulance drivers for the purposes of skill comparison. The Conciliation and Arbitration Commission rejected the principle of comparable worth, and all such cases were ruled out because of the threat they pose to the stability of the wage fixing system. The NSW Nurses Association (with ACTU support) was eventually more successful in having nursing achieve professional rates of pay in 1988, with the concomitant acceptance of nursing as a profession. It ought to be thought-provoking at the least to consider that it was easier to have nursing recognised in an Industrial Tribunal as 'professional' than to have it recognised as being equivalent to the 'skilled' occupations of men.

The category of skilled work has been jealously guarded by male workers and their industrial representatives. Through the success of this strategy, there has been established an historical relationship between skill, men's work and masculinity. Hilary Rose has pointed out that in learning to recognise women's skills it has been necessary to tackle a cornerstone of patriarchal ideology, namely that where 'skill' is, women are not (Rose 1994, p. 37). For this reason, the classification of men's jobs as skilled and women's jobs as unskilled (or semi-skilled) often bears little relation to the amount of training or the ability required for them. As Phillips and Tayler commented in their influential paper on this subject: 'Far from being an objective fact, skill is often an ideological category imposed on certain types of work by virtue of the sex and power of the workers who perform it' (1980). How skill is conceptualised, recognised and practised has as much to with power relations as with its more obvious associations of manual dexterity, knowledge and technique (Braverman 1974; Game & Pringle 1983; Cockburn 1983). The work of healing is no exception. Yet nurses themselves had difficulty in describing what they did in terms of skill. When pushed to do so, nurses tended to conceptualise and articulate their skills in a way which reflected their dual orientations to medical and nursing priorities. Doctors, on the other hand, defined the skills of nurses very narrowly, and frequently in relation to medical priorities. Nursing skills were, by definition, inextricably linked to medical needs and nurses were judged by their ability to service those needs. As a result, many of the complex skills of the nurses in this study remained either unnamed, unrecognised, or both. This was revealed through observing nursing and medical actions and also at follow-up interviews with doctors, nurses and other health professionals connected to the ward.

MEDICAL PERCEPTIONS OF NURSING SKILLS

While it may have been true in the past that doctors considered nursing skills in relation to housekeeping tasks, today's doctors appear to have a more sophisticated view of the nature and variety of nursing skills. In large measure, medical perceptions of nursing skills appear to centre around the daily care of the patient and nurses' ability to observe the patient and gather

information. For instance, when I asked one doctor his view
on the role of the nurse, he replied:

> (Dr S) Well, they are members of the team . . . they are there
> for the day by day management of the patient, to provide
> care for the patient. The main focus is the medical one, but
> the nurse often has better opportunities and certainly more
> extended opportunities to gather information—for instance, I
> don't wash patients.
> (Interviewer) Would you like to?
> (Dr S) No.
> (I) Why not?
> (Dr S) It's hard work.
> (I) Your work is hard work.
> (Dr S) Yes, but it's of my choosing—and besides, it [washing
> patients] is unpleasant, or it can be. My sister is a nurse—she
> tells me that it can be satisfying, that she enjoys it. I suppose
> in a funny sort of way, it's like washing and cleaning a
> child—although I clean my own children—no I wouldn't like
> to do that.
> (I) Do you think that those sort of activities: washing,
> dressing, back care, can be therapeutic in themselves?
> (Dr S) You mean giving someone a bath or organising to get
> their hair done so they'll feel better?
> (I) Yes.
> (Dr S) Oh, you mean the communication?
> (I) Yes, the whole range of contact.
> (Dr S) I suppose they could be. Certainly patients feel better
> with certain nurses. Sometimes they'll ask to go to a certain
> ward because of a particular nurse and they relax when they
> know she is there.

And later:

> (I) Where does medical and nursing work intersect?
> (Dr S) At the patient's bedside. It is different work with
> different opportunities to gather information. We meet back at
> the team to pool information.

I suspect that this doctor was deflecting and avoiding the
issue when he answered that he did not want to wash patients
because it was 'hard work'. I further suspect that it was the
intimacy and the servicing (female) nature of the work which
made it 'unpleasant'. To an extent, this is confirmed by his
analogy with washing and cleaning his children and his

uncertainty about why he didn't mind doing that. It is possible that what we have here is a doctor who expresses 'the feminine' at home where it is safe to do so, at the same time as repressing the feminine in his public work and his public identity where a definite type of masculinity is necessary to maintain status within the organisation. It is as though there is a new division of masculine identity for 'modern' men between the public sphere and the private sphere where the boundaries between masculine and feminine identity are more relaxed. It is useful to recall here Chodorow's insights into the tenuousness of masculine identity and the need for men to define masculinity in opposition to all that is perceived as feminine or, in this case, as women's work. Caring is a constitutive activity through which women achieve their femininity and against which masculinity takes shape (1978:92–110).

The work of Mary Douglas adds another dimension to this issue. In her work, Douglas argues that all societies have elements of the sacred and profane and that an ordered separation between the two is essential for the proper functioning of any society. Societies respond to disorder by developing classification systems which define what is 'dirt' as 'matter out of place'. 'Where there is dirt there is system' (Douglas 1970:35). Social and bodily boundaries keep dirt separate and anything which breaches these boundaries will be regarded as pollution. Invariably, work which involves pollution will be regarded socially as dangerous and have low status. Because of their contacts with bodies and body products ('out of place'), nurses are regarded as being involved with 'dirty work' (Lawler 1991). This connection with pollution in addition to the association of nursing with femininity makes the connection between nursing and skill extremely problematic. It also makes clearer the doctor's definition of aspects of nursing work as 'unpleasant' and his desire to avoid such work.

On this occasion as well as on others, this doctor expressed respect for particular nurses who demonstrated specific nursing skills. There is, though, a strong sense that for him the key skills are those which serve the medical focus, especially in relation to information gathering. The other essentially nursing skills are interesting, even curious, but are peripheral to the main game. This echoes the point made by Rose that within public caring, even when the relational skills of women are acknowledged, it is not in terms of financial reward or status (1994:37).

We also see here the traditional association of nursing work with mothering. This presents the modern doctor, who cares for and bathes his own children, with something of a dilemma. How to conceptualise nursing when the traditional link of mothering = female, is broken, at least to some degree at home. While it may represent something of an intellectual dilemma, it is certainly not a practical one. Doctors are free to choose what work they will or will not do and they choose not to be involved in intimate care for patients despite the excellent opportunities for information gathering that these occasions represent. In this way they avoid the emotionally uncomfortable and gender-laden intimacy of tending another person as well as avoiding the status-threatening pollution of 'dirt' or 'matter out of place' represented by a non-kin, adult body being washed in a semi-public place. At the same time, this doctor's language represents an attempt to redefine the sexual division of labour with more emphasis on gender neutral terms like 'members of a team' who have different jobs to do and different opportunities for information gathering. Yet underlying these more gender neutral terms is a multi-layered and deeply ingrained system of gender symbolisms and gender practices. It is interesting to note that the language of 'teams' also emerged in the discourses of the bosses who were interviewed by Pringle in her study of secretaries (1988:55). The end result is still a division of labour which is gendered in quite fundamental ways, but which is represented by different metaphors and which requires different and deeper forms of analysis to explicate the connections. (See also Mackay 1993:162–6.)

This medical focus on the nurse as a source of information was also reflected in a conversation between a Specialist/Consultant (VMO) and a Registrar. The two were sitting together and going through the patient's notes doing some 'detective work'. They suspected that a patient consumed more alcohol than he admitted:

> (VMO) I see the son moved in with him seven weeks ago. It would be interesting to know why. You know dig[italis] toxicity can cause confusion. (A little later) This is the sort of bloke that it would be worth ringing up his club to check on what sort of intake he does have.
> (Reg) Oh yes.

(VMO) It's worth reading the nursing notes you know. You never know what useful bits of information you pick up.

Some minutes later, one of the nurses approached the desk. The Specialist began to ask the nurse some detailed questions about the patient's behaviour. Does he wash himself, feed himself, etc. When the specialist had finished questioning the nurse, she (the Specialist) physically turned away from the nurse to remark to the Registrar: 'That's real frontal lobe stuff'. They then went on to analyse the information obtained from the nurse in relation to a possible diagnosis. The nurse was not included in this aspect of the conversation. She stood there for a moment, waiting to see if she would be included, and then walked away. This incident impressed me as a quite clear example of the way that doctors 'worked' and constituted nursing skills in a particular and, in this case, limited way. This nurse had the requisite knowledge, experience and information to enter this conversation and contribute to the analysis. The fact that she was used for a limited purpose and then excluded, was a political decision (albeit an unconscious one) which reinforced the structure of the sexual division of labour through patterns of personal behaviour. There was, though, another level underlying the personal behaviour of the participants. This was a hierarchical structure of knowledge, which constituted nursing knowledge as 'information' and medical knowledge as the requisite for analysis and diagnosis. The fact that, in this case, the Specialist was female only serves to demonstrate that the sexual division of labour between doctors and nurses is constituted through relations of power with many dimensions, including dimensions of knowledge. It further indicates that discourses around the theme of a 'team' have different meanings from different standpoints.

While among doctors there was a common positioning of nurses as a source of information, different personal styles gave different meanings to the way this information was gathered. It appeared to me that the majority of doctors took the information from nurses and passed it on without bothering to attribute any credit to the nurses' skill. One particular incident which I observed illustrates this pattern vividly. I had been on the ward since early morning and had been aware of a general concern among the nurses for a young woman,

Megan, who had been admitted for treatment of severe asthma. To my eye she appeared pale and 'blocked up' in the nose but appeared otherwise okay. She seemed happy to read, chat and wander to the bathroom when she wanted. Beverly, a clinical nurse specialist and acting NUM (Nurse Unit Manager/Senior Sister), asked me to come and have morning tea with her. As we left the ward she said: 'I am very, very worried about that girl'. She appeared to want to use me as a sounding board. She was not able to easily articulate just why she felt this way. I asked her a few questions and she replied:

> (Bev) She is really at the end of the road as far as medication is concerned—yet she still tries to walk to the shower and toilet. She can just hardly breathe.
> (Interviewer) What could happen?
> (Bev) She could have a respiratory arrest.
> (I) Is that what worries you?
> (Bev) Yes, I feel it is a real danger.

When we returned to the ward she rang the RMO (Resident Medical Officer/Senior House Officer) who had been in the ward earlier and had noted nothing untoward himself. Bev explained that this patient was 'not good'. (I have heard experienced doctors say that when a nurse says this you ignore it at your peril.) She went on to support her observations by referring to the patient's poor peak flows and the fact that she was very breathless. She finished by emphasising that she was 'very concerned'. The RMO arrived almost immediately and examined her. He then ordered a portable X-ray and requested an urgent examination from the intensive care registrar. Then, ignoring Bev, he sat down to write up his notes. It was left to Bev to elicit some feedback. She approached him and asked:

> (Bev) Doctor, what is happening with Megan?
> (Dr) I have ordered a chest X-ray and rung Jim to come to examine her with a view to re-admission to ICU (Intensive Care Unit).
> (Bev) She's that sick? That's what I was worried about.
> (Dr) Yes, she needs ICU care.

In this conversation there was no recognition for the skilful (and possibly life-saving) observations made by this nurse. There was no 'thank you for calling me' or 'it's good you were on the ball and noticed the patient's deteriorating condition'.

Rather, the skills involved in this situation were to disappear in the institutional processes of requests and reportage. After the statement 'Called to the ward to see . . .' the anonymous nurse's role in this disappeared in the medical actions that would now unfold. The clinical history of this girl would centre on medical diagnosis and actions and credit for clinical success would be attributed to careful diagnosis and drug therapy.

However, there was one Specialist, a VMO/Consultant, who seemed to include the nurse (usually the NUM/Senior Sister) as 'different but equal' especially while on a medical round. I observed these interactions on several occasions. The retinue for the round would include the VMO, the NUM, the Registrar, the Resident, a couple of medical students, and sometimes the social worker and/or an occupational therapist. I observed that the VMO walked next to the NUM with everyone else following behind. Before reaching the patient's bed, he would scan the medical notes for information and then turn to the nurse and ask simply: 'How is she?' He did not want the nurse to provide him with test results. He had access to those. What he was asking for was a nursing perspective on the patient's condition. She would provide this and they would then discuss the situation. It seemed to me that at this point, he was entering the nursing discourse with a view to linking it to the medical discourse which would follow when they began to discuss test results and the possible need for more tests. It also seemed that, by a public demonstration of recognition for the nursing perspective, he was validating and valuing nursing skills. This probably contributed to the fact that I heard no word of complaint from the nurses concerning this doctor over the period of my presence in the ward. At the same time of course, both the VMO and the NUM were also constituting and consolidating the sexual division of labour. The very recognition of a separate nursing discourse constitutes nursing knowledge and practice as separate from medicine. The key point here concerns the degree to which the nursing perspective was accorded status and recognition. This would seem to represent an important gain for nursing and a consolidation of nursing achievements. It could also represent the potential for a process of 'coming together' of compatible strands of medical and nursing work into a less bifurcated framework.

UNNAMED AND INVISIBLE SKILLS

There were, however, many complaints about other doctors in this regard. It seems that not all doctors even valued nurses as useful sources of information. One particular enrolled nurse talked about what was for her an uncommon positive experience, then followed it up with an account of a more usual occurrence.

> (Ellen) I've been with a Registrar who must have observed me in the ward and has come to ask me about someone's incontinence or about their mobility or about their feeding and I really felt he took notice of what I've said and has followed that through, has come back and asked me again and has come looking for me when the VMO comes. Now mostly I've had the opposite experience to that where the VMO and Registrar roll in and maybe the resident tries to get me to come in on the round because he knows that I've been with these ladies for a long time, but yeh, the VMO and the Registrar speak to themselves, don't include the Sister on the round let alone me and therefore, yeh, you sometimes feel that the information that you could give them is lost.

She went on to talk about the personal effort that she had made to offer information that she considered important, even when not invited, or to interrupt a round to go and sit with an agitated patient even if she felt personally intimidated:

> (Ellen) So it probably has as much to do now with my confidence and for my not taking it personally when my presence isn't acknowledged, so I seem to have got over those hurdles.

I asked her to talk a bit more on how she thought about it so that she didn't take it personally. She answered:

> I think they have just become so used to the system and trying to get certain decisions made about this patient so that certain tests are done so that certain results are back by next round, they have neither the time nor the availability to be open to that, and yes I think sometimes it's just that they don't even see me, that they're so intent on, yes, having some type of report on this patient.
> (Interviewer) Do you get a sense of being looked through or looked past?

(Ellen) Yes, yes, so that I try to keep telling myself it's not that I've been looked at and rejected it's just that I haven't been seen in the first place.

At least one other study (Mackay 1993) has confirmed that few doctors speak directly to enrolled nurses. Another nurse spoke in similar terms when she talked about how it felt when her presence was not 'accepted':

> (Interviewer) How do they show you that you are not accepted?
> (Bev) Ignore me, talk over you or around you, but there are others, I mean Dr . . . (names three doctors). They make you feel like you are part of the team. They'll speak to you, they'll ask you about the patients. You feel that you're part of a team but there are still a few who look straight through you.

This description could be a metaphor for dominant medical attitudes toward nursing knowledge and skills: They aren't so much rejected as never seen in the first place. When they are seen, it is usually in an instrumental way, in terms of how they can be useful for medical practice. And yet, there were enough positive experiences to indicate that there were changes that were being brought from both sides; that while doctors and nurses continued to 'make' the sexual division of labour, they were doing it in ways that had the potential for either small or more fundamental changes. I stress the word 'potential' for there is also the potential for doctors and nurses to re-form their working relationship in ways that are more 'modern' and that take into account a less overtly gendered discourse but that would still operate within a bifurcated knowledge base and set of practices. In this latter case, it would also likely follow that the different knowledges and practices would continue to be valued differently at the personal, institutional and public levels. Central to the possible direction of future outcomes are nursing attitudes and practices in relation to their own skills.

CARE AS SKILLED WORK

There were many instances where nurses continued to 'not see' or to deprecate their own and other nurses' skills. Writing more generally about women and work skills, Cate Poynton has called this a process of 'minimising'—'women consistently underselling themselves and their skills by saying they "just" or "only" did all sorts of things or they did "a bit" of some highly skilled task' (1993:91). She further adds:

> It is important to understand why women represent their skills and hence themselves in such ways. When women minimise, it is not because the things they do are unimportant but because women themselves are regarded as unimportant. In other words, minimising has little to do with the importance of particular workplace activities and everything to do with the status of those who are responsible for those activities, in the workplace and in society at large. (1993:91)

These comments have a clear relevence for nurses' attitudes to their own skills. For instance, one of the things that the nurses did was to 'naturalise' their skills by equating skilled care with instinctive behaviour. When interviewing Leonie, I asked her to describe to me what she did in her job. She replied:

> (Leonie) Well you just look after the patients that you've got in your care as, I feel, as a mother looks after a child.

Yet at the same time, nurses had no hesitation in presenting their work in caring as equal or superior to medical work:

> (Ellen) I think they [doctors] probably have the same goal but I'm lucky enough to be more directly involved in carrying out that goal. I think because of their pressure of time and turnover of beds . . . their goal is to get that lady home as soon as she can . . . but I'm actually able to make it happen, I think, in a more direct way.

> (Lisa) Many doctors would probably disagree, but I see the nurse in a hospital situation as probably the most important. No, I don't mean inflated important but I mean the person who has the most to do with looking after the patient and in the long term in making the greatest difference.

> (Julie) I feel, actually, that we [nurses] are the primary caregivers.

The nurses on this ward valued what they did in terms of the practices of caregiving because they saw that it had results in good outcomes for their patients. For the nurses, good patient care was the result of good nursing and good nursing was pivotal for patient recovery. It seemed, however, that there was a huge semantic and ideological divide between the concept of good nursing and the concept of skilled work. The concept of skill has been so successfully colonised by masculine work associations (technology/machinery) and assumptions that it seems almost anathema to talk of skill and work in relation to care for vulnerable people. Feminist writers were among the first to make this connection. Clare Ungerson, for instance, articulated the important distinction between caring *about* someone and caring *for* that person (1983:31). While caring *about* (which is a feeling, an emotion) has little implication for how people spend their time, caring *for* someone involves servicing their needs and necessarily involves the consumption of time and effort on the part of the carer. It is work, whether or not it is recognised and rewarded with money. Ungerson pointed out that women are expected to care. They are expected to care for their own children, husbands, elderly relatives and by implication the children, husbands and elderly relatives of other women. There is a convenient elision between this generalised caring *about* with an expectation that women will care *for* and do it because it is natural for them to do so. This elision has had and continues to have profound ideological and material consequences for women, including the fact of poor remuneration and recognition of the true value of work in 'women's' occupations (1983:49). In nursing it has meant the masking and veiling of skilled work as 'the sorts of things a mother does for a child' by both doctors, hospital administrators and nurses themselves. The identification and naming of the skills of caring in nursing is now at least under way, as the concept of care as *work* emerges as a strong theme in recent nursing literature (Neil & Watts 1991; Smith 1992: James 1992). However, as we shall see, nurses were not limited in their skills to care and observation.

CLINICAL SKILLS

When asked directly to talk about an area of excellence in their work which they felt proud of, most nurses went quite literally blank. This forced me to review my interview methods with a view to coming at their attitudes and practices in a more indirect way. I then found that discourses around skill were, in a sense, woven into a total picture of work and knowledge. At one stage I was talking to a very experienced nurse about the intersection of medical and nursing work. After describing areas of overlap, she added:

> (Bev) We've got to do what they say but I have refused to do certain things.
> (Interviewer) What sort of things?
> (Bev) A classic example was (names a doctor, a VMO/Consultant) last week, came in on Monday to see a lady who had been admitted with a CVA (a cerebral vascular accident or 'stroke'). He left a message that her NG (naso-gastric) tube could be removed. I took one look at her and said 'no way that is coming out'. He had decided that her gag reflex was sufficient for her to swallow; as far as I was concerned, she was not ready for it.
> (I) Who did you say that to?
> (Bev) The staff.
> (I) Right.
> (Bev) And I took it on myself to make that decision.
> (I) Right.
> (Bev) And (names the doctor) came in the next day with the Registrar and the Resident and I told him that the NG tube was staying and I said I don't care, you might have seen a gag but I'm not convinced that it's strong enough.
> (I) What does a gag mean? Does it mean that she can swallow?
> (Bev) Yes, swallow her own secretions and later fluid and food. I've seen two CVA patients die from choking on their own secretions and I'm not going to see any more.
> (I) And did they respect your view on that and support it?
> (Bev) Well, nothing was said about it. I didn't get into trouble and plus I get on quite well with (names doctor, uses first name) and I think he knows me and respects my judgement.

She went on to say that, to make such a decision,

> (Bev) I've got to be a hundred per cent sure in my own mind and know exactly what I'm doing before I would take a decision like that to go against one of the doctors or sisters here.

At no point in this conversation did the word 'skill' appear, and yet this nurse's confidence in her own skill underlay the entire transaction. This incident was also significant because the nurse challenged the instructions of a senior doctor (a VMO or Consultant). It goes against the findings of Walby and Greenwell (1994:23) who concluded that while nurses may challenge the decisions of younger doctors, they accept the authority of a consultant or of doctors in the more senior grades. There were other instances which were illustrative of the relationship between skill, confidence and a redefining in action of doctor/nurse relationships. The first instance, which did not end happily, was related to me during an interview when I asked one of the nurses about the distinction between medical and nursing work. She proceeded to tell me about instances of overlap—particularly where a nurse performs the function of diagnosis.

> (Gail) You will get an experienced nurse playing the doctor. Now the basis of her knowledge isn't just what the textbook says, it will usually come from her own experience. When I was training I remember one registered nurse from accident and emergency (A and E) who was just terrific. This particular day this patient came into A and E, a big, strong, healthy bloke, a football injury, he'd had a kick in the guts. This nurse said put in an IV (intravenous line) before he goes down to X-ray. The RMO says no, he doesn't need one. She says, look, he's a big fellow, very fit, he's had a bad hit, if he's got a (ruptured) spleen he'll compensate for quite some time before showing any symptoms and then he'll go bang, and that was the terminology she used. So they took him down to X-ray without an IV line and the next thing he arrests and by the time the team got there and put the line in it was too late.

This is not to say that all junior doctors would be this feckless and that all senior nurses always know best. However, examples like this were numerous enough in this study to at least raise questions about the skill levels of some junior doctors *vis à vis* that of experienced senior nurses. The two salient points here are firstly, that the advanced clinical skills of these nurses are frequently unrecognised by the medical staff (though the achievement of clinical career pathways in Australia has gone some way to remedying this), and secondly, that hierarchical authority structures within hospitals operate to place patients at risk because of the lack of genuine teamwork inherent in the traditional division of labour between doctors and nurses. The next example illustrates how things could be different.

In this case, I had been invited on a round with one of the VMOs who was popular with the nurses and whom I have discussed above in relation to his interest in nursing perspectives on his patients. On this occasion both the VMO and the nurse (NUM) asked the patient a series of questions about how she felt and about her home situation. At the end of this, the NUM said:

> I don't think you are quite ready to go home yet. I would like to keep you here for another couple of days and in that time get the occupational therapist to go home with you to do an assessment. Then we can work out any problem areas for you at home and find ways around them.

At this point she paused, laughed and turned to the doctor with the comment: 'But, of course, I'm not the doctor.' He simply said: 'Well, sister is speaking for me. I feel the same way', and then he repeated the message.

This type of interaction was repeated with different patients and it was clear to me that both the doctor and nurse felt comfortable with the patients and with each other. However, it seemed to me that the quality of this interaction was also based on the confidence of equals. Between this doctor and nurse there was mutual respect, even fondness, and this also seemed to affect the patients who appeared more relaxed and cheerful. This was especially notable in comparison with the usual medical round which was distinguished by an authoritative medical hierarchy, silent nurses and nervous, apprehensive patients. Implicit in this easy confidence was a mutual recognition of their own and each other's skills. But while I am arguing that nursing attitudes and practices in relation to their own skills will be central to the future shape of the sexual division of labour, it will not be the only factor involved.

We have seen previously in relation to power and conflict that individual nurses and doctors act in ways that are permitted, encouraged or constrained by 'internal' factors like personality or by regulations, custom or an institutional culture which both reflects and constitutes the culture of the wider society. These elements of social structure are made by human agents at the same time as they limit and facilitate what these agents can make. In relation to this research, it is possible to see nurses making the sexual division of labour in ways that have the potential for both change and stability. This is not to say that nurses have a conscious strategy or long-term plan to overthrow the current division of labour. It is simply that by acting in ways that reflect their own knowledge base, skills and orientation, they are sometimes challenging medical discourse in quite fundamental ways. How these challenges are resolved will depend on the extent to which individuals and organised agents in groups are able to articulate and act on their interests so as to alter the nature of the interdependent structures of medical knowledge and the gender order. It will also depend on the relationship of practices within institutions (the gender regime) to those in the gender order as a whole. In the final chapter, which forms the conclusion to the book, I intend to examine these issues in relation to the historical and hospital studies. Before turning to this task, I want to examine the semantic domain of healing, which expresses and encapsulates the inherent tension between different knowledges and discourses within and between nursing and medicine and as such provides a 'window' into the dynamics at the heart of medical and nursing work.

Chapter 7

Healing

The words 'healer' and 'healing' have come, in recent years, to take on something of a mystical meaning. They conjure up images of traditional medicine men or women folk healers who use a mixture of herbal and supernatural remedies in an attempt to bring about dramatic cures. Healing may well involve dramatic rituals and incantations, however, what we are talking about here is actually something far simpler and less dramatic but just as interesting. It is an approach to health and illness which is marked by a belief in the interconnectedness of mind and body and on the restorative powers of nature which are within all living organisms, including ourselves. The Oxford Dictionary defines healing as 'restoration of wholeness' but before wholeness can be restored it has to be recognised as a possibility and as a goal worth working towards. We saw in chapter 2 the way that holistic models of health and healing were gradually overtaken by models based on reductionism and mechanics. This led to a focus in medical practice away from the complex interplay of mind/body/emotion and towards an ever narrowing concentration on physiological (mal)functioning. This has resulted in medical practices and occupational specialities which focus on disorder or 'pathophysiology' in isolation not only from emotions and the external environment but also in isolation from other physical aspects of the same body! In that chapter we also saw that while discourses of reductionism and mechanism became dominant, other marginalised discourses of holism and healing were not completely removed. They have survived and flourished in the Holistic Health Movement (Gordon 1984), in complementary health practice, but also, less obviously, within the practices and knowledge base of modern nursing and less obviously still, within modern medicine.

In this chapter I explore the conditions of possibility for, and evidence of, the continued existence of healing knowledge and practice within modern nursing and modern medicine in a modern teaching hospital. I also explore a possible link between healing discourses and the way doctors and nurses make the sexual division of labour on a daily basis. I look firstly at nursing work and secondly at medical work in relation to healing. In this context I will be using the term 'healing' to refer to an encompassing totality of approaches to sickness and health that must necessarily involve diagnosis, treatment and care. I have deliberately left these categories as wide and general as possible in order to draw out the variations in emphasis and the inclusions and exclusions which run through the different discourses. In other words, it will matter if doctors or nurses include, emphasise or marginalise certain concepts and approaches at the expense of others as they constitute discourses of healing.

HEALING AND NURSING WORK

In the sociological literature on health, there are numerous references to the dichotomous relationship between care and cure, and to the way in which these activities have been constituted as dualisms in the sexual division of labour between doctors (who cure) and nurses (who care) (Gamarnikow 1978; Colliere 1986; Reverby 1987; Benner & Wrubel 1989). In the first chapter, we saw that this split between care and cure is representative of a dualism between the mind and the body which emerged in the West from the scientific revolution of the seventeenth century and, in particular, from the contributions of Descartes. These hegemonic dualisms were then constituted into knowledge, discourses, practices, technologies and, ultimately, into institutions and occupations that were, and continue to be, gendered in fundamental ways. Essentially, these ways of knowing, acting and working happen through a constant interplay of agency and structure. The concept of caring as work, and work that is largely performed by women, has also been discussed in relation to discourses of pleasure and skill. The concept and activities of care are also relevant for a discussion of healing; for the care that nurses give so often goes beyond tending for a sick body. The actions of tending provide both the opportunity and the medium for a care which encompasses the patient's state of mind, their emotional state, as well as a concern with their physical environment.

This emphasis on the work of nursing and caring was predictably present when nurses articulated feelings about their own work. A high proportion of nurses used the word 'care' when asked to describe what they did. It was not infrequently expressed in a moving and profound way. It is also possible to discern a preoccupation with the immediate situation, as well as with longer term goals. For instance, when asked to talk about what she hoped to achieve in her work, one nurse responded:

(Ellen) I aim to make this patient as comfortable today as she can be. Now that's going to be different tomorrow. It's depending on her pain level, her emotional state, even the weather. You know looking out on a day like today is different to when the sun is out. If I can somehow pick those things up and help her to be as comfortable as she can be today, then tomorrow I think she's going to be, she's going to benefit from that. Now if she's getting over surgery and each day is a little more pain free, that's wonderful. It may not be the case. She may have something chronic and it's just a matter of her waking up tomorrow morning feeling a little bit better, a little bit happier in herself, feeling, 'I'm going to cope. I'm going to get to tonight afterwards'. It may be that she's dying and she feels, 'well, look, there was someone around yesterday to make sure things didn't get too much . . . there'll be someone around today'. I've just got this sense that help and care from the patient's point of view . . . whatever it is . . . to enable me to get back home to independent living, help to enable me to be comfortable back in my nursing home, if it's help to enable me to die in a dignified way . . . I just feel I've got some contribution to make, in making that patient feel as comfortable, as relaxed as is possible today.

There are a number of notable aspects to this nurse's description of her work. In this brief excerpt, and indeed, throughout the whole interview, the empathy of the nurse for her patients was almost palpable. The emphasis was on the immediate and the now and on comfort and pleasure for the patient. The disease process, test results and other objective measurements were of secondary interest to this major focus. It is also notable that concern and empathy were expressed within the widest possible framework of health. All aspects of the patient's internal and external environment were seen to have the potential to influence the patient's physical, mental and emotional state. Yet nurses did not limit their contribution to healing through caring. Nurses also saw healing as an active, central and even autonomous part of their work. This was particularly marked in the three areas of *pain relief*, *wound management* and the *care of the dying patient*. I will deal with each of these in turn.

Pain relief

The practice of pain relief is an area of nursing work where a high proportion of nurses considered that they were expert in both their judgement and practice. In some instances, they felt able to assert that their skills were superior to those of the doctors, as in the following example:

> (Susie) The thing that springs to my mind, being a paediatric nurse and having worked with adults, is the administration of pain relief for patients. When you are a nurse dealing with a patient all the time—and I think nurses are discerning enough to be able to tell which patient is becoming dependent and which is really in pain—the medical staff impede nurses relieving patients' pain by refusing to order any more drugs. Nurses are supposed to help the patient get better—but how can patients get better when they are suffering intense pain?

The nurse then went on to talk openly about nurses' non-compliance in this area. She claimed that it was not uncommon for nurses in her specialist area to disregard medical orders and give, for example, a larger dose of a particular pain-killing drug than had been ordered. The practice is most likely to involve a junior doctor with, in the view of the nurse, insufficient experience in the area, and it is known in the nursing language of her work area as a 'bonus' or a 'present'. This was verified with other nurses present who were familiar with these terms[1].

The practice was also confirmed during a conversation with an intensive care nurse who worked with both adults and babies. She talked about occasions when she had been distressed on behalf of the babies under her care, who were unable to move or cry out because of the drugs which caused complete paralysis while they were being artificially ventilated. She related an incident where a doctor began a surgical procedure on a baby (a 'cutdown') without administering sedation or pain relief. Because of the ventilator, this baby was unable to cry or move, but the nurse observed that its heart rate increased and she assumed from this that it was experiencing pain. She drew this to the attention of the doctor who made no comment and continued with the procedure. The nurse then administered sedation to the baby, observed the effect (lowered heart rate) and then told the doctor what she had done. He replied: 'I thought the heart rate had calmed down a bit', but made no other comment. She followed up her initiative by warning the other nurses in the unit to be on guard for a repeat of the event, but she chose not to officially report the incident in case it resulted in a formal restriction (by medical or nursing administration) on her discretionary power. In this instance, the nurse took individual, direct action, based on confidence about her judgement and expertise in the area of pain relief, for a patient who was completely powerless.

That such events take place with reasonable frequency was also confirmed in the course of a conversation with a hospital staff doctor. Discussing the role of nurses in a specialist area, he made the comment that they did not just suggest treatment but would actually initiate it, especially in relation to symptom or pain relief:

> (Brian) They [the nurses] will sometimes ring you and say: 'Can you come up and chart such and such medication—I've already given her some Maxalon' . . . I don't like that. I don't like it at all, but they've been allowed to get away with it.

In relation to pain relief, nurses also emphasised the importance of touch. In doing so, they were calling on a framework of healing that was generally marginal or outside the dominant medical model. Information regarding these techniques was communicated verbally amongst the nurses and rarely shared with the doctors:

(Denise) I use massage a lot. You know, like a lady last night had a sore back, instead of just going and rubbing her back like you normally do, I just stood there for about ten minutes and just massaged her back and it was fine.

(Meg) I tend not to take pharmaceuticals myself, I try a massage first or a hot bath or heat treatment or physiotherapy before I have to turn to drugs and therefore if my patient is in pain, instead of giving them panadol, I'll give their back a rub or I'll massage their neck or I'll get hot water and massage their feet.

Touch was also used to reassure and comfort patients:

(Ellen) Even my physical presence can sometimes make a difference to a lady who is very demented. I have tried on a couple of occasions to just slide in and sit beside her (during doctors' rounds) because I know if I can sit there and hold her hand and look at her . . . I'm thinking of one example, in particular, while all these men have just descended on her, she's sitting beside the bed so even physically they're all up higher than her, if it's someone like Dr S who's, you know, a different colour again, speaking away about her . . . I know one day there was this one old darling, I could see how agitated she was getting, I tried to slide in and just sit with her and hold her hand, I know that could have been valuable.

However, many of the nurses also emphasised the power of touch and the fact that they needed to be constantly sensitive to patients' own feelings and needs in this area:

(Kay) Touch is part of caring but it has to be appropriate. Some people welcome it where others would feel invaded. Knowing when and how much to touch is a skill you have to acquire.

It became clear to me that this was an area of quite profound skill, though one which was not only unrecognised but rarely even spoken of.

Wound healing

The area of wound healing was one where a significant number of nurses considered themselves 'expert'. This expertise was frequently recognised by other nurses who would call for advice from certain nurses who were recognised as holding expert knowledge in this area. In an interview with one of these 'experts', I was able to explore this notion and some of the ways that different doctors and nurses responded to it. This nurse explained to me that:

> (Kath) Because of my orthopaedic background, I have become very interested in wound management . . . You know how you can heal them really quickly and it was always a challenge for me and so I sometimes get asked by the nursing staff to come and have a look at a wound and . . . 'What would you do about this wound?' I might say: 'Well, first of all, I'd debride the black stuff on it . . .' and then whatever else I thought that it needed to heal.[2]

Significantly, it was not just nurses who sought her advice. She went on to describe the way that different doctors, both junior and senior, also sought her advice and expertise:

> (Kath) I did have one Resident one day specifically request that when I was going to debride a wound [that she would like] to come and watch because she'd never done it before and liked to know how to do it.

In addition:

> I have one orthopaedic surgeon that will refer patients to me that he's having a particular problem with as far as wound healing is concerned. There is a lady that's in the community actually at the moment that I'm looking after. She's got Raynaud's Disease and he did an operation on her foot, put in a pin and then the whole side of her foot broke open and wouldn't heal. So he told her to contact me and that I'd look after her and *so he goes along with whatever I say can happen to that wound.* And when we had paediatrics he did the same thing with a little girl that had some peripheral vascular problem and had half a toe amputated and he was going to have to do the rest but said, you know, go in and see what you can do and we were able to save the rest of it which was great. But he's the only one that sort of does that, but then again I suppose he's the only one that has funny wounds like that. (Emphasis added)

This statement seemed to me to be of some significance. Here was an area, that of wound healing, which has always been recognised as being central to the practice of medicine and here was a nurse, quietly telling me that not only could she do the job better than many doctors, but that at least one Specialist/Consultant recognised this and referred his most difficult patients to her. Yet this expertise remained relatively silent and unacknowledged within the public and institutional arena. Not only did this expertise remain silent but so too did the framework of knowledge and practice which underpinned the skill. This seemed to me to be a very clear instance of the resilience of healing knowledge, and yet at the same time, it revealed the silent power of the dominant paradigm to make use of but keep marginalised the more traditional, holistic approach. It also revealed the way that institutional arrangements could permit the power of the dominant paradigm and occupation to remain silent while being so effective. As an employee, this particular nurse could be requested to undertake a variety of 'jobs', a situation she happily complied with. Nevertheless, the fact remained that she 'owned' none of them. While she took charge of the wounds, the patients themselves remained under the 'ownership' of the doctor. Ultimately, the successful outcome of the healed wound was submerged into the overall success of the total procedure. In this way, the individual agency and the meaning of the actions of both the nurse and the doctor were shaped and constrained by institutional arrangements and structures.

This relationship and set of arrangements did, however, seem to be the exception. It was more common for 'surgical' nurses to experience different approaches to wound healing as a potential area of overt and covert conflict with doctors. Some nurses expressed frustration at doctors ordering what they considered to be inappropriate dressings when another type of dressing would have been more effective. What they did about this then depended on the individual nurse, the perceived support from nurse administration and, to a certain extent, whether it was a public or private hospital. In one example, a nurse made a direct suggestion to the surgeon about an alternative dressing:

> (Kay) I just explained to him that I wanted to do the dressing in a certain way and explained my reasons for it. I think he had started off wanting to do something else but he listened

and agreed that my way was the best. Generally doctors now realise that we have the knowledge to decide these things . . . but we have to have a sound knowledge base to support it. By this I don't necessarily mean tertiary education.

It became apparent that the confidence and assertiveness displayed by individual nurses was related to a number of factors, and that these included confidence in their own skills, recognition from their peers, and recognition and support from nursing administration. It is interesting to note the answer that the Director of Nursing gave me when I asked her a question concerning her definition of what made a 'good' nurse. Without hesitation she replied: 'a nurse who is confident about her skills and judgement'. It is possible that there is an important connection here between the possibility of emotions like confidence and the type of administrative support described earlier; that is, the setting up of several expert nursing committees, with the remit to investigate and make recommendations concerning changes to work practices initiated by nurses. Barbalet has argued that for individuals and groups to express 'future oriented' emotions like confidence, there needs to be an institutional expression of 'acceptance and recognition' (1993:8). It can be argued that these hospital-wide nursing committees represented just such an expression. Indeed, it can be argued that these administrative structures have the potential as a 'space' to foster and nourish nursing discourses.

Knowledge and practice unique to nursing was also revealed in the specific area of wound healing to do with pressure area sores. (See Walby and Greenwell, 1994, for another exploration of these issues.) This was an area that medical staff frequently left to the management of nurses and where nurses consequently found less conflict. It was therefore one of the most interesting and revealing areas of the research. Here, nurses continue to hold and verbally communicate a 'secret' knowledge concerning treatments, often concocted from natural ingredients, for the purpose of facilitating wound healing. These concoctions may include any combination of substances, such as those high in vitamin B (vegemite) or protein (egg, fish oil) and may sometimes involve the direct application of oxygen. Towards the end of my period of attachment to the hospital ward, I asked the Nursing Unit

Manager/Senior Sister (NUM) about the survival of these practices. She replied:

> (Kay) It's funny that you should mention that. Only last week
> I had a query from the kitchen regarding the number of raw
> eggs that were being requested from the ward. After asking
> around I found that one of the nurses had been using her
> favourite recipe on a stubborn pressure sore on a lady who
> had come in from a private hospital. It was actually having a
> good effect.

Care of the dying patient

Where a patient is dying, nurses have a language and set of
practices which relate to their ability to 'know' when death is
going to occur (see Benner 1984; Benner & Wrubel 1989, on
intuition in nursing). On one occasion during the study there
was an elderly female patient who was not responding to
treatment. I recorded the following incident at the nurses'
station:

> 11 a.m.: Registrar came up to review patient. Bev and Ellen
> [nurses] were standing around the desk. Registrar looked up
> and exclaimed to them: 'She just won't get better'. Both
> nurses explained to him: 'But you have to understand, she
> wants to die, she's had enough'.

Later, the Registrar tentatively put the same view to the VMO/
Consultant on a ward round: 'The nurses think she has thrown
in the towel'. The consultant nodded but made no comment.

This was only one of many examples where nurses used a
language which took into account a patient's conscious or
unconscious desire to die. It followed that there were cases
where nurses considered that further medical intervention to
prolong life was inappropriate. In another incident, a nurse
was instructed to put up a 'dopamine' drip on a dying patient.
The patient died during the procedure. When the nurse spoke
to me immediately after the incident, she was uncharacter-
istically sad and angry. To begin with, she commented that the
doctor had ordered the drip '24 hours too late'. Her main
complaint, however, concerned the intrusion of the action:
'What use was I to her? She should have had her daughter
with her then. Instead the daughter was waiting outside while
I fiddled around with that useless drip'.

The issue of tests and examinations on dying patients was the one which created the most frequent, potential source of conflict between the nursing and medical staff. This is consistent with other studies (see Mackay 1993: 146–9 and Walby & Greenwell 1994: 43–5). The nursing goal appeared to follow the Nightingale admonition to 'structure the environment' so that the patient could die without pain and with privacy and dignity. It appeared, however, that with the exception of doctors from palliative care, it was difficult for doctors to decide when to give up trying to 'save' a patient. One nurse made the comment: 'They [doctors] see death as a failure. They can't accept that so they do all these things trying to justify why the patient dies'. Another went further when she claimed: 'They like to watch how people are dying'.

Two related and yet contrasting incidents in this area emerged during the interviews. The first concerned a nurse who was recalling an event which occurred when she was a junior nurse, and the second was a more recent event which involved a senior and very experienced nurse.

> (Gail) It was the only time I really lost my cool in a ward in front of patients . . . They put her [the patient] through a whole lot of tests that day. I couldn't stand it. The doctor came in, he had all these little chappies following, medical students and so on. Janet [the patient] was in a single room and she was drifting 'in' and 'out'. She wasn't deeply unconscious but she was 'in' and 'out' and they came in and this little chappie was sort of chatting about her over the bed but she wasn't truly gone, she was in and out and he was talking prognosis and the rest of it and as a second year nurse I was getting crankier and crankier because I couldn't do anything about it so that was very frustrating and then he started to poke her in the liver area and saying to the students . . . and it was painful and it was back in the days when we didn't have a great deal of . . . well the pain control treatments were bloody appalling in comparison with what they are now . . . she was audibly groaning . . . and then he started saying to the students . . . 'feel this, feel this' and I can remember going outside the room because she was in pain—I was in tears—and I ran smack bang into the NUM. 'Thank Christ it's you', I said. She said, 'What's the matter with you' and I told her and she went in and said: 'I'm sorry but you'll have to stop this, you haven't got the

family's permission' and she got rid of the lot of them. I didn't feel powerful enough as a second year nurse, but it was great what she did though I think that was the worst experience I've had.

(Kay) There was an oncology patient, very young, who was, I considered, days away from death. Some of the medical staff involved realised that, some didn't. One morning, I went to the patient and found the patient being examined by a Psychiatric Registrar who was trying to do his medical fellowship. I saw what was happening and immediately asked him to leave the patient. He came outside and I then explained that the examination was over and that the patient would not be seen by any more people. He replied that for me to enforce that he would have to be told by the person who sent him to the patient [another Registrar]. I contacted this person who said: 'But the patient has actually had a massive cardiac effusion, he might go another twenty years and never see that'. And that was his justification. It wasn't justification enough for me.
Interviewer: Were you able to enforce it?
(Kay) I did enforce it. I then made contact with the VMO who was unaware of what was happening and then had a formal apology from the people concerned, which I thought was interesting [laughs]. Not all patient advocacy issues are resolved like that.

Again the ability and the inclination to take such action were not unrelated to structural factors. Nurses are sometimes spoken of as though they constitute an undifferentiated mass, yet it is apparent that factors such as seniority and experience are central for the type and range of 'agency' that nurses are able to give expression to. The nurse involved in the last incident herself felt that confidence was related to 'tertiary education, age and experience'.

These and numerous other examples constitute evidence that nurses do call on other frameworks of knowledge (explicitly and implicitly) as a base to their practice, and that these are revealed in the different ways they conceptualise and describe their work. Through speech and action nurses constitute ways of knowing and ways of working which sometimes challenge medical prerogatives. Their discourses reveal that they are aware in these instances that their knowledge framework and its ensuing practice places them in a situation of direct or indirect conflict with the dominant medical paradigm and its practitioners. In many such situations, particularly in the three areas just discussed, nurses will not simply complain but will challenge and override medical jurisdiction. In this way, the sexual division of labour is reconstituted in ways that create the potential for instability and more fundamental change.

That is not to say that nurses are always consistent in such behaviour. In fact, I found that nurses operate with what I have called a 'duality of focus', that is, they operate within a central contradiction between servicing scientific medicine and trying to provide holistic care for their patients. There is also evidence to show that this 'duality of focus' can at times place them in a situation of conflict with doctors which will be resolved in different ways depending on both individual and organisatioal factors.

HEALING AND MEDICINE: HOW NURSES SEE DOCTORS

There is also evidence which suggests that nurses are increasingly differentiating between doctors and groups of doctors. Most were reluctant to generalise. One exception was Gail who, while conceding that change was occurring, commented:

> I think some of the changes in the female/male ratio mix in medicine maybe are making a really slow difference, but it is making a difference. Maybe the female doctors are improving some of the poor attitudes that we've had over quite some time. I think they're getting better. I'd give them another 40 years at least to catch up.

On the whole, though, nurses in this study distinguished carefully between individual doctors and certain categories of doctors. Even Gail was later to qualify her generalisation about doctors in the following terms:

> (Gail) I wouldn't work with surgeons for a million dollars.
> Interviewer: Why?
> (Gail) On the whole, they treat you like dirt. Our physicians are like another race. They treat you with real respect.

and:

> (Kay) On the whole, the oncologists give more time to their patients. They really try to be there for them.

As far as individual doctors were concerned, nurses used expressions like:

> (Kay) Oh, he's a very caring person, he's a wonderful doctor [Dr S].

and:

> (Julie) You must meet Dr L. She's a fabulous doctor.

I attempted to observe, interview or at least speak with all the doctors specifically mentioned, either positively or negatively, by the nurses. Without exception, all the doctors referred to in a positive sense worked in a way that was noticeably 'against the grain' of mainstream medical and hospital practice. I shall enlarge upon this observation in more detail below.

MECHANISTIC/HOSPITAL MEDICINE

There were many examples from the discourse and practice of doctors which illustrate the dominant, mechanistic and objectifying process of scientific medicine. For our purposes here, two will suffice. The first involved a conversation between a Medical Registrar (MR) and a Psychiatric Registrar (PR) who had been called in to assess a patient. This female patient had been living with a potentially fatal illness (lymphoma) for over 10 years. It was now progressing to a stage where she was having difficulty in swallowing. The patient had also recently stated that not eating and hence dying was a way out for her. This represented a dilemma for the medical staff who then felt that they had to decide if her difficulty in swallowing had a 'psychological' or a 'real' physical cause:

> MR: It's hard to know if we need to dilate her [throat] again or if depression is the problem.
> PR: Is she anxious?
> MR: Very. And incredibly manipulative. Beginning of last week, I thought ECT [electro-convulsive therapy] might be the way to go.

Clearly, the patient was not co-operating with the medical paradigm any longer, and her refusal to eat was seen as a form of 'manipulation', which itself needed to be 'treated'.

The second incident involved an elderly woman who was dying, and who was very distressed. The nurses had arranged for the VMO to see her with a view to prescribing morphine to 'ease her out'. This was carried out, and she was now more peaceful. Suddenly, a Registrar arrived with an offsider to examine her. His main concern seemed to be to check whether he had been right about her diagnosis. He appeared to be quite pleased by what he read in her notes. I then recorded the following conversation between the doctor and the nurse who was to look after the patient for the afternoon:

> (Doctor) She has aortic stenosis with quite a large amount of reflux.
> (Nurse) She can hardly breathe.
> (Doctor) That is because of . . . [more technical detail].
> (Nurse) She is very distressed. She says that if she is dying she wants to go quickly.
> (Doctor) Her condition is complicated by . . . [more technical detail].

It became apparent that the conversation had no point at which the two participants could meet. The nurse was trying to present to the doctor a human being who was suffering, while the doctor continued to see an interesting condition. In another sense, it may be said that the nurse was describing what was happening *for* the patient while the doctor was relaying what was happening *to* her.

Even one of the 'better doctors' could not resist the teaching opportunity presented by a dying woman in a coma. Her daughter was asked to leave and the patient's head was suddenly turned from one side to the other to demonstrate the presence or absence of the 'doll's eye reflex' (to assess the level of coma). Her fingernails were then bent back to see if she responded to pain. (Strangely, one cannot help but feel a sense of guilt at revealing these techniques from a closed and secret world, but why shouldn't these practices be open to public scrutiny?)

In fact, the tensions involved in the use of patients as 'teaching material' emerged again and again. It was one of the most difficult predicaments for the nurses, who found it extremely hard to act as patient advocates in the context of the seemingly impenetrable legitimacy of medical education. The incidents I have described provide a small clue to understanding why the large teaching hospitals are seen as the 'high citadels' of medical dominance.

This is not to say that mechanistic discourses always went unchallenged between doctors. On this particular afternoon, Dr S (VMO/Consultant) arrived with a Registrar and a medical student to do a ward round. Before starting the round he had a long discussion with one of the Registrars about one of their patients. The Registrar was saying how difficult this case was. Both the medical student and VMO agreed. The VMO asked: 'Do you want me to tell you what is wrong with her?' He then explained her history and probable diagnosis in some detail. (This patient had some sort of neurological tumour but because of its location they were unable to perform a biopsy.) The Registrar suggested some other possibilities and then quipped: 'Yes, it's a very interesting case; pity we have to wait for an autopsy for the answers'. Both the medical student and Dr S were visibly taken aback. Dr S reacted with: 'Oh thanks'. (An interesting reaction in itself, meaning perhaps: 'Oh thanks for assuming that I can do nothing for my patient'.) The medical student appeared offended and stated: 'She is a very motivated and a really lovely lady'. To which the Registrar replied: 'Oh is she?' This was as close to a rebuke as both could venture without an explicit disagreement. In this exchange, the Registrar had been 'corrected' and there was an attempt on the part of the medical student to re-introduce the humanity and identity of the woman into the discussion. It reminded me that discourses, no matter how powerful and seemingly pervasive, are an achievement of practice and are therefore open to potential challenge from opposing discourses (Weedon 1987). In this case the dominant discourse of scientific medicine was challenged by a discourse of humanism. There were other, more explicit alternatives articulated and practised from within medicine. I will deal with these in some detail in the next section.

ALTERNATIVE DISCOURSES WITHIN MEDICINE

The research undertaken for this book has also revealed that alongside the dominant, mechanistic framework, there do exist examples of marginalised and occasionally opposing discourses of holism within hospital medical practice. I went on several 'rounds' with a VMO (referred to above) who had been described to me by several of the nurses as 'wonderful'. Apart from working with the NUM on as near an equal footing as imaginable, the doctor, a physician, talked through and around each patient's perception and experience of their illness and even discussed their home situation—when they would like to go home, how they would manage, who would do their shopping, etc. It was apparent that this doctor was attempting to deliver holistic care, and to do so in such a way that included nurses and the patients themselves in the process. When I commented on the extent of interest in the patient's home situation, the doctor responded: 'Oh yes, we treat the whole person'. Now, it could be argued that this was an illustration of a process of incorporation of opposing discourses into the dominant one, with the result of an even more powerful and comprehensive dominant discourse, but we need to be open to the possibility that something more was going on.

This possibility was supported at a follow-up interview, where the doctor revealed a wide, social view of health and therapeutics. He did, however, himself marginalise his own practice within the dominant medical discourse. He explained that his area (rheumatic disorders) was not as 'important' as other areas in medicine, such as cardiology and oncology, but he liked it because it was an area in which he could really get to know and get close to his patients. Even his surgery (where the interview took place) had the air of an old-fashioned GP's surgery, with its connotations of a long-term personal interest in the patient, and it seemed only natural that I should have to wait for over an hour for our interview while he saw a single patient—his final one for the day.

The possibility for opposing discourses from within medicine was also presented to me with great clarity by an Aboriginal doctor who sat at the nurses' station and began (unusually) to ask me about my research. At some point in the conversation the term 'medical model' was raised and he responded with the statement that there ought to be 'no one model' and that doctors needed to be far more flexible in relation to individual patients. His own dictum was 'do no harm' and 'that means often simply not interfering in people's lives'. To explain what he meant, he used the example of a current patient, aged 80 (Mr T), who was regularly picked up by police and brought to the hospital for some food, care and the chance to dry out. The doctor stated that the last thing he would do would be to tell the old chap to give up his beer. There were other things he could offer which were much more useful in terms of nutrition and basic care. He said that every now and then on one of these regular visits, a 'bright young thing' (recent medical graduate) would order a blood test for Mr T, notice all the asterics (abnormalities) on the results and then go on to order 'all sorts of unnecessary tests'. He said that there was no point in any of this. He went further and asked: 'Did any one of them ask Mr T if he was satisfied with his health?' I suggested that his was a somewhat unique and certainly a minority view. He laughed and agreed that this might be so. He then talked about Aboriginal culture and developed an analogy concerning his people who had houses built for them without fireplaces.

> These are people who have gathered around fires for 40 thousand years—so of course they pulled up floor boards and made their own fireplaces. See, nobody had asked them if they wanted houses without fireplaces. Well, medicine is the same. It's no good doing things to people if it's not what they want. My first aim is not to do any physical, emotional or spiritual harm.

Regrettably, this was my only contact with this particular doctor who moved on to another hospital shortly after this meeting. I was struck with the way he was attempting to integrate an Aboriginal world view with its traditional, holistic approach to health and healing with the practice of modern medicine.

The issue of marginalised discourses within medical practice was brought home even more starkly in relation to palliative care medicine which, it may be recalled, is an area of overt and covert conflict between nurses and doctors. My research shows that it is also an area of potential and real conflict within medicine, and one that is occasionally exploited by nurses who seek, and find, allies within medicine over certain issues. The discourses of doctors working in palliative care frequently stand in marked contrast with those in mainstream medicine. Some examples provide some idea of the difference between them:

> (Dr L) This is low-tech medicine. I really like the fact that simple medication, managed well, can give fantastic results. I like to think that, as a palliative care doctor, I don't rely on tests much. I don't treat people as numbers. My job is to treat the *whole person*—and that often includes family and friends—I know that sounds like a truism, and that all doctors should do it, but it's often not the case [my emphasis].

And:

> Pain relief can change someone who is in bed crying to someone who is walking around wanting to go home. I have a very basic knowledge of drugs but that's all you need if you also have an attitude which allows you to listen to what people are saying.

When asked to explain why she liked palliative care, this doctor replied:

> (Dr L) I like palliative care . . . because I don't care if your liver function test is through the roof—I care if you're feeling nauseated or not.

These discourses clearly go against the grain of mainstream medicine with its emphasis on objective tests, measurements and results. They also go against the grain of individualism with this doctor including family and friends as an integral part of the patient's world. Chris Weedon talks about the way that some discourses support the *status quo*, while others challenge existing practices from within and 'contest the very basis of current organisation and the selective interests which it represents' (1987:41). She goes on to point out that, 'Such discourses are likely to be marginal to existing practice and dismissed by the hegemonic system of meanings and practices as irrelevant or bad' (1987:41). In this context, it is worth noting that there have been disputes over 'ownership' of patients between palliative care and oncology, in cases where palliative care patients have been readmitted to hospital. (It was explained to me that if patients came in 'under' the jurisdiction of oncology, there was the possibility of conducting more tests. The palliative care team tried to protect patients from these.)

The reality of a different form of daily practice also appears to have implications for the way doctors view nurses. Within the dominant discourse, nurses are seen primarily as sources of information, as well as the means by which medical orders are carried out. Within the more marginalised discourses, however, nurses are viewed on a much more equal footing. One particular doctor in palliative care even went so far as to acknowledge areas of expertise which she lacked in comparison to nurses. Indeed, her whole view of being a doctor appeared to be imbued with an ethic of care which she saw as coming from the same impetus as nursing. When I raised the issue of how she worked with nurses she began by saying: 'I really admire nurses. My mother was a nurse and she is my role model'. She went on to add:

> A nurse is an equal member of the team—though this has stirred up medical opinion elsewhere in the hospital. But their view of the patient is just as valid as mine.

When I asked this doctor what she did in her work that the nurses didn't do, she replied:

> (Dr L) Nothing really. It's funny, I've never really thought about it but I can't think of anything—we discuss everything together and tell each other our decisions. Just the legal prescribing, that's my job.

IMPLICATIONS FOR HEALTH CARE

We have seen that nurses articulate and practise a wide range of discourses in their daily work. These include discourses of pleasure, power, conflict, skill and healing, and it is clear that these are by no means exhaustive. The presence of these discourses indicates that nurses do not simply comply with or complain about their lack of power in a given situation. Their responses will vary from covert action through to direct and overt action to call attention to, and sometimes eventually change, an unsatisfactory situation. Crucial to the type and

degree of action taken is the level of perceived and actual
support from peers and from nursing administration, as well
as their own level of confidence, maturity and education.
We have seen that threads of the marginalised discourses
of holistic healing do exist within and alongside the dominant
mechanical and objectifying discourses of scientific medicine.
The holistic/organicist remnants are most strongly evident in
the discourses of nurses who practise and articulate these
discourses in their daily work. As they are constituted by
nurses, the holistic discourses of 'bedside healing' represent a
conflict of interest with the dominant paradigm which is sometimes overt and conscious and sometimes covert and invisible.
I suggest that the survival of discourses of healing constitutes
real evidence of resistance to the dominance of reductionist and
mechanistic bio-medical knowledge and practice. The extent to
which these healing discourses are articulated and practised
depends on both individual agency and structural factors (such
as administrative support) which serve to inhibit or encourage
such diversity and potential opposition.

The extent of the expression of these discourses will also
depend on the scope or space for holistic approaches within
particular practice areas. We have examined three such areas—
that of pain relief, wound healing and care of the dying
patient—where nurses have created and expanded a space
where they articulate and practise a discourse of healing. These
healing discourses have revealed both an alternative, oppositional knowledge and practice framework and a level of
autonomy in certain areas which has been generally unrecognised.

We have also examined the survival of marginalised discourses within medicine itself. It is apparent that certain
individual practitioners work noticeably 'against the grain' to
continue a tradition which reaches back to Hippocrates.[3] It is
further suggested that there is a direct relationship between the
extent to which healing discourses have been subordinated and
marginalised and the degree of medical hegemony in the hospital environment. There are indications that the marginalised
discourses of holism have a far weakened structural 'need' for
hierarchy and professional ownership and control. Within those
situations where alternative discourses existed with some
presence, there was a genuine emphasis on equality among all
categories of hospital staff and between staff and patients.

There was also a mutual respect for different kinds of knowledge and different kinds of care. One instance of this was seen in the area of palliative care where healing discourses flourish and where the sexual division of labour was seen to be weak.

These observations have implications for the future direction of health care in general, and for political strategies aimed at destabilising the sexual division of labour and creating the conditions of possibility for more equal and co-operative ways of working together. Rather than relying solely on the 'importation' of ideas and knowledge from disciplines outside of nursing, it may be that nurses have a rich store of knowledge and practice that has the potential to provide the basis for the future direction of their practice and occupational status. I stress the word 'potential', for at the moment these discourses are fragmentary and sometimes contradictory, but they do nevertheless indicate the richness of a tradition which leads a largely underground existence. This is an issue of politics as well as being an issue about conflicting knowledges. In the sense that certain structures restrict the ability of nurses to practise the art of healing, it can be said that the power relations inherent in the sexual division of labour work against their interests. There are indications that this also works against the interests of their patients. The word 'potential' also suggests that the possibilities are suspended, as indeed they are, in the nexus between agency and structure. There are also significant implications for the way power relationships between doctors and nurses are theorised and for sociological theory at a more general level. These and other issues will be explored in the following, concluding chapter.

Chapter 8

Implications and possibilities

In this book I have undertaken a re-examination of the history and the dynamics of the working relationship between nurses and doctors. Such a re-examination was both necessary and overdue because of the unsatisfactory treatment of nursing in both the mainstream sociological and feminist literature. I considered that it was necessary to move to an account where there was more space for the voices and active agency of nurses themselves in the making of their occupation. The active agency of nurses has been a key theme throughout the book. In relation to the historical themes, we saw that the dynamic between structure and agency had the effect of constituting modern nursing as a paid occupation for women with the *potential* for the development of autonomy and skill in the field of healing. Yet this very potential meant that nursing developed within a contradiction. This was the contradiction between the goal of nursing practice—health and healing—and the political reality of the position of nursing in the network of scientific, medical power. At the same time we saw that it was this same contradiction which provided the potential for fundamental and ongoing resistance to medical dominance. As a result, the complex interplay of structure and agency involved in the constitution of modern nursing resulted in a dominance of medicine over nursing in nineteenth century Britain which was both *unstable* and *contingent*.

In relation to current work arrangements, we saw that in

the hospital ward this unstable and contingent dominance continues today. In particular, we saw that the oppositional discourses discussed in the historical themes have indeed survived. In nursing, they represent a significant stream of discourse which permeates and shapes much of what nurses do. However, they are also a cause of tension in nursing because of the 'duality of focus' with which nursing is constituted. This was expressed by one nurse in the conflicting imperatives expressed concerning 'getting through the 2.00 p.m. observations', and yet wanting to sit and talk with a lonely and anxious patient who clearly needed the comfort of contact.

The existence of the oppositional discourses within nursing was also seen to be a cause of tension and conflict with doctors. This was demonstrated across many areas of work, but particularly in the areas of wound healing, pain relief, and in the care of the dying patient. In several instances we were witness to nurses taking direct action to resist medical prerogatives in situations where there was a perception that the wider interests of the patient were being compromised. However, it was also clear that the desire and ability of nurses to resist medical prerogatives was contingent on structural factors such as support from nursing administration, peer support (for example through nursing committees) and wider structural influences such as the effects of feminism and the availability of tertiary education for nurses. Nevertheless, these holistic discourses were not always a source of conflict with doctors. The evidence from the hospital ward echoed the discussion of the historical themes, which revealed that discourses of healing continued to exist *sotto voce* within medical knowledge and practice. However, it was apparent that the doctors who attempted to deliver holistic care were positioned, and positioned themselves, on the margins of mainstream medicine in areas where the approach was not perceived as a threat to the dominant discourse. Even so, there were still instances of conflict, for instance between doctors in palliative care, and doctors from oncology, where there is sometimes a concern for knowing and watching 'how people are dying'. It was a significant finding of the research that the few instances of genuine, non-hierarchical teamwork witnessed between doctors and nurses occurred in those instances where holistic discourses were dominant. This is not to say that the discourse determined the work arrangements; rather that the non-hierarchical work arrangements created the conditions of possibility for the expression of a healing focus and practice.

IMPLICATIONS

The findings presented in this book have various implications. I will discuss them within the following three categories: firstly, the implications for a feminist analysis of nursing and the sexual division of labour between doctors and nurses; secondly, the implications for sociological theory more generally and; thirdly, the implications for health care policy and the structure of the health care workforce.

Implications for feminist analyses of nursing and the sexual division of labour

The evidence in this book adds another dimension to the critical literature on nursing which has emerged from feminist traditions. While analyses of patriarchy and medical dominance have been important to balance accounts based solely on voluntarism and functionalism, they have led to a somewhat negative concentration of the ubiquity and pervasiveness of male, medical power, at the expense of accounts which incorporate the active role of nurses in constituting their occupation. Modern nursing was not simply 'imposed on relatively passive women' from above, nor was it the result of the 'sell out' of the nineteenth century nurse leaders such as Nightingale. Rather, I have demonstrated that the constitution of modern nursing was, in a very real sense, an exemplar of the interrelationship of structure and agency in social action. In particular, we have seen that while the ideological effects of structures of class and gender limited and shaped the type of occupation that it was possible to make, the agency of individuals and groups worked to extend and reshape those limits in ways that made future power relationships and structures less than completely stable.

This was especially visible in relation to discourses of healing and the practice of bedside healing. We have seen that while doctors *attempted* to constitute nurses solely as hand-maidens to scientific medicine, nurses actively *resisted* these attempts to limit their knowledge and their territory to the status of medical assistants. Indeed, nurses fought on several fronts for an institutional place for nursing where a nursing language and culture could be established and protected. This goal was motivated by more than just professional concerns—the usual and only motivation inevitably presented to explain the actions of past nursing leaders. These findings presented here have implications beyond sociological interpretations of nursing history. They have significant implications for socio-logical and feminist analysis of the current status of nursing and for nursing-related issues. In particular, they indicate that it is time that analyses of nursing and the sexual division of labour moved beyond nursing stereotypes such as nurses as passive victims, nurses as complainers, nurses as unassertive game players and nurses as power hungry professionalisers, to develop techniques of study which permit an examination of what nurses actually do, say and know in a variety of situa-tions. The findings of this study indicate that nurses are active agents in the making of their occupation, even if they 'make' it in ways which sometimes perpetuate hierarchy and authority relations. We have also seen them 'making it' in ways which resist, extend and structure the territory of the knowledge and practice of nursing as well as the possibilities of the nurse/doctor relationship.

In order to more adequately understand the sometimes contradictory actions of nurses, it has been necessary to look beyond the behaviour of nurses and doctors, to the underlying and dynamic development of feminine and masculine *identity*. The study has shown that 'being a nurse' includes, for many nurses, both the pleasures of caring and the exhaustion of 'care overtime' because of the inability or unwillingness of many doctors to demonstrate and experience care and nurturance toward patients. It indicates that any attempt to re-conceptual-ise the nurse/doctor relationship must include a recognition of the psychodynamics of gender construction.

These findings also have implications for theorising the nurse/doctor relationship. Rather than viewing the relationship as either a complementary, functionalist one, or one where nurses are subordinated through the structure of medical dominance, I have suggested that the relationship is more dynamic, complex and uneven. In many situations, doctors will call on the power of their position to subordinate nurses to the dominant discourse. In others, nurses will challenge and override medical authority. In others again, nurses and doctors will find common ground and will work together much more as a team with genuine humour, goodwill and pleasure. In arguing this position, I have placed the struggle between discourses at the heart of the process of power between doctors and nurses. In so doing, I have not wanted to replace other accounts, but rather to enrich a feminist understanding of the processes and forms of power in this area of research.

IMPLICATIONS FOR SOCIOLOGICAL THEORY

This book has found Turner's 'theoretical strategy of inclusion' useful for analysing social relationships and events (1992:235). This approach has enabled the writer to include neglected dimensions of struggle and power in the construction of a sociological account of nursing and the nurse–doctor relationship. It has also demonstrated that seemingly incompatible theoretical positions may, in fact, complement each other, to the extent that they are used not to cancel each other out but rather as tools to investigate or solve a specific empirical problem. This is not to say that theoretical coherence and integrity are not important. Rather, it is useful to note that there are many concurrent projects in sociology and, while theoretical development within particular 'schools' is one of these, it is also possible that dialogue and synthesis across schools may lead to the construction of more powerful theoretical tools for the deciphering of social relationships and processes.

The book has also shown the importance of an adequate conceptualisation of the interconnectedness of structure and agency for analysing social action. Giddens's theory of structuration and Connell's theory of practice have been used to underpin and guide both the direction and method of the research. Without such a theory, it has been all too easy to analyse nursing either from a perspective of the 'great women' and 'bad doctors' or, on the other hand, from a perspective which views the sexual division of labour as structurally determined and so impossible to change unless the structures of class and gender are (somehow) removed.

Finally, the attempts to resolve theoretical problems connected with structure and agency and the operation of power have also demonstrated the usefulness of aspects of post-structuralism for the analysis of nursing. Of particular relevance has been the concept of discourse. In this book, the concept has been given a dual meaning. 'Discourse' has referred to both the common sense meaning of language and practice, as well as the Foucauldian sense of a 'network' which has its own history and conditions of existence. Not only are these two conceptions consistent, they are indeed *bound together* as aspects of the structure/agency duality discussed above. While discourse as a network structures and conditions what can be said, what *is* said has the capability of transforming the network and the conditions of possibility for future language and practice. This conceptualisation has been especially important for analysing the operation of power in situations where there is no obvious conflict of interest and where the dominant discourse appears to go unchallenged. In many of these instances, an analysis of the language of the oppressed group has revealed situations where marginalised, oppositional discourses have either surreptitiously or openly challenged the discursive 'hegemony'.

Implications for health workforce education and structure

The analysis of competing knowledges and discourses of healing within and between the occupations of nursing and medicine presented in this book has far-reaching implications for policies on health care delivery and on the structure of the health workforce. At the very least, it raises questions concerning the suitability and appropriateness of a health division of labour which is based on a division of healing tasks based on the 'care' and 'cure' dichotomy. We have seen through the historical and ward study that, at various points in the history of health care, healers and medical workers of both genders and across all categories practised caring, holistic 'bedside healing'. This changed as the discourses of mechanistic, scientific medicine became dominant and became recognised as the legitimate expression of the healing arts. Those occupations which continued to cling to the subordinate marginalised discourses of healing became de-legitimised as 'alternative' or, more commonly, as 'quackery'. The practitioners in mainstream medicine who continued to practise bedside healing either died out or became peripheral to the more technologically driven, high status specialities within the occupation. As regards modern nursing, we saw that nursing was constituted in a public way as an 'assistant' within the dominant discourse of scientific medicine. Yet, we have seen that nursing has also fought for, and clung to, some of the marginalised, holistic healing discourses.

Perhaps more importantly, we have also seen that it is this stream of knowledge and practice within nursing which is the main contact that hospitalised, sick people have with holistic, bedside care. Occasionally they meet it in mainstream medicine, especially if they are dying.[1] But more commonly, it is nurses who continually and quietly compensate for the lack of a holistic approach from doctors; and there is ample evidence to show that patients want this kind of care. For those that can afford it, many turn to the private services of 'alternative' practitioners. Willis has shown that, over the last two decades, there has been a discernible increase in demand for, utilisation of and availability of the services of the complementary health practitioners (1989:262). More recently, a survey of parents whose children were being treated for cancer revealed that almost fifty per cent were also practising some sort of 'alternative' therapy (Sawyer et al. 1994). The authors of this study conclude:

> There is a continuing need to consider how to better provide, within the context of orthodox medical treatment, those elements of their children's care which parents currently seek from alternative therapies. (1994:320)

It is clear that many doctors have been aware of and concerned about these trends for some time. One analysis of the reasons for the popularity of alternative approaches (written for a medical audience) concluded that:

> [R]easons for the success of alternative medicine should therefore be sought in its preparedness to enter areas of

human discomfort which conventional medicine tends to
ignore as trivial or beyond hope, in its reputed rapidity of
benefits, its intimate and touching style, and its congruence
with social aspirations for holism and balanced ecology. It
also constitutes a criticism of some features of current medical
practice. (Maddocks, quoted in Willis 1989:273)

Yet, while alternative practitioners continue to proliferate
in the private sphere, public health care continues to be dominated by a form of medicine which continues to separate the
unity of mental, emotional, spiritual and somatic aspects of
healing. This is also the medicine which receives the vast bulk
of public funding for services and research.

I have shown that it survives and proliferates *because* it is
balanced by the silent knowledge and care provided by nurses.
It is only possible for doctors to concentrate on the body
because someone else is taking care of the other, neglected
aspects of the sick person. Moreover, it is not even the whole
body that is the concern of modern medicine. It is the
malfunctioning part. The rest of the care of the body is handed
over to nurses for the necessary time-consuming and intimate
care. But at the same time, who would want to return to the
days before the development of scientific medicine when bedside medicine was dominant, but when treatment was
frequently less than efficacious? This is, of course, the common
reply to criticisms of modern medicine—'this is the price you
have to pay for the dramatic advances in treatment'. But is it?
Is it not possible for health professionals to provide good
'evidence based' treatment at the same time as empathetic care?
In fact the two seem to be bound up together. It seems to me
that there are only two ways to go in order to achieve this
goal.

The first is to accept that notwithstanding some obvious
problems, the sexual division of labour between doctors and
nurses works reasonably well. Such a view accepts the division
between nurses who care and doctors who diagnose and cure.
Within such a perspective there may be arguments concerning
the need for 'society' to give greater value to care and to more
justly recognise and reward women's work. There is something
to be said for this. The majority of nurses do a fine job in
caring for their patients. There are many who would argue that
there simply are not enough men around who would or could

work in the same way. Better to fight for a fairer recognition of the skills involved in care and in this way the work of caring for the sick would, over time, undergo a change in status and power. It could be argued that this process will be accelerated anyway given the fact of tertiary education for nurses combined with the large numbers of women who are now graduating from medicine for the first time in history. In this scenario the nurses continue to provide the empathy and care; they are just more properly recognised and rewarded for their work.

The second position is more radical. From this more critical position it is possible to envisage the first scenario as a more equally rewarded sexual division of labour but one which remains, at base, solid as a rock. While more women enter medicine, the majority remain at the periphery doing part-time work and 'locums'. While nursing becomes professionalised, lower paid and less formally educated 'care assistants' of whatever official designation will take over the bedside work which will always be there while ever people become sick, injured or are dying. From this perspective it is possible to separate the gender of the operatives from the nature of the work. For instance, it is entirely possible for women to become immersed in mechanistic, objectifying medicine and to join its expert operatives. Their gender is no guarantee of an empathetic, caring approach. While women may have a predisposition to empathy (if the object relations theorists are correct), and while some knowledge frameworks are more conducive to holistic care than others, it is ultimately the daily reality of intimate contact which forges the bond of human connectedness between the sick person and their carer.

This leads me to question the long term viability and desirability of a division of labour which is to a significant extent based on the underdevelopment and overdevelopment of emotional responses to sick and needy people and on the under involvement and over involvement of doctors and nurses in intimate daily care. While re-valuing the skills of care would certainly be helpful (setting aside the issue of how and if this might be achieved), we are still left with the binary opposition of care and cure. Ultimately we need to do more than equalise or reverse the emphasis of the constituent parts of binary oppositions. We need to transcend them. Chodorow's observations on the psychic construction of femininity and masculinity are relevant here. If she is right about the need for men to become 'mothers' through changing patterns of child care as a precondition for the possibility of the emergence of new types of feminine and masculine identity, then this same argument applies to the feminine identity of nurses, the masculine identity of doctors and the division of labour between them. While it would help for nurses and doctors to have more contact during their training, and, while it would help for doctors to obtain 'better skills in communication' (Stevens 1994), these are not solutions which go far enough. The solution lies in a fundamental restructuring of the health workforce. *In particular, I propose that doctors be nurses.*

While this may be a radical idea, it is not a new one. The reader may recall a discussion in an earlier chapter of Dr Richard Bright who worked at Guy's Hospital during the nineteenth century. His biographer notes that his concern with patient care led him to believe that a doctor's training should include nursing. According to Bright, 'doctoring' included both treatment and care and involved

> learning how to take pressure off protruding bones by
> rubbing in lead or applying plaster, by positioning cushions
> and using Dr Arnott's water pillows; learning how to treat a
> bedsore; knowing how diluted brandy or laudanum would
> stimulate healing, how nitric acid with distilled water would
> clear pus, how linseed poultices would remove scabs. (Bright
> 1983:193)

All of these (and their modern counterparts), are concerned with the day-to-day comfort and care of the sick and injured and are crucial for creating the optimum conditions for healing and recovery. Yet, I would be surprised if any of these issues were given two minutes in modern medical school curricula. Making nursing a pre-condition for medicine would ensure that these practical, basic, all important issues of patient care would become, once again, an integral part of 'doctoring'.

How might this work? There is a worldwide trend to changing medical degrees to post-graduate qualifications. While some universities favour a foundation degree of a scientific nature, others favour basing post-graduate medical degrees on a foundation of a liberal Arts degree. Rather than basing a medical qualification on either of these, I suggest that aspiring doctors ought first to undertake a degree in nursing. This should be a degree with elements of both arts and science and with a strong emphasis on an ecological and holistic approach to health and illness, health education, public and community health, as well as the clinical theory, experience and skills required. After a year's practice as nurses, graduates could then choose either to continue to work with their present qualification (as a 'first rung' or 'generic' health worker) or to go on to post-graduate studies in nursing (clinical or community nursing), complementary modalities, medicine, public health or other specialisations. In this way, it would be possible to retain the effective aspects of modern medicine, integrated with a perspective which emphasises holism, illness prevention and the relationships between health, illness, individual life history and social structure. Over time, these existing categories might change and merge into different forms altogether. A more incremental way to approach this goal would be to keep all health- and medicine-related students together for the first few years of their vocational qualifications.[2]

The requirement to nurse and care for people in order to treat them may not suit all aspiring doctors. Some may choose to become research scientists instead. In my view, this would be no bad thing. Unless all health workers, including doctors, are prepared to touch and lift and clean and dress, as well as examine and prescribe and treat, the sexual division of labour may be modified, but will continue to divide this central aspect of human experience, both for patients and practitioners. This itself constitutes a wound in human consciousness and practice. It also locks health practitioners into nineteenth century conceptions of appropriate gender attributes and behaviour. With the proposal I have advanced, there is at least some possibility that this wound might itself be healed and transcended. Both patients and practitioners might, as a consequence, look forward to a more humane, effective and less gender proscriptive health care system.

Notes

CHAPTER 1   A NEW FRAMEWORK

1. As many will recognise, I am drawing on Marx here, who wrote: 'Men make their own history, but they do not make it just as they please; they do not make it under circumstances chosen by themselves, but under circumstances directly encountered, given and transmitted from the past.' (Marx & Engels 1970: 96 *The Eighteenth Brumaire of Louis Bonaparte*)
2. Some may consider that the thesis concerning a relationship between women healers and witchcraft allegations has been comprehensively disproved by David Harley in an influential article in *Social History of Medicine* (1990). In fact, the thrust of Harley's argument concerns the lack of evidence of a connection between allegations of witchcraft and *midwives*, not women healers. In any case, the Ehrenreich and English position continues to be highly influential both culturally and academically through numerous feminist studies of women's health and studies of the occupational and sexual division of labour in health care. For this reason it deserves critical consideration.
3. Pamela Smith has applied this concept to an analysis of nursing work, in particular, to the work involved in caring (1992).
4. This aspect of her work is reminiscent of the histories of some members of the *Annales* group of historians. This group of historians are identified by their association since 1946 with the journal *Annales: Economies, sociétés, civilisations*, and since 1947 with the Sixième Section of the École Pratique des Hautes

Études in Paris which has since become an independent institution known as École des Haute Études en Sciences Sociales (Clark 1990).

5. However, it is important to note that Giddens has been heavily criticised in relation to this and other issues. Turner has outlined these criticisms, including the claim that Giddens's account of structure depends on a vague notion of 'systems of generative rules' and 'enabling conditions', so that any idea of structure as constraint is, in effect, excluded (1992:86).

6. Foucault also shares this view. In an interview from the 1970s, he comments that '. . . power would be a fragile thing if its only function were to repress . . .'; and later, 'Far from preventing knowledge, power produces it'. He even goes so far as to say: 'That is why the notion of repression which mechanisms of power are generally reduced to strikes me as very inadequate and possibly dangerous' (1972:59). Here, Foucault is following Nietzsche and his 'school', who conceptualise power as producing positive as well as negative effects (Hoy 1986:130).

7. Hoy makes the point that Lukes's view is similar to the Frankfurt School's notion of domination, since Critical Theory also assumes that those subject to power may not consciously be aware of their real interests in a given situation (Hoy 1986:125).

8. Benton's solution to the 'paradox of emancipation' is to replace the concept of interests with that of the objectives of both A and B. This has its own problems, most particularly the fact that it then becomes very similar to Weber's conception of power which was the probability of individuals realising their wills in the face of the resistance of others. This then excludes an analysis of power in relation to collective forces and social arrangements and is therefore at base a more sophisticated version of a one-dimensional view of power (Lukes 1974: 22).

9. 'One might almost say that he has two theoretical consciousnesses (or one contradictory consciousness): one which is implicit in his activity and which in reality unites him with all his fellow-workers in the practical transformation of the real world; and one, superficially explicit or verbal, which he has inherited from the past and uncritically absorbed' (Gramsci 1971:333).

10. Gramsci argues: 'A human mass does not "distinguish" itself, does not become independent in its own right without, in the widest sense, organising itself; and there is no organisation without intellectuals, that is without organisers and leaders . . .' (1971:334).

CHAPTER 2   NURSES MAKING NURSING

1. The idea of dominion over the earth existed in Greek philosophy
    and the Christian religion; that of the earth as a nurturing mother
    also existed in Greek and other pagan philosophies (Merchant
    1982:3). Of course, the idea of a nurturing earth also existed,
    and in many instances continues to exist in many non-Western
    cultures including that of the Australian Aborigines.
2. It is important to note that there is a logical flaw in any approach
    which claims a capability for a total and all-encompassing un-
    derstanding of anything. Given this important caveat concerning
    the term 'holistic', it is useful to define the distinguishing features
    of a holistic approach to healing as, firstly, an approach which
    does not focus on the sick part at the expense of the integrity
    of the person; secondly, an approach which maintains a bond
    between the healer and the person to be treated and, thirdly, an
    approach in which the sick person is empowered (where possible)
    to play an informed and active part in his or her own recovery.
3. I use the terms 'regular'/'irregular' and 'formal'/'informal' (prac-
    titioners) interchangeably and descriptively with no derogatory
    intent.
4. The full title of the Royal Commission is: 'First Report of the
    Commission to Inquire into and Report Upon The Working And
    Management of The Public Charities of The Colony' in Votes
    and Proceedings of The Legislative Assembly During the Session
    of 1873–74, Vol. VI Government Printer, Sydney, 1873

CHAPTER 3   PLEASURE

1. Turner's study was based on 22 unstructured interviews (chosen
    from 60 interviews) with nurses from private and public hospitals
    in Adelaide, Australia, in 1985.
2. Nevertheless, it should be borne in mind that this process might
    not always run the same course, for the two issues that I saw
    resolved in this way may well have been at the complaint stage
    for some time before their resolution.
3. Clearly, these domains interrelate. This is especially the case with
    discourses of power which are present in all of these domains
    but for the purpose of analysis I have treated them separately
    when an exercise of power is both overt and conscious in the
    relationship or event.
4. Over a period of time, the obvious camaraderie and friendship
    between the nurses began to have an effect on me. Indeed, I was

able to observe a tendency in myself to 'go native'. I began to feel a sense of 'belonging' in the ward and in the hospital as a whole. I also started to have fantasies about leaving my academic job and working in the hospital full time. I was aware from the literature that this was a common experience, and one which indicated that I had probably crossed the line of observer 'marginality' into an area where I was far too 'at home'. Fortunately, it occurred at the end of the period of fieldwork.

5. Throughout the following chapters I use the term 'nurse' for all grades of nursing staff. In Australian hospitals there is no separate category designated with the title 'sister'. Upon graduation, all registered nurses are entitled to use the term 'sister' but it appears that it is being used less and less in Australian hospitals. It is most commonly used by older doctors and nurses, especially when they don't know or do not want to use the first name of a particular nurse.

6. I also refer to this encounter in the chapter on Healing. However, in this context I want to focus on the erotic dimensions of the encounter.

7. See the evidence presented in this and the following chapter, especially the section on 'Care of the dying patient'.

8. For example: 'Ability to care for the helpless is woman's distinctive nature. Nursing is mothering. Grown up folks when very sick are all babies' (*Hospital*, 8 July 1905:237).

9. It most certainly also happens between human beings and animals although Rose does not discuss this.

CHAPTER 4   POWER

1. The 'doctor/nurse game' is a concept which derives from an article by Stein (1967) who described a 'game' which, he claims, is played out between doctors and nurses. The main features of this game are that the nurse must be assertive and make positive suggestions regarding patient care *while not appearing to do so*. In other words, she must couch suggestions regarding patient care in such a way that the doctor can pick them up and act on them as though they were his own initiative. For his part, the doctor must learn how to request such information from nurses while not actually appearing to do so. Stein goes on to argue that there are rules and sanctions for poor 'gamesmanship'. Many nurses are now familiar with this concept, and conscious of their own behaviour in this regard.

2. I was present at this meeting and took notes of the proceedings.

CHAPTER 5   CONFLICT

1. Primary nursing is patient-centred rather than task-centred and is characterised by each patient having a single, identified, qualified nurse who is responsible for their care during the entire period of their hospital stay.

CHAPTER 7   HEALING

1. The information in this case was gathered at a group interview from nurses who were not associated with the hospital involved in the extended period of ethnographic research. The nurse in question was, however, from a major capital city teaching hospital.
2. 'Debride' refers to a technique whereby all dead and necrotic tissue is removed, usually by cutting. It is a delicate operation which requires manual skill and visual judgement so that only dead tissue is removed and healthy, living tissue is not injured.
3. Wolpe has analysed the holistic movement in medicine in the US as an exemplar to show how holistic physicians use a strategy of ideological challenge to orthodox medicine. He calls this challenge 'the holistic heresy' (Wolpe 1990: 913–923).

CHAPTER 8   IMPLICATIONS AND POSSIBILITIES

1. It may well be the case that there are other areas of medical practice which are also conducive to the practice of holistic care from doctors. Such areas might include paediatrics and geriatrics, as well as care from some general practitioners. Beyond this conjecture, it may be that this is an area which, while outside the scope of this book, is worthy of future research.
2. While a discussion of the education and training of other health professions is beyond the scope of this book, it is worth noting that at some universities there is already a degree of integration in the undergraduate courses for health professionals. For example, at the University of Newcastle (Australia), there are 'common core' subjects jointly undertaken by Occupational Therapy, Nutrition and Dietetics and Nursing students.

Bibliography

PRIMARY SOURCES: GREAT BRITAIN

Nightingale Collection, London School of Economics

Nightingale, F. 1860 *Notes on Nursing: What It Is and What It Is Not* Harrison and Sons, London
——1863 *Notes on Hospitals* Longmans, Green
——1865 Rules for admission and training nurses at St Thomas's Hospital, London.

St Bartholomew's Hospital, London; Minutes of the Board of Governors
The Archives, St Bartholomew's, London
St Thomas's Hospital, London; Minutes of the Court of Governors (Held at the Greater London Record Office, London)

PRIMARY SOURCES: AUSTRALIA

Official documents

Government Printer 1873 'First Report of the Commission Appointed to Inquire into and Report Upon The Working And Management of The Public Charities of The Colony' *Votes and Proceedings of The Legislative Assembly During the Session of 1873–74, Vol. VI* Government Printer, Sydney

188 NURSES AND DOCTORS AT WORK

SECONDARY SOURCES

Abel-Smith, B. 1975 *A History of the Nursing Profession* Heinemann, London

Ackerknecht, E. H. 1967 *Medicine at the Paris Hospital 1794–1848* The John Hopkins Press, Baltimore

Arch, M. & Graetz, B. 1989 'Work Satisfaction, Unionism and Militancy Amongst Unions' in *Community Health Studies*, Vol. XIII, No. 2

Armstrong, D. 1983a *Political Anatomy of the Body* Cambridge University Press, Cambridge

——1983b 'The fabrication of the nurse–patient relationship' *Soc. Sci. Med.* vol. 17, no. 8, pp. 457–460

Atkinson, P. 1977 'The reproduction of medical knowledge' Dingwall, R., Heath, C., Reid, M. & Stacey, M. *Health Care and Health Knowledge* Croom Helm, London

——1981 *The Clinical Experience* Gower Westmead, Farnborough, Hampshire, England

Attridge, C. & Callahan, M. 1989 'Women in women's work: Nurses, stress and power' eds L.K. Hardy & J. Randell *Recent Advances in Nursing: Issues in Women's Health* Churchill Livingstone, Edinburgh

Bacchi, C. 1990 *Same Difference. Feminism and Sexual Difference* Allen & Unwin, Sydney

Bacon, F. 1597 *Essays* (1922 edition, Blackie & Son Ltd, London)

Baly, M. 1980 *Nursing and Social Change* Heinemann Medical Books, London

——1986 *Florence Nightingale and the Nursing Legacy* Croom Helm, London

Barbalet, J.M. 1993 'Confidence: a macrosociology of time and emotion', *Journal for Theory of Social Behaviour* vol. 23, no. 3, pp. 229–47

Barrett, M. 1991 *The Politics of Truth. From Marx to Foucault* Polity Press, Cambridge

——1992 'Words and Things: Materialism and Method in Contemporary Feminist Analysis' in Barrett, M. & Phillips, A. *Destabilizing Theory: Contemporary Feminist Debates* Polity Press, Cambridge

Barrett, M. & Phillips, A. 1992 *Destabilizing Theory: Contemporary Feminist Debates* Polity Press, Cambridge

Beechey, V. 1979 'Women and Production: A Critical Analysis of Some Sociological Theories of Womens' Work' in Kuhn A. & Wolpe, A.M. *Feminism and Materialism*

Benjamin, J. 1990 *The Bonds of Love* Virago, London

Benner, P. 1984 *From Novice to Expert. Excellence and Power in Clinical Nursing Practice* Addison-Wesley, California

Benner, R. & Wrubel, J. 1989 *The Primacy of Caring: Stress and Coping in Health and Illness* Addison-Wesley, New York

Benton, E. 1974 'Vitalism in 19th century scientific thought: A typology and reassessment' *Stud. Hist. Phil. Sci,* vol. 5, no. 1, pp. 17–48

Benton, T. 1981 '"Objective" interests and the sociology of power' *Sociology* vol. 15, no. 2, pp. 161–184

Berliner, H.S. 1982 'Medical modes of production' eds A. Treacher & P. Wright *The Social Construction of Medicine* Edinburgh University Press, Edinburgh

Blumer, Herbert 1969 *Symbolic Interactionism* Prentice-Hall, New Jersey

Bologh, R.W. 1990 *Love or greatness: Max Weber and Masculine thinking—a feminist inquiry* Unwin Hyman, London

Bottomore, T. 1984 *The Frankfurt School* Tavistock, London

Braverman, H. 1974 *Labor and Monopoly Capital: The Degradation of Work in the Twentieth Century* Monthly Review Press, New York

Bright, P. 1983 *Dr Richard Bright. 1789–1858* The Bodley Head, London

Brown, T.B. 1974 'From mechanism to vitalism in eighteenth century England' *Journal of Hist. Biol.,* vol. 7, no. 2, pp. 179–216

Bryant, C. G. A. & Jary, D. (eds) *Giddens' Theory of Structuration: A Critical Appreciation* Routledge, London

Buckenham, J. E. & McGrath, G. 1983 *The Social Reality of Nursing* ADIS Health Science Press, Balgowlah

Burman, P. 1988 *Killing Time, Losing Ground* Wall & Thompson, Toronto

Burton, C. 1985 *Subordination: Feminism and Social Theory* George Allen & Unwin, Sydney

Bury, M. R. 1986 'Social constructionism and the development of medical sociology' *Sociology of Health and Illness* vol. 8, no. 2, pp. 137–169

Capra, F. 1983 *The Turning Point. Science, Society and the Rising Culture* Fontana, London

Chodorow, N. 1978 *The Reproduction of Mothering. Psychoanalysis and the Sociology of Gender* University of California Press, Berkeley
——1994 'Gender, relation and difference in psychoanalytic perspective' in *The Polity Reader in Gender Studies* Polity Press, Cambridge

Clark, Alice 1919 *Working Life of Women in the Seventeenth Century* George Routledge & Sons Ltd, New York

Clark, Stuart 1990 'The *Annales* historians' ed. Q. Skinner *The Return of Grand Theory in the Human Sciences* Canto Edition, Cambridge University Press, Melbourne

Clarke, M. (1978) 'Getting Through the Work' in Dingwall, R. &

McIntosh, J. (eds) *Readings in the Sociology of Nursing* Churchill Livingstone, Edinburgh

Cockburn, C. 1983 *Brothers: Male Dominance and Technological Change* Pluto Press, London

Colliere, M. F. 1986 'Invisible care and invisible women as health care providers' *International Journal of Nursing Studies* vol. 23, no. 2, pp. 95–112

Connell, R. W. 1983 *Which Way Is Up?* Allen & Unwin, Sydney

——1987 *Gender and Power* Allen & Unwin, Sydney

Coward, R. 1992 *Our Treacherous Hearts* Faber & Faber, London/Boston

Dandeker, C. 1989 *Surveillance, Power and Modernity* Polity Press, Cambridge

Davidoff, L. 1983 'Class and Gender in Victorian England' in Newton, J., Ryan, M. & Walkowitz, J. (eds) *Sex and Class in Women's History* Routledge & Kegan Paul, Melbourne

Davidoff, L. & Hall, C. 1987 *Family Fortunes. Men and Women of the English Middle Class, 1780–1850.* Century Hutchinson Pty Ltd, Australia

Davies, C. (ed.) 1980 *Rewriting Nursing History* Barnes & Noble Books, New Jersey

——1995 *Gender and the Professional Predicament in Nursing* Open University Press, Buckingham, Philadelphia

Delphy, C. 1977 'Proto-feminism and anti-feminism' in *The Main Enemy: A Materialist Analysis of Women's Oppression* Women's Research and Resources Centre, London

Dews, P. 1987 *Logics of Disintegration* Verson, London

Dickenson, M. 1993 *An Unsentimental Union: The NSW Nurses Association 1931–1992* Hale and Iremonger, Sydney

Dingwall, R., Rafferty, A. M. & Webster, C. 1988 *An Introduction to the Social History of Nursing* Routledge, London

Donnison, J. 1977 *Midwives and Medical Men* Heinemann, London

Douglas, M. 1970 *Purity and Danger: an Analysis of Concepts of Pollution and Taboo* Penguin, Harmondsworth

Doyal, L. 1979 *The Political Economy of Health* Pluto Press, London

Dreyfus, H.L. and Rabinow, P. 1982 *Michel Foucault: Beyond Structuralism and Hermeneutics* The University of Chicago Press, Chicago

Duden, B. 1991 *The Woman Beneath the Skin: A Doctor's Patients in Eighteenth-Century Germany* Harvard University Press, London

Ehrenreich, B. & English, D. 1973 *Witches, Midwives and Nurses: A History of Women Healers* The Feminist Press, Old Westbury

——1979 *Complaints and Disorders: The Sexual Politics of Sickness* The Feminist Press, Old Westbury, NY

Ehrenreich, J. (ed.) 1978 *The Cultural Crisis of Modern Medicine* Monthly Review Press, New York

Engel, G. L. 1977 'The need for a new medical model: A challenge for biomedicine' *Science* 196, pp. 129–36

Fagerhaugh, S. Y. & Strauss, A. 1977 *Politics of Pain Management: Staff–Patient Interaction* Addison-Wesley, Menlo Park

Farrington, B. 1949 *Francis Bacon: Philosopher of Industrial Science* Schumann, New York

Fernbach, D. 1981 *The Spiral Path* Gay Men's Press, London

Forster, M. 1986 *Significant Sisters. The Grassroots of Active Feminism 1839–1939* Penguin, Australia

Foucault, M. 1970 *The Order of Things: An Archaeology of the Human Sciences* Tavistock, London

———1971 *Madness and Civilization* Tavistock, London

———1972 *The Archaeology of Knowledge* trans. A.M. Sheridan, Routledge, London

———1973 *The Birth of the Clinic* Tavistock, London

———1977 *Discipline and Punish: The Birth of the Prison* Allen Lane, London

———1980 *Power/Knowledge, Selected Interviews and Other Writings 1972–1977* Harvester Press, Brighton

———1981 'The Order of Discourse' (1971) (translated McLeod, I.) in Young, R. (ed.) *Untying the Text: A Post-Structuralist Reader* Routledge & Kegan Paul, London

Fox, N. J. 1993 *Postmodernism, Sociology and Health* Open University Press, Buckingham

Fraser, N. 1989 *Unruly Practices: Power, Discourse and Gender in Contemporary Social Theory* Polity Press, Cambridge

Freidson, E. 1970 *Professional Dominance: The Social Structure of Medical Care* Aldine, Chicago

———1975 'Dilemmas in the doctor/patient relationship' in Cox, A. & Mead, A. (eds) *A Sociology of Medical Practice* Collier-Macmillan, London

Gamarnikow, E. 1978 'Sexual division of labour. The case of nursing' *Feminism and Materialism* eds A. Kuhn & A.M. Wolpe, Routledge & Kegan Paul, London

Game, A. & Pringle, R. 1983 *Gender at Work* Allen & Unwin, Sydney

Gardner, H. & McCoppin, B. 1989 'Emerging Militancy? The Politicisation of Australian Allied Health Professionals' in Gardner, H. (ed.) *The Politics of Health* Churchill Livingstone, Melbourne

Gelfand, T. 1981 'Gestation of the clinic' *Medical History* 25, pp. 169–180

Giddens, A. 1973 *The Class Structure of the Advanced Societies* Hutchinson, London

——1976 *New Rules of Sociological Method: A Positive Critique of Interpretative Sociology* Hutchinson, London

——1977 *Studies in Social and Political Theory* Hutchinson, London

——1979 *Central Problems in Social Theory* Macmillan, London

——1984 *The Constitution of Society: Outline of the Theory of Structuration* Polity Press, Berkeley

——1987 *Social Theory and Modern Sociology* Polity Press, Cambridge

——1991) *Modernity and Self-Identity* Polity Press, Cambridge

Gillespie, R. 1990 *Handmaidens and Battle-Axes* Silver Films, Sydney

Gilligan, C. 1982 *In a Different Voice* Harvard University Press, Cambridge, Mass.

Ginzberg, R. 1989 'Uncovering Gynocentric Science' in Tuana, N. *Feminism and Science* Indiana University Press, Bloomington

Glaser, B. G. & Strauss, A. L. 1967 *The Discovery of Grounded Theory* Aldine De Gruyter, New York

Goffman, E. 1961 *Asylums: Essays on the Social Situation of Mental Patients and Other Inmates* Penguin Books, Harmondsworth

——1963 *Behaviour in Public Places* Free Press, New York

Gordon, J. 1984 'Holistic health centers in the US' *Alternative Medicines: Popular and Policy Perspectives* ed. J. W. Salmon, Methuen, New York

Gramsci, A. 1971 *Prison Notebooks* International Publishers, New York

Hammersley, M. & Atkinson, P. 1983 *Ethnography: Principles in Practice* Tavistock Publications, London

Harding, S. 1986 *The Science Question in Feminism* Cornell University Press, New York

Harley, D. 1990 'Historians as Demonologists: The Myth of the Midwife-witch', *The Society for the Social History of Medicine,* 1, pp 1–26

Hazelton, M. 1990 'Medical Discourse on Contemporary Nurse Education. An Ideological Analysis' *ANZJS,* vol. 26, no. 1, March, pp. 107–125

Hochschild, A. R. 1983 *The Managed Heart* University of California Press, California

Holton, S. 1984 'Feminine Authority and Social Order: Florence Nightingale's Conception of Nursing and Health Care' *Social Analysis,* no. 15, August, pp. 59–72

Hoy, D. C. 1986 *Foucault, A Critical Reader* Basil Blackwell, Oxford

Hughes, D. 1988 'When Nurse Knows Best: Some Aspects of Nurse/Doctor Interaction in a Casualty Department' *Sociology of Health and Illness,* vol. 10, no. 1

Hughes, Everett C., Hughes, Helen McGill and Deutscher, Irwin 1958 *Twenty Thousand Nurses Tell Their Story* Lippincott, Philadelphia

Hughes, M. J. 1943 *Women Healers in Medieval Life and Literature* Books for Libraries Press, New York

Hurd-Mead, K. C. 1938 *A History of Women in Medicine* Milford House, Boston

Jaggar, A. M. 1983 *Feminist Politics and Human Nature* N. J. Rowman & Allanheld, Totowa

James, N. 1992 'Care = organization + physical labour + emotional labour' *Sociology of Health and Illness* vol. 14, no. 4, pp. 488–509

Jewson, N. D. 1974 'Medical knowledge and the patronage system in eighteenth century England' *Sociology* vol. 8, no. 3, pp. 369–85

——1976 'The disappearance of the sick man from medical sociology 1770–1870' *Sociology* vol. 10, no. 2, pp. 225–44

Johnson, T. 1972 *Professions and Power* Macmillan, London

Johnston, K. 1987 *Shaping the Educational Agenda: A Study of Ideology and Education* unpublished PhD Macquarie University, Sydney

Jordanova, L. J. (ed.) 1986 *Languages of Nature* Free Association Books, London

Katz, F. E. 1969 'Nurses' in Etzioni, A. (ed.) *The Semi-Professions and their Organization: Teachers, Nurses, Social Workers* Free Press, New York

Keller, E. F. 1985 *Reflections on Gender and Science* Yale University Press, New Haven

Ker-Conway, J. 1993 *The Road from Coorain* William Heinemann, Australia

King, D. 1987 'Social Constructionism and Medical Knowledge: The Case of Transsexualism *Sociology of Health and Illness*, vol. 9, no. 4, pp. 351–377

King, L. S. 1958 *The Medical World of the Eighteenth Century* University of Chicago Press, Chicago

——1974 'George Cheyne, mirror of eighteenth century medicine' *Bul. Hist. Med.* vol. 48, no. 4, pp. 517–39

Kuhn, T. S. 1962 *The Structure of Scientific Revolutions* University of Chicago Press, Chicago

Kuhn, A. & Wolpe, A. M. (eds) *Feminism and Materialism. Women and Modes of Production* Routledge & Kegan Paul, London

Laclau, E. & Mouffe, C. 1985 *Hegemony and Socialist Strategy* Verso, London

Lane, J. 1985 'The doctor scolds me' *Patients and Practitioners, Lay Perceptions of Medicine in Pre-Industrial Society* ed. R. Porter, Cambridge University Press, Cambridge

Lawler, J. 1991 *Behind the Screens. Nursing Somology and the Problem of the Body* Churchill Livingstone, Melbourne

LeFanu, W. R. 1972 'The lost half century in English medicine' *Bull. Hist. Med.* vol. XLVI, pp. 319–49

Lewin, E. & Olesen, V. 1985 *Women, Health and Healing* Tavistock, New York

Lloyd, G. 1984 *The Man of Reason* Methuen, London

Lorber, J., Coser, R. L., Rossi, A. & Chodorow, N. 1981 'On *The Reproduction of Mothering*: A Methodological Debate' in *Signs: Journal of Women in Culture and Society* 6(3), Spring, 482–514

Loudon, I. 1986 *Medical Care and the General Practitioner 1750–1850* Clarendon Press, Oxford

Lukes, S. 1974 *Power: A Radical View* Macmillan, London

Macdonell, D. 1986 *Theories of Discourse: An Introduction* Basil Blackwell, Oxford

MacIntyre, S. & Oldman, D. 1985 'Coping with migraine' in Black, N. et al. (eds) *Health and Disease: A Reader* Open University Press, Milton Keynes

McMahon, R. & Pearson, A. eds 1991 *Nursing As Therapy* Chapman & Hall, Australia

Mackay, L. 1989 *Nursing a Problem* Open University Press, Milton Keynes

——1993 *Conflicts in Care* Chapman & Hall, London

McNay, L. 1992 *Foucault and Feminism: Power, Gender and the Self* Polity Press, Cambridge

Maggs, C. 1983 *The Origins of General Nursing* Croom Helm, London

——1987 *Nursing History: The State of the Art* Croom Helm, London

Marx, K. 1970 *A Contribution to the Critique of Political Economy* Progress Press, Moscow

Marx, K. & Engels, F. 1970 *Selected Works* Progress Publishers, Moscow

Merchant, C. 1982 *The Death of Nature* Wildwood House, London

Moore, N. 1918 The History of St Bartholomew's Hospital 2 vols C. Arthur Pearson Ltd, London

Navarro, V. 1977 *Social Security and Medicine in the USSR* Lexington Books

——1977 *Medicine Under Capitalism* Prodist, New York

——1978 *Class Struggle, the State and Medicine* Martin Robertson & Co. Ltd, London

Neil, R. & Watts, R. eds 1991 *Caring and Nursing. Explorations in Feminist Perspectives* National League for Nursing, New York

Nettleton, S. 1995 *The Sociology of Health and Illness* Polity Press, Cambridge

Nicolson, M. & McLaughlin, C. 1988 'Social constructionism and medical sociology: A study of the vascular theory of multiple sclerosis' *Sociology of Health and Illness*, vol. 10, no. 3, pp. 234–261

Noske, B. 1989 *Humans and Other Animals* Pluto Press, London

Parry, N. & Parry, J. 1976 *The Rise of the Medical Profession* Croom Helm, London

Parsons, T. 1951 *The Social System* Free Press, Glencoe

Pearson, A. (ed.) 1988 *Primary Nursing. Nursing in Burford and Oxford Nursing Development Units* Croom Helm, Beckenham

Pelling, M. & Webster, C. 1979 'Medical Practitioners' *Health, Medicine and Mortality in the Sixteenth Century* ed C. Webster Cambridge University Press, Cambridge

Peterson, M. J. 1978 *The Medical Profession in Mid-Victorian London* University of California Press, London

Phillips, A. & Tayler, B. 1980 'Sex and skill: Notes towards feminist economics' *Feminist Review,* 6, pp. 79–88

Porter, R. (ed.) 1985 *Patients and Practitioners: Lay Perceptions of Medicine in Pre-Industrial Society* Cambridge University Press, Cambridge

——1987 *Disease, Medicine and Society in England 1550–1860* Macmillan, London

Porter, S. 1995 *Nursing's Relationship with Medicine* Avebury, Aldershot

Poynton, C. 1993 'Naming women's workplace skills: Linguistics and power' in Probert, B. & Wilson, B. *Pink Collar Blues. Work Gender and Technology* Melbourne University Press, Melbourne

Pringle, R. 1988 *Secretaries Talk. Sexuality, Power and Work* Allen & Unwin, Sydney

Pringle, R. & Watson, S. 1992 '"Women's interests" and the post-structuralist state' in Barret M. & Phillips, A. *Destabilizing Theory. Contemporary Feminist Debates* Polity Press, Cambridge

Purvis, T. & Hunt, A. 1993 'Discourse, Ideology, Discourse, Ideology, Discourse, Ideology . . .' *The British Journal of Sociology,* vol. 44, no. 3, September 1993, pp. 473–501

Rather, L. J. 1965 *Mind and Body in Eighteenth Century Medicine* University of California Press, Berkeley

Raymond, J. 1986 'Female friendship: Contra Chodorow and Dinnerstein' *Hypatia* 1 (2), Fall, pp. 24–36

Reverby, S. 1987 'A caring dilemma: Womanhood and nursing in historical perspective' in *Nursing Research* vol. 36, pp. 5–11

Rivett, G. 1986 *The Development of the London Hospital System 1823–1982* King's Fund Publishing Office, London

Roberts, S. J. 1983 'Oppressed group behaviour: implications for nursing' *Advances in Nursing Science,* July 1983

Rose, H. 1994 *Love, Power and Knowledge* Polity Press, Cambridge

Rosenberg, C. E. (ed.) 1979 *Healing and History. Essays for George Rosen.* Science History Publications, USA

Rossi, F. 1968 *Bacon: From Magic to Science* Routledge & Kegan Paul, London

Royal College of Nursing 1992 *The Value of Nursing* London
Russell, C. & Schofield, T. 1986 *Where It Hurts* Allen & Unwin, Sydney
Salmon, J. W. 1984 *Alternative Medicines. Popular and policy perspectives* Tavistock, New York, London
Salvage, J. 1985 *The Politics of Nursing* Heinemann, London
——1988 'Professionalization—or a struggle for survival? A consideration of current proposals for the reform of nursing in the United Kingdom' *Journal of Advanced Nursing* 13:515–19
——1992 'The new nursing: Empowering patients or empowering nurses?' *Political Issues in Nursing* eds J. Robinson, A. Gray & R. Elkan, Open University Press, Buckingham
Sawyer, M. G., Gannoni, A. F., Toogood, I. R., Antoniou, G. & Rice, M. 1994 'The use of alternative therapies by children with cancer' *Medical Journal of Australia* vol. 160, no. 6 pp. 320–322
Scott, J. 1988 'Deconstructing Equality Versus Difference: Or, the Uses of Post-Structuralist Theory for Feminism' *Feminist Studies* 14, 1, pp. 33–51
Sheridan, A. 1982 *Michel Foucault. The Will To Truth* Tavistock, London
Short, S. & Sharman, E. 1989 'Dissecting the Current Nursing Struggles in Australia' in Lupton, G. & Najman, J., *Sociology of Health and Illness* Macmillan, Australia
Short, S. D., Sharman, E. & Speedy, S. 1993 *Sociology for Nurses* Macmillan, Australia
Shyrock, R. H. 1936 *The Development of Modern Medicine* The University of Wisconsin Press, Wisconsin
Sigsworth, E. M. 1972 'Gateways to Death? Medicine, Hospitals and Mortality, 1700–1850' in Mathias, P. (ed.) *Science and Society* Cambridge University Press, London
Smart, B. 1985 *Foucault, Marxism and Critique* Routledge & Kegan Paul, London
Smith, D. E. 1984 *The Everyday World As Problematic. A Feminist Sociology* University of Toronto Press, Toronto
Smith, G. 1985 'Prescribing the rules of health: Self help and advice in the late eighteenth century' *Patients and Practitioners* ed. R. Porter, Cambridge University Press, Cambridge
Smith, P. 1992 *The Emotional Labour of Nursing. How Nurses Care* Macmillan, London
Stein, L. I. 1967 'The doctor-nurse game' *Archives of General Psychiatry* 16, pp. 699–703
Stevens, M. M. 1994 'Improving communication with parents of children with cancer' Medical Journal of Australia vol. 160, no. 6, p. 325
Svensson, R. 1996 'The Interplay between Doctors and Nurses: A

Negotiated Order Perspective', *Sociology of Health and Illness*, vol. 18, no.3, pp. 379–98

Thompson, E. P. 1968 *The Making of the English Working Class* Penguin, Harmondsworth

——1978 *The Poverty of Theory & Other Essays* Merlin Press, London

Tong, R. 1994 *Feminist Thought* Routledge, London

Tuana, N. 1989 *Feminism and Science* Indiana University Press, Bloomington

Turner, B. 1986 'The vocabulary of complaints—Nursing professionalism and job context' *ANZJS* 22, 3, pp. 368–386

——1987 *Medical Power and Social Knowledge* Sage, London

——1992 *Regulating Bodies. Essays in Medical Sociology* Routledge, London

Ungerson, C. 1983 *A Labour of Love. Women Work and Caring* eds J. Finch & D. Groves, Routledge & Kegan Paul, London

Versluysen, M. 1980 'Old wives' tales? Women healers in English history' *Rewriting Nursing History* ed C. Davies, Barnes and Noble Books, New Jersey

Waddington, I. 1973 'The role of the hospital in the development of modern medicine: A sociological analysis' *Sociology* vol. 7, no. 2, pp. 211–224

——1977 'General Practitioners and Consultants in Early Nineteenth Century England. The Sociology of an Intra-Professional Conflict' in Woodward, J. & Richards, D. (eds) *Health Care and Popular Medicine in Nineteenth Century England* Holmes and Meier, New York

——1984 *The Medical Profession in the Industrial Revolution* Gill and Macmillan, Dublin

Waitzkin, H. 1981 'A Marxist analysis of the health care systems of advanced capitalist societies' *The Relevance of Social Science for Medicine* eds L. Eisenberg & A. Kleinman, D. Reider Publishing Co., Dordrecht, Holland

——1983 *The Second Sickness* The Free Press, Collier Macmillan, London

Walby, S. 1990 *Theorizing Patriarchy* Blackwell, Oxford

——1992 'Post-post-modernism? Theorizing social complexity' *Destabilizing Theory. Contemporary Feminist Debates* eds M. Barrett & A. Phillips, Polity Press, Cambridge

Walby, S. & Greenwell, J. with Mackay, L. & Soothill, K. 1994 *Medicine and Nursing Professions in a Changing Health Service* Sage, London

Ward, D. 1991 'Gender and Cost in Caring' in Neil, R. M. & Watts, R. (eds) *Caring and Nursing* National League for Nursing, New York

Weedon, C. 1987 *Feminist Practice and Poststructuralist Theory* Basil Blackwell, Oxford

Wicks, D. 1994 Nurses, Doctors and Bifurcated Knowledge: Healing the Sexual Division of Labour, unpublished PhD, Macquarie University, Sydney

——1995 'Nurses and doctors and discourses of healing' *ANZJS* 31, 2, August

——1997 'Nursing and sociology: An uneasy relationship' in Germov, J. *Second Opinion* Oxford University Press, Melbourne

Williams, C. 1989 *Gender Differences At Work* University of California Press, Berkeley

Williams, K. 1980 'From Sarah Gamp to Florence Nightingale: A critical study of hospital nursing systems from 1840–1897' *Rewriting Nursing History* ed. C. Davies, Croom Helm, London

Willis, E. 1983 *Medical Dominance* Allen & Unwin, Sydney

——1989 'Complementary healers' in Lupton, G. M. & Najman, J. M. *Sociology of Health and Illness Australian Readings* Macmillan, Melbourne, Sydney

Witz, A. 1992 *Professions and Patriarchy* Routledge, London

——1994 'The Challenge of Nursing' in Kelleher, D. Gabe, J. & Williams, G. (eds), *Challenging Medicine,* Routledge, London

Wolpe, P. R. 1990 'The holistic heresy: Strategies of ideological challenge in the medical profession' *Soc. Sci. Med.* vol. 32, no. 8, pp. 913–923

Wright, P. & Treacher, A. 1982 *The Problem of Medical Knowledge* Edinburgh University Press, Edinburgh

Young, I. 1980 'Socialist Feminism and the Limits of Dual Systems Theory', *Socialist Review* 10, nos 2–3

Index